PTE ACADEMIC
Testbuilder

MACMILLAN

Macmillan Education
Between Towns Road, Oxford OX4 3PP
A division of Macmillan Publishers Limited

Companies and representatives throughout the world

ISBN 978-0-230-42785-3

First published 2012

Designed by xen

Picture research by Emily Taylor

The authors and publishers would like to thank
the following for permission to reproduce their
photographs:

Alamy/Arco Images p91(tr), Alamy/Mary Evans Picture
Library p121(tr);
Bartholome, E. M. and Belward A. S., 2005, GLC2000;
a new approach to global land cover mapping from
Earth Observation data, International Journal of
Remote Sensing, 26, 1959 – 1977 p119(bc);
Corbis p14(br), Corbis/H. Armstrong Roberts/
ClassicStock p54(cr), Corbis/Atlantide Phototravel
p14(tr), Corbis/The Francis Frith Collection p54(br),
Corbis/Andrew Holbrooke p118(br), Corbis/ Image
Source p121(cr), Corbis/Viviane Moos p89(br), Corbis/
Ocean p14(cr), Corbis/Kris Ubach and Quim Roser/
cultura p91(cr);
Getty Images/Apic p54(tr), Getty Images/ Frans
Lemmens p91(br), Getty Images/Bob Stefko p121(br).

Printed and bound in Thailand

2016 2015 2014 2013 2012
10 9 8 7 6 5 4 3 2 1

CONTENTS

CONTENTS

INTRODUCTION

The PTE Academic Testbuilder is more than a book of practice tests; it offers students 'tests that teach'. This teaching function is achieved in part through sections of Further Practice and Guidance. These sections review the exam tasks and provide information about each exam section, tips on completing that section of the exam, and detailed study of various aspects of the tasks. The exam tasks are designed to reflect the actual PTE Academic exam as closely as possible. The PTE Academic is a computer-based exam, and so some adaptation has been made to some tasks for them to appear in printed form. The On-Screen feature which appears on some pages explains how the printed task differs from the computer-based version.

Using the PTE Academic Testbuilder

Either:

- Do each part of the exam under 'exam conditions'. This means not allowing yourself to use a dictionary and making sure that you stick to any time limits. Then either check your answers, or look at the relevant Further Practice and Guidance section. When you have completed that section, you can go back and think about your answers again before checking your final answers against the key.

Or:

- Before doing an exam section, particularly for the first time, you may like to look at the Further Practice and Guidance section first. Read the What's Tested section and the Tips. They will help you understand what is required in that part of the exam. You might then do the A Detailed Study section before attempting the exam task. Then check your final answers against the key.

PTE (Pearson Test of English) Academic

PTE Academic is a computer-based test of English. It is designed to measure the academic English abilities of candidates who wish to demonstrate their level of achievement to professional and government organizations and education institutions.

Part 1: Speaking and Writing

(approximately 77–93 minutes)

Section 1: Personal introduction

In this section, you are given a prompt and are asked to introduce yourself orally. You speak about yourself for up to 30 seconds. This is not assessed but is sent to institutions along with your score report.

Section 2: Read aloud

In this section, you are given a text (up to 60 words) and are asked to read the text aloud. You do six to seven of these items, depending on the combination of items in your test.

Section 2: Repeat sentence

In this section, you hear a sentence. You are asked to repeat the sentence exactly as you heard it. You do ten to twelve of these items, depending on the combination of items in your test.

Section 2: Describe image

In this section, you are given an image (picture, graph, table, etc.). You are asked to describe in detail what the image is showing. You do six to seven of these items, depending on the combination of items in your test.

Section 2: Re-tell lecture

In this section, you hear a lecture. You are asked to retell the lecture in your own words. You do three to four of these items, depending on the combination of items in your test.

Section 2: Answer short question

In this section, you are asked a question, the answer to which is a word or short phrase. You do ten to twelve of these items, depending on the combination of items in your test.

Sections 3–4: Summarize written text

In these sections, you read a text (up to 300 words). You are then asked to summarize the text in one sentence. You are given ten minutes to write each summary sentence.

Section 5: Summarize written text / Write essay

This section is either a *Summarize written text* task or a *Write essay* task (see Section 6), depending on the combination of items in your test.

Section 6: Write essay

In this section, you are given a prompt to read. You are then asked to write an essay (200–300 words). You are given twenty minutes to write your essay.

Part 2: Reading

(approximately 32–41 minutes)

Multiple-choice, choose single answer

In this section, you read a text (up to 300 words). You are then given a multiple-choice question with three to five answer options. You choose the one correct answer option. You do two to three of these items, depending on the combination of items in your test.

Multiple-choice, choose multiple answers

In this section, you read a text (up to 300 words). You are then given a multiple-choice question with five to seven answer options. You choose all the correct answer options. You do two to three of these items, depending on the combination of items in your test.

Re-order paragraphs

In this section, you are given a text (up to 150 words) divided into paragraphs. The paragraphs are in the wrong order. You have to drag and drop the paragraphs into the correct order. You do two to three of these items, depending on the combination of items in your test.

Reading: Fill in the blanks

In this section, you read a text (up to 80 words) which has blanks in it. You drag words from a box and drop each word onto the correct blank to complete the text. You do four to five of these items, depending on the combination of items in your test.

Reading and Writing: Fill in the blanks

In this section, you read a text (up to 300 words) which has blanks in it. You click on each blank and a drop down list appears. You choose the correct word from each list to complete the text. You do five to six of these items, depending on the combination of items in your test.

Part 3: Listening

(approximately 45–57 minutes)

Section 1: Summarize spoken text

In this section, you listen to a short lecture. You are then asked to write a summary of that lecture (50–70 words) for a fellow student who was not present at the lecture. You do two to three of these items, depending on the combination of items in your test.

Section 2: Multiple-choice, choose multiple answers

In this section, you listen to a recording on an academic subject. You are then given a multiple-choice question with five to seven answer options. You choose all the correct answer options. You do two to three of these items, depending on the combination of items in your test.

Section 2: Fill in the blanks

In this section, you listen to a recording while you read a transcription of that recording. The transcription has up to seven blanks in it. As you listen, you type in the missing words you hear. You do two to three of these items, depending on the combination of items in your test.

Section 2: Highlight correct summary

In this section, you listen to a recording. You read three to five paragraphs and select the paragraph which is the best summary of the recording. You do two to three of these items, depending on the combination of items in your test.

Section 2: Multiple-choice, choose single answer

In this section, you listen to a recording on an academic subject. You are then given a multiple-choice question with three to five answer options. You choose the one correct answer option. You do two to three of these items, depending on the combination of items in your test.

Section 2: Select missing word

In this section, you listen to a recording. The final word or group of words has been replaced by a beep. You are given three to five answer options. You choose the correct answer option to complete the recording. You do two to three of these items, depending on the combination of items in your test.

Section 2: Highlight incorrect words

In this section, you listen to a recording while you read a transcription of that recording. The transcription contains up to seven deliberate errors. You click on the words in the transcription which do not match the recording. You do two to three of these items, depending on the combination of items in your test.

Section 2: Write from dictation

In this section, you hear a sentence. You are then asked to write the sentence exactly as you heard it, using correct spelling. You do three to four of these items, depending on the combination of items in your test.

Marking the Practice Tests

Candidates for PTE Academic receive a score report, which includes an Overall Score, Communicative Skills scores and Enabling Skills scores. Communicative Skills consist of Listening, Reading, Speaking and Writing. Enabling Skills consist of Grammar, Oral Fluency, Pronunciation, Spelling, Vocabulary and Written discourse. Each item on the exam contributes to these scores in a complex way, depending on the particular skills being tested.

For classroom practice, it is recommended that you adopt a simplified scoring scheme. Scores on PTE Academic range up to 90. For those sections of the exam where there are clear right and wrong answers (e.g., *Part 1, Section 2: Answer short question*), calculate the number of correct answers as a percentage and then convert into a mark out of 90. For each section of the exam which judges performance in a more qualitative way (e.g., *Part 1, Section 6: Write essay*), award students a score based on their overall performance. A score of 43–58 indicates that a student should be able to perform language tasks at B1 level, 59–75 indicates B2 level, and 76–84 indicates C1 level. For example, a student whose performance on *Part 1, Section 2: Read Aloud* is what you would expect from someone capable of performing language tasks at a high B2 level may be given a score of 74 or 75. The average of these scores should give you an approximate indication of how a student is likely to perform on PTE Academic.

A note on language

PTE Academic tests ability in international academic English. In this book, individual texts follow either British or American spelling conventions. The Further Practice and Guidance sections follow American spelling conventions. On the Audio CD, you will hear a range of native speaker voices, including British, American and Australian speakers.

TEST 1

PART 1: SPEAKING AND WRITING

SECTION 1: PERSONAL INTRODUCTION

Read the prompt below. In 25 seconds, you must reply in your own words, as naturally and clearly as possible. You have 30 seconds to record your response. Your response will be sent together with your score report to the institutions selected by you.

Please introduce yourself. For example, you could talk about one or more of the following:

- Your interests
- Your plans for future study
- Why you want to study abroad
- Why you need to learn English
- Why you chose *this* test

For Further Guidance, see page 9.

SECTION 2: READ ALOUD

Look at the text below. In 40 seconds, you must read this text aloud as naturally and clearly as possible. You have 40 seconds to read aloud.

(Allow 40 seconds for each separate text.)

A History rubs shoulders and often overlaps with many other areas of research, from myths and epics to the social sciences, including economics, politics, biography, demography, and much else besides. Some histories are almost pure narratives, while others go in for detailed, tightly-focused analyses of, for example, the parish records of a Cornish village in the 16ᵗʰ century.

B There are many kinds of pond, but nearly all are small bodies of shallow, stagnant water in which plants with roots can grow. Water movement is slight and temperatures fluctuate widely. The wealth of plants ensures that during daylight hours oxygen is plentiful. However, at night, when photosynthesis no longer takes place, oxygen supplies can fall very low.

C Before the time of Alexander the Great, the only eastern people who could be compared with the Greeks in the fields of science and philosophy were from the Indian sub-continent. However, because so little is known about Indian chronology, it is difficult to tell how much of their science was original and how much was the result of Greek influence.

D While far fewer people these days write letters and therefore have less use for stamps, there are still a few categories of stamp which attract collectors. Stamps in common use for an indefinite period – until the price goes up – are called "definitive" issues, while a more collectible type of stamp is the "commemorative" issue, honoring people, events and anniversaries.

E In the second quarter of the 19ᵗʰ century, a rapidly growing middle class created a great demand for furniture production. Yet at this stage, while machines were used for certain jobs, such as carved decoration, there was no real mass production. The extra demand was met by numerous woodworkers. Mass production came later and the quality of domestic furniture declined.

F In the Middle Ages, the design and use of flags were considered a means of identifying social status. Flags were, therefore, the symbols not of nations, but of the nobility. The design of each flag resembled the "devices" on the noble's Coat of Arms, and the size of the flag was an indication of how high the owner stood in the nobility.

You can hear model answers on the CD1, track 1.

SECTION 2: REPEAT SENTENCE

You will hear some sentences. Please repeat each sentence exactly as you hear it. You will hear each sentence only once.

 1.2 Play the CD to listen to the recording that goes with this item.

PERSONAL INTRODUCTION

WHAT'S TESTED

The Personal Introduction section is not scored. The purpose of this section is to give you an opportunity to show admissions officers a little about your personality. Additionally, it is used to verify your identity by the institutions that receive your scores.

First, you will be given 25 seconds to read the prompt. Then, you will have 30 seconds to respond. An on-screen status box will let you know when to begin recording, how much time remains, and when the recording time is up. You cannot re-record your Personal Introduction.

TIPS

- Remember that your goal for this section is to make a positive impression on the admissions officers.

- Be prepared. You should know what you are going to say before you arrive at the testing center.

- Practice what you intend to say in front of a mirror. If you can, record yourself and listen to your delivery. Does it sound natural? Are you conveying the impression you want? Keep practicing until you feel completely confident about what you will say. You will not be able to read a prepared speech, but if you have practiced what you want to say, you will sound confident and natural. Relax, speak clearly, and avoid sounding as if you have memorized a speech. Your aim should be to sound naturally confident, not rehearsed.

- You will have 30 seconds to record your Personal Introduction. Be sure your speech lasts the required length of time. If it does not, then either you will run out of time while you are still speaking, or you will finish too soon, and have to sit in uncomfortable silence until the recording ends.

A DETAILED STUDY

To help you focus on what you will say, practice answering the following questions orally to form a personal introduction. Use a timer and keep your response within the 30-second time limit.

- What is your name?
- How old are you?
- Where are you from?
- What year of school are you in now, or where do you work?
- What are you planning to study, and why?
- Why should the institutions you are applying to accept you? What qualities do you possess that will be of interest to them?

Think of any other points you would like the admissions officers to know about you. Practice your Personal Introduction until you are satisfied with it and feel confident about delivering it on test day. Be sure you have practiced with a timer and that your introduction is neither too long nor too short.

Example Answer

Hi, my name's Kim Jae-sun. I'm eighteen, I'm from Seoul, South Korea, and I'm in my final year of high school. I plan to study computer science in college, because it's an area I would like to work in after I graduate. One reason a school would be interested in me is that I belong to an electronics club. We build robots and remote-controlled toys. If the school I'm accepted at doesn't have a club like this, I could start one.

SECTION 2: DESCRIBE IMAGE

A Look at the pie chart below. Describe in detail what the pie chart is showing. You will have 40 seconds to give your response.

Where do you get the news?

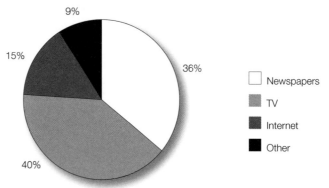

B Look at the graph below. Describe in detail what the graph is showing. You will have 40 seconds to give your response.

Unemployment rates by age and qualification

For Further Guidance, see page 12.

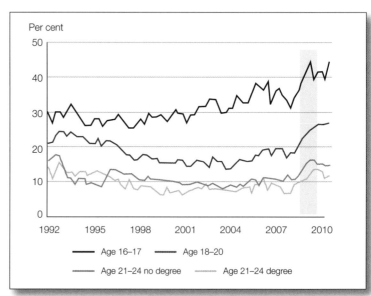

C Look at the graph below. Describe in detail what the graph is showing. You will have 40 seconds to give your response.

Carbon dioxide emissions per resident, 2008 (Tonnes)

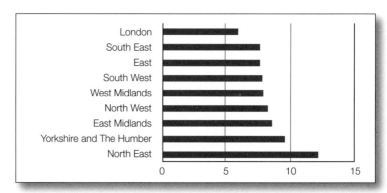

D Look at the graph below. Describe in detail what the graph is showing. You will have 40 seconds
to give your response.

Households with access to the Internet, UK

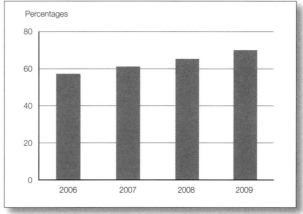

E Look at the graph below. Describe in detail what the graph is showing. You will have 40 seconds
to give your response.

Overseas residents' visits to the UK
and UK residents' visits abroad

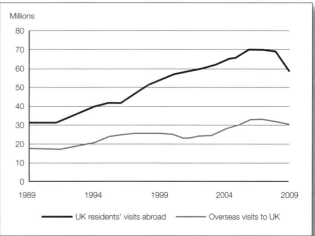

F Look at the graph below. Describe in detail what the graph is showing. You will have 40 seconds
to give your response.

Population: by gender and age, mid-2010

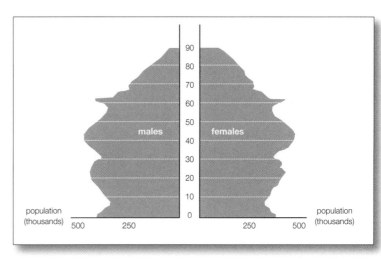

You can hear model answers on the CD1, track 3.

DESCRIBE IMAGE

WHAT'S TESTED

The purpose of this task is to assess your ability to describe an image related to an academic theme drawn from the humanities, natural sciences, or social sciences. Only speaking skills are assessed. You will see an image (a graph, picture, map, chart, or table). You will have 25 seconds to study the image. When you hear the tone, you should begin describing in detail what is shown in the image. You will have 40 seconds to give your response. There are six or seven images.

TIPS

- Identify the type of image. Is it a graph, picture, map, chart, or table? The approach for handling each image type is slightly different.

- Take notes if you need to. Use the Erasable Noteboard Booklet and pen provided. Do not write full sentences; briefly list any important features you see.

- For graphs, charts, and tables, be sure you understand what is being measured and in what units it is being reported.

- Try to determine what the main point of the image is. You should be able to answer the question, *"What is the image mainly showing?"*

- Maps and pictures will often have obvious features highlighted. Use words and phrases that describe the locations of features within the image, for example, *on the left/right*, *next to*, *above*, *below*, and so on. If objects are particular colors, these may help you identify them, for example, *the countries marked in yellow*. The same is true for sizes and shapes, for example, *the large square*, *the smaller circle*.

- Graphs, charts, and tables often show trends or changes. Use words and phrases that describe the trend or movement. For example, *increase*, *decrease*, *rise*, *fall*, *remain stable/steady*, and so on. Use phrases to describe the speed at which the changes happen, for example, *a sudden increase, a slow decline*.

- Pie charts show proportions. The size of the "slices" indicates the relative size of whatever is being measured or counted. The actual numerical values for the slices are usually provided. Be sure to mention these values. If the slices are equally sized, say so, using words and phrases such as *equal, the same, about the same, similar*. If the slices are different – the usual case – use comparatives and superlatives to describe them, for example, *the smaller of the two export categories, the largest group of people, the most popular option, the least common answer*, and so on.

- For all graphs, charts, and tables, look for a pair of extreme values – for example, the highest and lowest, the largest and smallest, the most expensive and cheapest – identify them by name and describe them using the values for their measures or counts.

- While you are speaking, if you lose your train of thought, or find yourself at a loss for words, do not remain silent. The microphone turns off automatically if there is no sound for three seconds. If you need to pause to think or check your notes, use pause fillers such as *um, uh, Let me see*, and so on. Saying something – anything – is better than saying nothing because once the microphone turns off, you cannot turn it on again.

A DETAILED STUDY

The exercise below will help you practice describing a graph. Look at Graph B on page 10 again and answer the following questions.

1   What kind of image is it?

....

2   What is the image mainly showing?

....

3 How did the unemployment rates in 1992 compare to those in 2007?

....

4 What happened to the unemployment rates in 2010?

....

5 What general trend is shown in the unemployment rate for 16–17 years olds?

....

Now check your answers.

SECTION 2: RE-TELL LECTURE

A You will hear a lecture. After listening to the lecture, please retell what you have just heard from the lecture in your own words. You will have 40 seconds to give your response.

 1.4 Play the CD to listen to the recording that goes with this item.

B You will hear a lecture. After listening to the lecture, please retell what you have just heard from the lecture in your own words. You will have 40 seconds to give your response.

 1.5 Play the CD to listen to the recording that goes with this item.

C You will hear a lecture. After listening to the lecture, please retell what you have just heard from the lecture in your own words. You will have 40 seconds to give your response.

 1.6 Play the CD to listen to the recording that goes with this item.

For Further Guidance, see page 15.

You can hear model answers on the CD1, track 7.

SECTION 2: ANSWER SHORT QUESTION

You will hear some questions. Please give a simple and short answer to each one. Often just one or a few words is enough.

 1.8 Play the CD to listen to the recording that goes with this item.

RE-TELL LECTURE

WHAT'S TESTED

The purpose of this section is to assess your ability to make an oral presentation based on information taken from an academic lecture. Both speaking and listening skills are assessed. You will listen to a lecture on an academic topic and then retell what you have heard in your own words. The lectures are each between 60 and 90 seconds long. There are either three or four lectures; the number will depend on which form of the PTE Academic you are given. There will always be at least three lectures. You will have 40 seconds to retell each lecture.

TIPS

- Study the picture if there is one. It will give you a general idea about the context of the lecture. From the picture, try to predict what the lecture will be about. You will have three seconds to get ready for the start of the lecture.

- Take notes. Use the Erasable Noteboard Booklet and pen provided. Do not try to write down every word you hear. Unless you are able to write quickly and accurately, you will probably fall behind and miss important information. Instead, focus on key words.

- Writing quickly is a key skill to master. Use abbreviations whenever possible. Ignore articles (e.g., *a, an, the*) unless they are necessary. Omitting the vowels from words is one way to increase writing speed.

- Key words include names, numbers, dates, times, and words and phrases that are stressed. Words and phrases that are repeated are usually central to the main idea.

- Focus on understanding the main idea of the lecture and the key points that support it. If the speaker draws a conclusion, be sure you have identified it. Try to identify the overall purpose of the lecture.

- Listen for clues to the speaker's attitude, opinion, or stance. Be aware of the speaker's tone of voice and delivery, and try to detect any emotions that are being conveyed.

- When the lecture ends, you will have approximately 10 seconds to review your notes. Use this time to organize what you will say. When you hear the tone, begin speaking. You will have 40 seconds to complete the task.

- While you are speaking, if you lose your train of thought, or find yourself at a loss for words, do not remain silent. The microphone turns off automatically if there is no sound for three seconds. If you need to pause to think or to check your notes, use pause fillers such as *um, uh, Let me see, a*nd so on. Saying something – anything – is better than saying nothing because once the microphone turns off, you cannot turn it on again.

A DETAILED STUDY

The exercise below will help you practice listening to identify key information. Listen to Lecture A from page 14 again and answer the following questions in your own words. If necessary, listen to the lecture a further time.

1 What is the lecture mainly about?

....

2 Who is Frank O. Gehry?

....

3 What does the speaker say about modern architects?

....

4 What did Frank O. Gehry want to do?

....

5 How did the computer help Frank O. Gehry?

....

6 How did Frank O. Gehry feel about architecture?

....

7 What will the speaker talk about next?

....

8 How does the speaker probably feel about Frank O. Gehry?

....

Now check your answers.

SECTION 3: SUMMARIZE WRITTEN TEXT

Read the passage below and summarize it using one sentence. You have 10 minutes to finish this task. Your response will be judged on the quality of your writing and on how well your response presents the key points in the passage.

How do we measure efficiency? To economists – or to a certain type of economist – it is simply a question of profitability, even when it concerns what most people consider a social provision such as public transport. What is lost when railway lines and bus routes to small, out-of-the-way communities are cut in the name of efficiency? After all, if a line or a route is only used occasionally by a few people, it would be much cheaper to rip up the lines and let everyone use their cars.

For many governments, the way to turn inefficient national services into profitable businesses has been to sell off these services – and their responsibilities – to private enterprises. Cost, in terms of profit and loss, is of course an important factor, but other factors need to be considered when dealing with the livelihoods of whole communities, however small. Among these are the social, environmental, human and cultural costs incurred by cutting off more remote communities from greater opportunities, including economic activities that benefit society as a whole.

Taking away such links – the usual result of privatization – may well lead to economic benefits in the short term, but, as the last twenty to thirty years have shown, also leads to long-term social and cultural damage. Of course, no business with its eye on profits is going to "waste" money supporting underused services. Only large collective bodies such as national and local governments can do that. These services are, after all, a social provision, not businesses.

....

....

....

....

SECTION 4: SUMMARIZE WRITTEN TEXT

Read the passage below and summarize it using one sentence. You have 10 minutes to finish this task. Your response will be judged on the quality of your writing and on how well your response presents the key points in the passage.

Is the purpose of history to promote a strong national identity and support national myths? Certainly, it has been used in this way for centuries, and this is often reflected in the history curriculum. We can all remember history at school as being a matter of learning lots of facts and dates, and long lists of kings and queens – a grand narrative of how we got from a not so civilized past to the great nation we are today. Putting aside the fact that national identity is a complex and divisive question – especially in countries like the UK, which is comprised of several nationalities – this approach to history emphasizes a broad understanding, rather than a detailed understanding.

Yet history is, or should be, a critical, skeptical discipline: some historians see their work as disproving myths, demolishing orthodoxies and exposing politically-motivated narratives which claim to be objective. What students need to develop are more critical and analytical skills; in other words, to think for themselves. They can do this by studying certain historical problems in depth. This involves being critical of the narratives presented by historians and skeptical of the myths preserved in the national memory.

....

....

....

....

SECTION 5: SUMMARIZE WRITTEN TEXT

Read the passage below and summarize it using one sentence. You have 10 minutes to finish this task. Your response will be judged on the quality of your writing and on how well your response presents the key points in the passage.

Tradition and commerce often clash in many cultures. In Trinidad, it is the Carnival that is the cause of current friction. The complaint, as you would expect, is that traditional skills and creativity are being lost in the rush to make profits. And the profits are large: the two-day festival, which attracts up to 40,000 tourists each year, is estimated to generate somewhere between $27 million and $100 million.

A particular problem for the traditionalists is that the extravagant colorful costumes people wear in the bands or processions are now largely being imported, especially from China. These costumes are cheaper and more revealing (another cause of complaint) than those made locally. Critics say these imports are a threat to traditional creations and, worse, mean sending work elsewhere. Others see turning the Carnival into a profitable and exportable industry as a progressive move, benefiting the country as a whole.

A large number of people are in two minds. On the one hand, the changes are a reflection of what people – mainly tourists – want, and bring in money. On the other, there is a desire to preserve traditions. The transformation of the bands and processions into businesses has disrupted the social order, which used to be made up of friends getting together to relax, eat and drink, and make costumes. Both sides agree, though, that the country needs to make better use of the skills of the people in the Carnival business and that the country's resources must appeal to a wider market.

....
....
....
....

SECTION 6: WRITE ESSAY

You will have 20 minutes to plan, write and revise an essay about the topic below. Your response will be judged on how well you develop a position, organize your ideas, present supporting details, and control the elements of standard written English. You should write 200–300 words.

When computers first appeared on the scene, it was thought they would make us more productive in providing goods and services, smarter and possibly happier. Skeptics claim that the opposite is true as computers have proved disappointing in terms of productivity, and have made us less happy and more stupid because information is not knowledge.

Which of these points of view do you agree with most? Support your argument with reasons and/or examples from your own experience and observations.

....
....
....
....
....
....
....
....
....
....
....
....

For Further Guidance, see page 19.

SUMMARIZE WRITTEN TEXT

WHAT'S TESTED

The purpose of these sections is to assess your ability to write a one-sentence summary of the key points from a reading passage. The passages are up to 300 words long and cover a variety of academic topics drawn from the humanities, natural sciences, and social sciences. You will summarize either two or three reading passages. You will have 10 minutes to summarize each passage. Each summary should be a single sentence of no more than 30 words.

TIPS

- Skim the entire passage to get an idea of its general content. You should be able to answer the question "*What is the passage mainly about?*" Your answer should be a few words, at most. Write this down.

- Scan the entire passage for key words and phrases. Words and phrases that are repeated throughout the passage are usually important. Make a note of these.

- Read the entire passage carefully. Use context clues within the passage to work out any unknown vocabulary.

- Most academic writing has a logical structure. Passages are written in paragraphs. A passage can have a single paragraph, or several, depending on the nature of the topic and the specific focus of the passage. Each paragraph will usually present one main idea, which is supported with various arguments and evidence.

- If there are multiple paragraphs, the first paragraph will typically be an introduction to the topic, and will often include a brief description of what will be discussed. The last paragraph will typically close with a conclusion. Pay special attention to the introduction and the conclusion.

- Each paragraph will have its own topic sentence expressing the main idea. Typically, the topic sentence is the first sentence of the paragraph. The rest of the paragraph generally supports the main idea by presenting a number of arguments, details and other evidence.

- The task of summarizing a multi-paragraph passage is sometimes made easier by briefly summarizing each paragraph first, and then combining these summaries into a single summary. Make a brief summary of each paragraph as you finish reading it. You do not need full sentences at this point.

- Use your notes, as well as the information in the introductory and concluding paragraphs, to write your final summary.

- Keep your summary to a maximum of 30 words. The response box has an indicator that will tell you how many words you have written. If you are getting close to your word limit, but still need to write more, edit your sentence to remove unnecessary words, especially adjectives. These can often be omitted.

A DETAILED STUDY

The exercise below will help you practice identifying topic sentences in a reading passage.

Read Section 3 on page 17 again and <u>underline</u> the topic sentences. Then, write a brief summary of each paragraph. Finally, summarize the entire text in a single sentence of 30 words or less.

Paragraph 1 summary sentence:

....

....

Paragraph 2 summary sentence:

....

....

Paragraph 3 summary sentence:

....

....

One-sentence summary of entire text:

....

....

Now check your answers.

PART 2: READING

MULTIPLE-CHOICE, CHOOSE SINGLE ANSWER

A Read the text and answer the multiple-choice question by selecting the correct response.
Only one response is correct.

"Rightly is they called pigs," said Rowley, a farm laborer looking at the wallowing animals before passing on to the cow sheds, in Aldous Huxley's novel *Chrome Yellow*. Those who heard his words commented on his wisdom.

This raises all sorts of questions about language and how we perceive the world, questions that range from the philosophical to the politically correct (PC) use of language and the question of causing offence – for example, calling someone a pig.

Those who believed in being PC tried to adjust language to take into account people's sensitivities in the areas of race, sexuality and disability, and a theologian has recently written that we should do the same for the animal kingdom. To call them "wild" or "beasts" is, he says, "derogatory and offensive". I'm all in favor of animal welfare, but, in arguing his case, he says that language is the means by which we understand and conceptualize the world around us.

But is it? Isn't it the other way round? To put it another, very simple, way: do you believe that the language you use has made you think of the world in a certain way, or that you have an idea of the world as it is and your place in it, and you use language to understand and describe it?

Is Rowley's wisdom based on his many years working with farm animals, and what he has seen is just pigs being pigs and there's nothing more to be said? Or has he decided that the name "pig" suits these creatures because they behave piggishly? If we cleaned them up, taught them table manners and made them wear a tie, would we have to call them something else?

What is the main reason for the writer mentioning Rowley?

1 Because he is a farm laborer.

2 To illustrate his view about the use of language.

3 To support the idea that we should be politically correct when talking about animals.

4 To bring some humor into his text.

B Read the text and answer the multiple-choice question by selecting the correct response.
Only one response is correct.

These days you can fit hundreds of books into one e-book reader or smartphone, and this has led publishers, writers and readers alike to ask whether this means the death of the printed book and a drastic change in how we read. Or, as some hope and believe, will the electronic book format simply complement traditional book publishing?

The fact that a book can be downloaded from almost anywhere in the world has blurred the lines between author, reader, format and distribution, and this has caused some head-scratching at some of the world's biggest publishing companies. Such companies must adapt, and quickly, to the new market; but many are nervous of the risks and often shareholders are not willing to break new ground.

For many writers, however, e-publishing provides new freedoms and opportunities. Many e-books are published by writers who do not have a readership through mainstream publishers, and this allows them to deal with material that mainstream publishers would consider too controversial or otherwise unmarketable.

The market is very much driven by the consumer, and publishing companies are going to have to deal with this new situation sooner or later. It is quite a complicated situation, but it doesn't have to be either/or. The book as we know it has been around for about 500 years and, once things settle down, there is no reason why the e-book and the traditional printed book should not exist happily side by side.

Which of the following statements is true according to the text?

1 E-publishing has created new possibilities for writers.

2 Publishing companies have been unable to adapt to the new market.

3 E-books will radically alter our reading habits.

4 Most e-books are not by conventionally-published writers.

5 Sales of e-books are likely to overtake sales of traditional books.

For Further Guidance, see page 23.

MULTIPLE-CHOICE, CHOOSE SINGLE ANSWER

WHAT'S TESTED

The purpose of this task is to assess your ability to read an academic text for a variety of purposes, including reading for the main idea, reading for specific details, reading for the writer's purpose, analyzing discourse, making inferences, and assessing the quality and usefulness of a text. The texts are up to 300 words long and cover a variety of academic topics drawn from the humanities, natural sciences, and social sciences. Each text has one multiple-choice question; there will be between three and five answer options to choose from, only one of which will be correct. You will have either two or three items in this part. The individual questions are not timed. You will have a fixed time of between 32 and 41 minutes to complete the entire Reading part, depending on which form of the PTE Academic you receive.

TIPS

- Read the question before you read the text. This will tell you what information you will be reading for.

- Scan the answer choices to further help you focus on the information you will be reading for.

- Skim the text to get an idea of its general content and the main idea. You should be able to answer the question *"What is the passage mainly about?"* in your own words.

- Read the entire text again carefully. Pay attention to details that support the main idea.

- Read the question and the answer options again. Select the correct answer if you know it. If you are not sure about the answer, eliminate any options that are obviously incorrect, and choose from those that remain.

- If you do not know the answer, and are unable to eliminate any options, guess. Never leave the question unanswered. If you leave the question unanswered, it will be marked as incorrect. By guessing, you have the possibility of answering correctly.

A DETAILED STUDY

Read Text B on page 21 again and answer the following questions.

1 Where is the idea of new possibilities for writers mentioned?

  a Paragraph 1

  b Paragraph 2

  c Paragraph 3

  d Paragraph 4

2 Where does the author discuss how publishers have adapted to new conditions?

  a Paragraph 1

  b Paragraph 2

  c Paragraph 3

  d Paragraph 4

3 Where does the author first describe how e-books might affect reading habits?

  a Paragraph 1

  b Paragraph 2

  c Paragraph 3

  d Paragraph 4

4 Where is the relationship between authors of e-books and their publishers discussed?

   a Paragraph 1

   b Paragraph 2

   c Paragraph 3

   d Paragraph 4

5 Where does the author make a prediction about the sales of e-books and traditional books?

   a Paragraph 1

   b Paragraph 2

   c Paragraph 3

   d Paragraph 4

Now check your answers.

MULTIPLE-CHOICE, CHOOSE MULTIPLE ANSWERS

A Read the text and answer the question by selecting all the correct responses.
More than one response is correct.

The *flaneur* is almost extinct now. It is not just that men – and they usually were men – no longer have the time or the inclination to idly stroll the city streets, taking in the sights and sounds at a leisurely pace while the crowd hurries to and fro about its business. Cities have changed their nature too and, for the most part, people today walk as little as possible.

Baudelaire, the 19ᵗʰ century French poet, was probably the first to describe the *flaneur* in his essay *The Painter of Modern Life*, and he himself would often saunter and loiter in the arcades of Paris absorbing the frantic bustle going on around him. The *flaneur* is the detached, ironic observer in the midst of the crowd, rambling through the city seeing where the streets take him. There is no specific aim in mind; it is not like the evening promenade that still occurs in many Mediterranean towns, where the purpose is to see and be seen. Besides, promenaders usually amble arm in arm with a chaperone. The *flaneur* is a solitary walker.

As mentioned above, cities have changed and are far less congenial for walking nowadays. Baudelaire's Paris of arcades and narrow, crooked streets disappeared with Baron Haussmann's wholesale redevelopment of the city. These days, despite the provision of public spaces such as parks, city dwellers would rather go to the countryside, and hike up and down hills and valleys where the air is fresh and there are no crowds.

Which of the following words have the same meaning in the passage as "walk"?

1 pace	**3** saunter	**5** promenade	**7** loiter
2 amble	**4** bustle	**6** stroll	

B Read the text and answer the question by selecting all the correct responses.
More than one response is correct.

What do we mean by the term "intellectual", and what is a "public intellectual"? It is an odd fact of English culture that it is largely a term of abuse and, when asked to name one, we almost always turn to the continent, particularly France. A typical intellectual in France, we think, will hold down a job as a professor – preferably of philosophy – have a column in a mass circulation daily newspaper, be involved in politics and appear on the cover of *Vogue*.

Our aversion to intellectuals, or to the term, may go back to when we were at school where nobody likes a "swot". In fact, almost any kind of braininess is disparaged: scientists are mad-haired "boffins", tech-savvy kids are "nerds", and people can be "too clever by half". Indeed, we would claim that we are naturally practical thinkers and too full of common sense to produce such highbrows – a situation not helped by many of the people who we consider to be intellectuals denying the fact.

One problem is that of definition: what qualifications are required and what sort of activities does someone have to engage in before they can be called an intellectual? One possible definition is that public intellectuals should be independent of those in power and critical of received ideas. Furthermore, he or she must be someone who raises embarrassing questions in public, contests dogma, and who cannot be persuaded to join governments or corporations.

Let's take a thinker from last century whose theories still have an impact today and see if the definition fits: John Maynard Keynes was an economist who worked for the Treasury and wrote influential books on monetary policy, an art collector, and a member of the Bloomsbury group of writers, artists and intellectuals. Perhaps we need to adjust our definition slightly!

According to the text, which of the following are true of English attitudes towards intellectuals?

1 They never join forces with those in authority.

2 Most people would not be able to name an intellectual.

3 In general, the English do not admire/respect intellectuals.

4 Even some English intellectuals do not like to be called intellectuals.

5 They are not clear about what an intellectual is or does.

RE-ORDER PARAGRAPHS

> **ON-SCREEN**
>
> Remember that in the exam, you will re-order the paragraphs
> by dragging and dropping them with your mouse.

A The paragraphs have been placed in a random order. Restore the original order.

Jumbled paragraphs	Correct paragraph order (1–4)
a The construction of new houses came to a standstill during the war, and this, together with growing demand, led to an estimated shortage of close to a million houses when the war was over.	
b In the absence of housing regulations, including the availability of loans to the less well-off, poor-quality housing was built by private enterprise to meet the growing demand at rents that people could afford.	
c Before the First World War, most housing in Britain was provided on a rental basis as the cost of housing was beyond the means of the average family and mortgages were hard to come by.	
d This created a dilemma, since wartime inflation had pushed up wages and the cost of building materials with the result that private enterprise was no longer able to provide the houses needed at rents which people could afford.	

B The paragraphs have been placed in a random order. Restore the original order.

Jumbled paragraphs	Correct paragraph order (1–4)
a Others, however, believe that the fossil evidence suggests that, at various stages in the history of life, evolution progressed rapidly, in spurts, and that major changes occurred at these points.	
b An evolving group may have reached a stage at which it had an advantage over other groups and was able to exploit new niches in nature. Climate change may also have produced a "spurt", as might the extinction of other groups or species, leaving many niches vacant.	

c Today, many years later, many believe that evolution has progressed at the same steady rate and that the absence of transitional forms can be explained by Darwin's argument that there are huge gaps in the fossil record and that transition usually occurred in one restricted locality.	
d Paleontologists still argue about the origins of major groups, though new fossil finds since Darwin's time have cleared up many of the disparities in the fossil record. Even during Darwin's lifetime, some transitional forms were found.	

C The paragraphs have been placed in a random order. Restore the original order.

Jumbled paragraphs	Correct paragraph order (1–4)
a One of the Tibetan names for this mountain translates as "Mountain So High That No Bird Can Fly Over It". It was first measured in 1852 and was called Peak XV until 1865, when it was named after the British Surveyor of India, Sir George Everest.	
b About 200 million years ago, the Indian subcontinent broke away from a vast southern super-continent called Gondwanaland. It drifted north-east across the sea and collided with the Asian landmass. These two huge landmasses buckled, rather like cars in a head-on collision, and rose up to form the world's tallest mountain.	
c Mapping the Himalayas and Everest wasn't easy. Foreigners were not welcome, so Himalayan traders were recruited to infiltrate the area and gather enough information to allow accurate maps to be made.	
d Fossilized fish remains have been found high up on the slopes of Everest proving that the world's highest mountain once lay at the bottom of the sea. How did this happen?	

For Further Guidance, see page 28.

RE-ORDER PARAGRAPHS

WHAT'S TESTED

The purpose of this task is to assess your ability to understand the organization and cohesion of an academic text. The texts are up to 150 words long and are divided into either four or five paragraphs that have been placed in random order. You will arrange the paragraphs in the correct order by dragging them on-screen. There are either two or three texts. The individual texts are not timed; you will have a fixed time of between 32 and 41 minutes to complete the entire Reading part, depending on which form of the PTE Academic you receive.

TIPS

- Skim each of the paragraphs to get a general idea of the topic.
- Identify the paragraph that is the topic paragraph or main idea. This probably goes first.
- Note any paragraphs that begin with conjunctions such as *However, Nevertheless, But, Also, Furthermore,* and so on. Such sentences cannot go first.
- Paragraphs that contain pronouns such as *he, she, it, they, them* are probably referring to something mentioned in an earlier paragraph.
- Look for any obvious clues to the logical order or chronology of events, for example, sequencing words such as *first, second, lastly, finally, next, then, after,* and so on.
- Keep track of your time using the on-screen timer.

A DETAILED STUDY

The exercise below will help you focus on how to place jumbled paragraphs of text in the correct order. Look at Text A on page 26 again and answer the following questions.

1 Which paragraph definitely cannot go first? Why?

....

2 Which paragraph probably goes first? Why?

....

3 Which paragraph most logically goes second? Why?

....

4 Which paragraph most logically goes third? Why?

....

5 Which paragraph most logically goes last? Why?

....

Now check your answers.

READING: FILL IN THE BLANKS

> **ON-SCREEN**
> Remember that in the exam, you will fill the blanks by
> dragging and dropping the words with your mouse.

A In the text below some words are missing. Choose the correct word to fill each blank from the box below. There are more words than you need to complete the exercise.

This exciting new M.A. in Creative Writing is designed for graduates who wish to examine and expand their work. Through workshops, seminars, and **(1)** .... tutorials, students will discover new writing strategies and refine their writing. The course **(2)** .... students the practical expertise needed for researching and structuring texts, and **(3)** .... traditions and genres, as well as the critical and creative proficiencies **(4)** .... to develop a career in creative writing or in a related **(5)** ....

single	understanding	field	individual	offers	necessary	wanted

B In the text below some words are missing. Choose the correct word to fill each blank from the box below. There are more words than you need to complete the exercise.

As we know from tsunamis, when water is moving at 50 or 60 kilometers an hour it becomes deadly. Even if a wave only **(1)** .... up to the knees, the **(2)** .... can knock a person down. Water flows around some obstacles, while slamming into large **(3)** .... , such as walls, which stand in its way. It also gathers **(4)** .... , like rocks and trees, as it flows, causing even more destruction when it crashes into buildings.

energy	materials	objects	force	rise	debris	comes	rubbish

C In the text below some words are missing. Choose the correct word to fill each blank from the box below. There are more words than you need to complete the exercise.

Wind-blown **(1)** .... of sand from dunes may carry far inland, covering fields and diverting streams. More seriously, drifting sands can bury whole buildings and transform **(2)** .... land into desert. However, dunes can be made more stable by the artificial **(3)** .... of marram grass, a plant so robust that it can find **(4)** .... even in sand. The grass spreads over the **(5)** .... of the dune, protecting it against wind, while its roots bind the sand together.

summit	grains	rich	fertile	surface	nourishment	clouds	planting

D In the text below some words are missing. Choose the correct word to fill each blank from the box below. There are more words than you need to complete the exercise.

Employers often offer employees perks in addition to cash wages, for example, membership of a health insurance or company pension **(1)** .... If they do, they must **(2)** .... that they are fair in providing these benefits in order to **(3)** .... discrimination. For instance, if an employer **(4)** .... an entitlement to low-interest loans in male, but not female, employees' contracts, the female employees could take the employer to court on the basis of unequal **(5)** ....

consideration	avoid	allowance	scheme	treatment	includes	allows	ensure

E In the text below some words are missing. Choose the correct word to fill each blank from the box below. There are more words than you need to complete the exercise.

Thomas De Quincey once said that there is no such thing as forgetting – a rather frightening **(1)** .... If we could remember everything all the time, not to **(2)** .... those things we feel **(3)** .... or guilty about, life would be unbearable. Naturally, we remember shocking and dramatic events better than any **(4)** .... The things we most often forget are names, numbers, dates, **(5)** .... learned by cramming for exams, and things we don't understand.

others	say	mention	information	ashamed	know-how	theory	thought

READING AND WRITING: FILL IN THE BLANKS

> **ON-SCREEN**
> Remember that in the exam, a drop-down menu will appear when you click
> on each blank with your mouse. You will select an answer from each menu.

A Below is a text with blanks. Select the appropriate answer choice for each blank.

Most of us **(1)** .... to have, or like to think we have, a sense of humor. It makes us better
company and is an effective way of dealing with the various annoyances and frustrations that life brings,
whether **(2)** .... by people or by circumstances. We assume that it gives us the ability
to laugh at ourselves, even when others make **(3)** .... of us. Now, what is the difference
between humor and satire, and is it true, as many people seem to think, that humorists are on the whole
optimistic and sympathetic, while satirists are cynical and negative? I will be taking two writers – Henry
Fielding, a writer of comedy, and Jonathan Swift, a satirist – to examine what the differences might be
and how much a comic or satiric view of things is a matter of character and temperament, and to see
how much the lives these two men led coincided with their respective visions. However, first I'd like
to put **(4)** .... a theory of sorts that would seem to reverse the general idea that humor
is a positive and satire a negative view of the world. Humor is a way of accepting things as they are.
Confronted with human stupidity, greed, vice, and so on, you shrug your shoulders, laugh, and carry on.
After all, there is nothing to be done. Human nature is unchanging and we will never reform and improve
ourselves. Satirists, on the other hand, begin with the idea that making fun of the follies of man is a very
(5) .... way of reforming them. Surely, in believing this they, rather than the humorists, are
the optimists, however angry they may be.

1	demand	look	claim	deserve
2	caused	brought	made	effected
3	joke	conversation	fun	entertainment
4	up	in	down	forward
5	handy	effective	decent	logical

B Below is a text with blanks. Select the appropriate answer choice for each blank.

It's a risky, not to say foolhardy, business predicting the future, but some **(1)** .... trends are
so large they are impossible to ignore and the future becomes a little less difficult to see.
(2) .... of what the future might be like for the natural environment include population
(3) .... , acts of environmental vandalism such as deforestation, global warming, and
pollution.

Since the 1960s, the human population has roughly doubled and it is likely to rise by another third by
2030. This will of course lead to increased demands for food, water, energy, and space to live, necessarily
putting us in competition with other species – and, if the past is anything to go by – with obvious results.
Humans already use 40 % of the world's primary production (energy) and this is bound to increase, with
serious consequences for nature. We are fast losing overall biodiversity, including micro-organisms in
the soil and sea, not to mention both tropical and temperate forests, which are **(4)** .... to
maintaining productive soils, clean water, climate regulation, and resistance to disease. It seems we take
these things for granted and governments do not appear to factor them in when making decisions that
affect the environment.

One prediction that has been made is that, in the UK at least, warming and the loss of **(5)** ....
habitats could lead to more continental species coming to live here, and that in towns and cities, we will
have more species that have adapted to urban life and living alongside humans.

1	local	new	typical	global
2	Pointers	Indicators	Signposts	Premonition
3	development	growth	rises	explosion
4	crucial	favorable	decisive	effective
5	unusual	rare	uncommon	human

C Below is a text with blanks. Select the appropriate answer choice for each blank.

In any given population, about ten percent of the people are left-handed and this figure remains relatively **(1)** .... over time. So-called "handedness" **(2)** .... in families, but what causes it and why the proportion of left-handed to right-handed people is a constant are still a mystery.

One thing we do know is that hand dominance is related to brain asymmetry; and it seems to be generally agreed that the human brain is profoundly asymmetric, and that understanding how this works will tell us much about who we are and how our brains work. Brain **(3)** .... is distributed into the left and right hemispheres, and this is crucial for understanding language, thought, memory, and perhaps even creativity. For right-handed people, language activity is mainly on the left side. Many left-handers also have left-side language dominance, but a **(4)** .... number may have language either more evenly distributed in both hemispheres or else predominantly on the right side of the brain.

Because left-handedness is seen as a key to the complex anatomy of the brain, scientists are **(5)** .... for links to other conditions, including immune disorders, learning disabilities, and reduced life expectancy.

1 even	continual	similar	stable
2 happens	is	runs	occurs
3 function	memory	size	capacity
4 maximum	suggestive	significant	countable
5 researching	searching	detecting	inquiring

D Below is a text with blanks. Select the appropriate answer choice for each blank.

Computer viruses have been a **(1)** .... of life at least since the 1980s, if not before. They can cause companies to lose hours of working time and they can also spread panic among computer users everywhere. There are, however, several **(2)** .... types of computer infection – all loosely referred to as viruses – and they each work in a slightly different way. A particularly nasty one is the *worm*, which is a program designed to sneak its way into an entire computer network, and reproduce itself over and over again. Then there is the *Trojan*, which strictly **(3)** .... isn't a virus, but a piece of software that appears to do one thing, but actually does something malicious instead. When the **(4)** .... operator introduces it into the computer, the alien program will take over the machine. With *Trojans* you have to be particularly careful because they can often be introduced by way of a message advertising an anti-virus product.

So what motivates someone to introduce a virus into the computer systems of innocent victims? Perhaps it's simply the desire to prove that it can be done. Or because it gives the kind of pleasure you get from solving a difficult problem – nowadays people protect their computers with all sorts of security software, so it takes considerable **(5)** .... to break through all the defences and introduce a virus.

1 fact	threat	reality	theory
2 distinct	precise	distinguished	isolated
3 saying	telling	talking	speaking
4 incredulous	unsuspecting	sceptical	ignorant
5 qualifications	courage	skill	gift

For Further Guidance, see page 34.

E Below is a text with blanks. Select the appropriate answer choice for each blank.

Many Utopias have been dreamed up through the ages. From Plato's *Republic* to Thomas More's *Utopia* and beyond, serious thinkers have **(1)** .... societies where people live in peace and harmony. Most of these imaginary worlds have things in common: everybody is equal and plays a part in the running of the society; nobody goes without the **(2)** .... of life; people live mostly off the land; often there is no money, and so on. Another thing they have in common is that, to the average person, they appear distasteful or unworkable since they do not take into account ordinary human nature or feelings.

Architects have got in on the act, too. After the Great Fire of London, Christopher Wren drew up plans for a **(3)** .... of the whole city, including precise street widths. And in the 20th century there was Le Corbusier's *Radiant City* in which, if you weren't in a car or didn't have one, life would have been a nightmare.

Also in the 20th century, another famous architect, Frank Lloyd Wright, dreamed up a perfect city that got no further than the drawing-board. Wright believed that what was wrong with modern cities was, in his words, *rent*. Ideas, land, even money itself, had to be paid for. He saw this as a form of slavery and believed that modern city dwellers had no sense of themselves as productive individuals. Thus, Wright's city was to be made up of numerous individual homesteads, and the houses themselves were to be simple, functional and in **(4)** .... with the environment. Everyone would own enough land to grow food for himself and his family. No outsiders would be allowed to come between the citizen and what he produced, or to **(5)** .... both for money. Goods and services would all be exchanged, not bought and sold for profit.

1	seen	dreamt	envisioned	idealised
2	needs	wants	ingredients	essentials
3	redecoration	rearrangement	reconstruction	recomposition
4	contact	harmony	peace	community
5	usurp	rob	exploit	corrupt

F Below is a text with blanks. Select the appropriate answer choice for each blank.

It is surprising how many people still believe that advertising has little or no influence on what they buy. It is more surprising still when these same people **(1)** .... to using a particular brand of, say, washing powder, toothpaste or cigarettes, and say they wouldn't change if you paid them – even after they've been shown that another brand is either just the same, better or cheaper. The fact is, people **(2)** .... themselves that they have never *consciously* made a deliberate decision to buy a product based on an advertisement they have seen. They may, however, own up to doing so when they come to buy a product they have never owned before and shop around for the best **(3)** ....

But there's no **(4)** .... away from ads. They're everywhere, and they're designed very cleverly and carefully to play on your emotions. And it works: you remember the ads that make you laugh, or feel sad, or simply annoy you. Often you find yourself buying something simply – you tell yourself – to try it out, but how did this brand of this product get into your head? Another reason for supposing advertising works is the question: why would so many hard-headed business people spend so much money on something that didn't?

1	divulge	reveal	admit	declare
2	believe	persuade	confess	credit
3	money	saving	package	deal
4	escaping	getting	breaking	going

FILL IN THE BLANKS

WHAT'S TESTED

The purpose of this task is to assess your ability to analyze contextual cues to correctly complete incomplete sentences in an academic reading text. The texts are up to 300 words long and cover a variety of academic topics. Each text has up to six blanks; each blank can have up to five options. For each blank, you have to choose the option that best completes the sentence. You will read either five or six texts. The individual texts are not timed; you will have a fixed amount of time of between 32 and 41 minutes to complete the entire Reading part, depending on which form of the PTE Academic you receive.

TIPS

- Skim the text, skipping over the blanks, to get an idea of its general content and the main idea. You should be able to answer the question *"What is the passage mainly about?"* in your own words.

- Read the first sentence containing a blank carefully. Using vocabulary and grammatical cues from the words surrounding the blank, determine what kind of word is needed – that is, what part of speech is required (e.g., adjective, adverb, plural noun, preposition). Check the options and eliminate any that are clearly the wrong part of speech. Choose from among what remains.

- Look for any obvious clues to the logical order or chronology of events, such as *first, second, lastly, finally, next, then, after*, and so on, and eliminate any answer options that are illogical. Choose from among what remains.

- Some items test your knowledge of idioms and collocations. Check whether any of the options form a common expression, and if so, whether this makes sense in the given context.

- If you do not know the answer, and are unable to eliminate any options, guess. Never leave the question unanswered. If you leave the question unanswered, it will be marked as incorrect. By guessing, you have the possibility of answering correctly.

- Keep track of your time using the on-screen timer.

A DETAILED STUDY

The exercise below will help you to understand all of the answer options for Text D on page 32. For each group of sentences, select the appropriate word from the box for each blank. If you are unsure about which word to choose, refer to the text before and after the blank for clues.

fact   threat   reality   theory

1   The authorities said the

chemicals didn't pose a .... to life.

2   We have to take into account the .... of the situation.

3   I know that what you say is true in .... , but will it work in practice?

4   Sadly, it seems that crime is just a .... of life these days.

distinct   precise   distinguished   isolated

5 Dr. Cho's team reports that they have successfully .... the gene that causes the disease.

6 English essayist Joseph Addison famously wrote, "Man is .... from all other creatures by the faculty of laughter."

7 He was .... with his language, choosing his words carefully.

8 While there are two types of camels, both are quite ....

saying   telling   talking   speaking

9 Mr. Harris is not an employee here, strictly .... , but we do hire him quite often on a freelance basis.

10 I keep .... them my answer is no!

11 Maria was .... she might go to UCLA next semester.

12 Our professor is quite strict and there's definitely no .... during his classes.

incredulous   unsuspecting   sceptical   ignorant

13 Credit card information is captured from .... customers who swipe their cards in what they believe to be an ordinary machine.

14 When Jack said he'd seen an alien, I was absolutely ....

15 It's not that he's unintelligent – he's simply .... in that particular area.

16 Mark offered his version of the events, but I have to say I'm .... about it.

qualifications   courage   skill   gift

17 I thought you showed a lot of .... when you told the boss she was wrong.

18 It takes considerable .... to ride a unicycle while juggling four balls!

19 You've got a real .... for explaining things in a simple way.

20 My dad left school at 16 and doesn't have any ....

Now check your answers.

PART 3: LISTENING

SECTION 1: SUMMARIZE SPOKEN TEXT

A You will hear a short lecture. Write a summary for a fellow student who was not present at the lecture. You should write 50–70 words.

You will have 10 minutes to finish this task. Your response will be judged on the quality of your writing and on how well your response presents the key points presented in the lecture.

1.9 Play the CD to listen to the recording that goes with this item.

....

....

....

....

....

....

....

B You will hear a short lecture. Write a summary for a fellow student who was not present at the lecture. You should write 50–70 words.

You will have 10 minutes to finish this task. Your response will be judged on the quality of your writing and on how well your response presents the key points presented in the lecture.

1.10 Play the CD to listen to the recording that goes with this item.

....

....

....

....

....

....

....

C You will hear a short lecture. Write a summary for a fellow student who was not present at the lecture. You should write 50–70 words.

You will have 10 minutes to finish this task. Your response will be judged on the quality of your writing and on how well your response presents the key points presented in the lecture.

1.11 Play the CD to listen to the recording that goes with this item.

....

....

....

....

....

....

....

For Further Guidance, see page 37.

SUMMARIZE SPOKEN TEXT

WHAT'S TESTED

The purpose of this task is to assess your ability to write a summary of a spoken academic lecture. Both listening and writing skills are assessed. There are either two or three lectures; the number depends on which form of the PTE Academic you are given. There will always be at least two. The lectures are between 60 and 90 seconds long. After each lecture ends, you will have 10 minutes to write a summary of what you have heard. Your summary must be between 50 and 70 words. The test automatically advances to the next lecture after 10 minutes.

TIPS

- The aim of the task is to write a summary for a fellow student who was absent from the lecture. Your summary should convey the key points.

- Pay careful attention to the on-screen word counter. Write between 50 and 70 words only. If you write either fewer or more, your score will be decreased. If you write fewer than 40 or more than 100, your score will be zero.

- Take notes. Use the Erasable Noteboard Booklet and pen provided. Do not try to write down every word you hear. Unless you are able to write quickly and accurately, you will probably fall behind and miss important information. Instead, focus on key words.

- Writing quickly is a key skill to master. Use abbreviations whenever possible. Ignore articles (e.g., *a, an, the*) unless they are necessary. Omitting the vowels from words is one way to increase writing speed.

- Key words include names, numbers, dates, times, and words and phrases that are stressed. Words and phrases that are repeated are usually central to the main idea.

- Focus on understanding the main idea of the lecture and the key points that support it. If the speaker draws a conclusion, be sure you have identified it. Try to identify the overall purpose of the lecture.

- Begin to review your notes and organize your summary as soon as the lecture ends. You will have 10 minutes to complete your summary. Pay attention to the on-screen timer, and manage your time wisely.

- Because you are limited to no more than 70 words, your summary must focus on key concepts and their supporting points. Avoid adding irrelevant details.

- Use standard spelling and punctuation. Do not use Internet or texting abbreviations (e.g., **LOL**) or emoticons (;-)) in your summary. Do not write everything in capital letters.

A DETAILED STUDY

The exercise below will help you take notes and summarize spoken text. Listen to each of the following extracts from a lecture in turn. Make notes as you listen. At the end of each extract, pause the CD and use your notes to summarize the extract in your own words.

🔘 **1.12 Play the CD to listen to the recording that goes with this item.**

Extract 1:

....

....

....

Extract 2:

....

....

....

Extract 3:

....

....

....

Now check your answers.

SECTION 2: MULTIPLE-CHOICE, CHOOSE MULTIPLE ANSWERS

A Listen to the recording and answer the question by selecting all the correct responses. You will need to select more than one response.

Which of the following are mentioned as influences on the English landscape garden?

1 The poet Alexander Pope

2 The Romantic Movement

3 A person's political affiliations

4 Italian classical painting

5 Gardens from classical Greece and Rome

 1.13 Play the CD to listen to the recording that goes with this item.

B Listen to the recording and answer the question by selecting all the correct responses. You will need to select more than one response.

Which of these countries still use woodblock printing on fabrics?

1 Japan

2 Peru

3 India

4 Egypt

5 China

6 Mexico

 1.14 Play the CD to listen to the recording that goes with this item.

C Listen to the recording and answer the question by selecting all the correct responses. You will need to select more than one response.

Which of the countries listed below continue to enforce punishments for failure to vote?

1 France

2 Bolivia

3 the UK

4 Australia

5 Austria

6 Greece

 1.15 Play the CD to listen to the recording that goes with this item.

SECTION 2: FILL IN THE BLANKS

A You will hear a recording. Write the missing words in each blank.

Almost everyone has heard of the London Stock Exchange, but **(1)** .... few know anything about the London Metal and Commodity Exchanges – yet these markets have a greater **(2)** .... on world economies because they set global prices for some of the essential raw materials for industry and food **(3)** ....

The LME provides three basic services to the world's non-ferrous metal trade. First, it is a market where large or small **(4)** .... of metal of a guaranteed minimum standard can be bought and sold on specific trading days. Second, it acts as a barometer of world metal prices. And third, it is a "hedging" medium: that is, it can help traders get some protection from price fluctuations that occur for economic, political or **(5)** .... reasons.

1.16 Play the CD to listen to the recording that goes with this item.

B You will hear a recording. Write the missing words in each blank.

It isn't necessary to have a **(1)** .... knowledge of, say, the intricacies of counterpoint, or even to be able to read music to understand it. Usually, getting the point of a piece of music, its emotional and dramatic **(2)** .... , is immediate or simply requires you to become more **(3)** .... with it. Of course, prolonged study of music and its **(4)** .... , as in any other field, will increase your understanding, but not necessarily your enjoyment. Now, I realize that it can require a good deal of willingness on our part to risk new sensations, and there is a lot of music that will seem unfamiliar and alien to you on a first **(5)** ....

1.17 Play the CD to listen to the recording that goes with this item.

C You will hear a recording. Write the missing words in each blank.

Before farming was introduced into Scotland, people lived by hunting, fishing, and **(1)** .... wild foodstuffs. This way of life meant that they usually didn't settle **(2)** .... in one place, but were to an extent nomadic, moving about in search of a livelihood, perhaps returning to the same places at certain times of the year. It is believed that the islands of Orkney were known to these people, but, so far, only a few flint **(3)** .... have been found to verify this. This is because coastal **(4)** .... has destroyed many ancient sites and these may have contained relics of some of these earliest pioneering **(5)** ....

1.18 Play the CD to listen to the recording that goes with this item.

SECTION 2: HIGHLIGHT CORRECT SUMMARY

A You will hear a recording. Choose the paragraph that best relates to the recording.

1

The speaker tells us that clichés are the enemy of literature and art. They are words, phrases and images that have become stale through overuse and therefore have nothing new to say to us. They are an enemy to clear and original thinking, although they are sometimes useful in advertising to get a simple message across.

2

While clichés in writing reveal lazy thinking and are to be avoided at all costs, in the graphic arts they become essential, helping to get the message across quickly, clearly and with emotional force. This is especially true of advertising and propaganda where the impact must be immediate.

3

Clichés are worn out, overused and over-familiar phrases, and the etymology of the word helps to explain this. Originally, a cliché or stereotype was a printer's term for a pre-set block of type with phrases used frequently in the newspapers. The word has since adopted a negative meaning and careful writers avoid them where they can.

 1.19 Play the CD to listen to the recording that goes with this item.

B You will hear a recording. Choose the paragraph that best relates to the recording.

1

Dolphins, whales and porpoises are all social animals, but some species are more sociable than others. This depends on the environment because a species adopts the lifestyle most suitable for this. Among dolphins, forming groups makes it easier for them to find food, reproduce and gain knowledge. They are safer, too, because dolphins can communicate danger when there are threats around.

2

The speaker explains that whales, dolphins, and porpoises have evolved differently and face different threats. River dolphin numbers are declining, while ocean dolphins are doing well in spite of the threats they face. The reason for this is that ocean dolphins are better adapted for finding food and avoiding predators.

3

Dolphins have adopted group living as a response to living in close contact with other animals in the ocean, some of which kill dolphins for food. Living in social groups makes it easier to hunt for food and, in a dangerous environment, it makes sense in terms of safety to move about in large numbers.

 1.20 Play the CD to listen to the recording that goes with this item.

For Further Guidance, see page 42.

HIGHLIGHT CORRECT SUMMARY

WHAT'S TESTED

The purpose of this task is to assess your ability to correctly identify a written summary of a recording. Both listening and reading skills are assessed. There are either two or three recordings. The recordings are between 30 and 90 seconds long. As the recording is playing, you will be able to read between three and five paragraphs relating to the recording (the number of paragraphs will depend on the specific content of the recording). When the recording has finished, you will choose the paragraph that correctly summarizes the recording you have heard. The individual tasks in Section 2 of the Listening part are not timed; you will have between 23 and 28 minutes to complete all of Section 2 of the Listening part, depending on which form of the PTE Academic you receive.

TIPS

- There is a 10-second pause before the recording begins. Use this time to skim the paragraphs. You will not have enough time to read them in detail, but by skimming them, you will have a better idea of what the recording will be about.

- Take notes. Use the Erasable Noteboard Booklet and pen provided. Do not try to write down every word you hear. Use abbreviations whenever possible. Ignore articles (e.g., *a, an, the*) unless they are necessary.

- Key words include names, numbers, dates, times, and words and phrases that are stressed. Words and phrases that are repeated are usually central to the main idea.

- Focus on understanding the main idea of the recording and on the key points that support it. If the speaker draws a conclusion, be sure you have identified it. Try to identify the overall purpose of the lecture.

- After the recording has finished, read each paragraph carefully. Eliminate any paragraphs that contain incorrect information or that contain information that was not mentioned in the recording. Eliminate paragraphs that do not contain the main points.

- If you do not know the answer, and are unable to eliminate any of the paragraphs, guess. Never leave the question unanswered. If you leave the question unanswered, it will be marked as incorrect. By guessing, you have the possibility of guessing correctly.

- Keep track of your time using the on-screen timer.

A DETAILED STUDY

The exercise below will help you identify the correct summary by focusing on information presented in the recording. Listen to Lecture B from page 41 again and answer the following multiple-choice questions. Then compare the information in each of the summary paragraphs on page 41 with your answers.

(🅟) **1.20 Play the CD to listen to the recording that goes with this item.**

1 The speaker describes whales, dolphins, and porpoises as ....

   a social animals

   b related to each other

2 An animal's group size is said to be related to ....

   a its proximity to other species

   b the environment it lives in

3 River dolphins have ....

   a complex social networks

   b groups of about 10 individuals

4 Oceanic dolphins form ....

   a groups of thousands

   b lifelong pair bonds

5 Sperm whales form groups based on their ....

   a sex and age

   b location

6 The speaker does not mention .... as a reason for forming groups.

   a gaining information

   b shared caring of young

7 The speaker mentions the discovery of a shoal of fish as an example of something that can be ....

   a communicated to a group

   b a sign of an impending attack

8 The speaker mentions a shark as an example of ....

   a an animal that lives alone

   b a predator

Now check your answers.

SECTION 2: MULTIPLE-CHOICE, CHOOSE SINGLE ANSWER

A Listen to the recording and answer the multiple-choice question by selecting the correct response. Only one response is correct.

What made the speaker take up geology as a profession?

1 The fact that he can travel to interesting places.

2 Because he sees geologists as detectives.

3 His childhood interest in fossils.

4 He regards building a picture of an unknown country as exciting work.

 1.21 Play the CD to listen to the recording that goes with this item.

B Listen to the recording and answer the multiple-choice question by selecting the correct response. Only one response is correct.

What is the speaker's view of creative writing classes?

1 In the end they can teach you to write well.

2 There are certain important aspects of writing they can teach.

3 It is better to read well than take writing classes.

4 They aim to develop a love of language in students.

 1.22 Play the CD to listen to the recording that goes with this item.

C Listen to the recording and answer the multiple-choice question by selecting the correct response. Only one response is correct.

What is the speaker's attitude to the report on narcissism?

1 He is amused by it.

2 He doesn't believe any of it is true.

3 He is angered by it.

4 He is skeptical of it.

 1.23 Play the CD to listen to the recording that goes with this item.

SECTION 2: SELECT MISSING WORD

A You will hear a recording about the brain. *At the end of the recording, the last word or group of words has been replaced by a beep.* Select the correct option to complete the recording.

1 ignored people speaking

2 participated in conversations

3 understood spoken language

4 understood foreign languages

5 used language

 1.24 Play the CD to listen to the recording that goes with this item.

B You will hear a recording about money. *At the end of the recording, the last word or group of words has been replaced by a beep.* Select the correct option to complete the recording.

1 notes

2 accounts

3 drafts

4 paper

5 charges

 1.25 Play the CD to listen to the recording that goes with this item.

SECTION 2: HIGHLIGHT INCORRECT WORDS

> **ON-SCREEN**
> Remember that in the exam, you will click on the words that are different with your mouse in order to highlight them in yellow.

A You will hear a recording. Below is a transcription of the recording. Some words in the transcription differ from what the speaker(s) said. As you listen, circle the words that are different.

When the European Economic Community was established in 1957, its aim was, in broad terms, to move towards closer political and economic co-operation. Today, the much bigger European Union has a far-reaching importance on many aspects of our lives, from the conditions we work under, to the safety standards we must adhere to, and the environment in which we live.

In order to achieve the free flow of goods and services, work and capital between the member countries, they needed to establish mutual politics in areas as diverse as agriculture, transport, and working conditions. When they had agreed on these policies, they became legal. Now, though, the EU is concerned with a far wider range of issues.

 1.26 Play the CD to listen to the recording that goes with this item.

B You will hear a recording. Below is a transcription of the recording. Some words in the transcription differ from what the speaker(s) said. As you listen, circle the words that are different.

Stem cells are the body's master cells, the rare material from which we are built. Unlike normal body cells, they can reproduce an indefinite number of times and, when manipulated in the right way, can turn themselves into any sort of cell in the body. The most versatile stem cells are those found in the embryo at just a few days old. This ball of a few dozen stem cells eventually goes on to form everything that makes up a human.

In 1998, James Thompson pronounced that he had isolated human embryonic stem cells in the laboratory. At last, these powerful cells were within the grip of scientists to experiment with, understand, and develop into fixes for the things that go wrong.

 1.27 Play the CD to listen to the recording that goes with this item.

For Further Guidance, see page 47.

SECTION 2: WRITE FROM DICTATION

You will hear some sentences. Write each sentence exactly as you hear it. Write as much of each sentence as you can. You will hear each sentence only once.

 1.28 Play the CD to listen to the recording that goes with this item.

1 ....

2 ....

3 ....

4 ....

HIGHLIGHT INCORRECT WORDS

WHAT'S TESTED

The purpose of this task is to assess your ability to find the differences between a recording and a transcription of the recording. Both listening and reading skills are assessed. There are either two or three recordings. The recordings are between 15 and 50 seconds long. As the recording is playing, you will read a transcription of the recording that contains up to seven words that do not match what the speaker says. You must identify the words that do not match by clicking on them with your mouse to highlight them.

TIPS

- There is a 10-second pause before the recording begins. Use this time to skim the transcription. You will not have enough time to read it in detail, but by skimming it, you will have a better idea of what the recording will be about.

- Before the recording begins, place the cursor on the first word of the transcription so that you are ready to follow the text and click on words that do not match as you listen.

- Watch the timer in the status box so that you will be ready to follow the text as soon as the recording begins.

- When the recording begins, follow the transcription with the cursor. Click on any words that do not match what you hear. Be sure you click ONLY on the words that you are sure are different.

- You will need to be able to read at the same speed that the recording is playing. If you are a naturally slow reader, you will need to practice reading more quickly on-screen.

- If you fall behind, do your best to find where the speaker is in the transcription. If you hear a slight pause, this often – but not always – indicates the speaker has finished one sentence and is about to start the next. In English, sentences always begin with capital letters. Scan the transcription for capitals during the pause.

A DETAILED STUDY

The exercise below will help you practice matching a recording with a transcription. Listen to the recordings while reading the transcriptions. Circle the words in each transcription that do not match the recording.

1　One way to think about voltage is to imaginary it as the pressure that pushes charges along a conductor.

2　The electrical resistance of a conductor would then become a measure of the difficulty of pushing those charges along.

3　Now, if we use an analogy of water flowing in a pipe, a long narrow pipe resists flow more than a short fat one does – a long narrow one has more resisting.

4　Currents work in the similar way: long thin wires have more resistance than do short thick wires.

5　Conversely, short fat wires have least resistance.

🔘 **1.29 Play the CD to listen to the recording that goes with this item.**

Now check your answers.

TEST 2

PART 1: SPEAKING AND WRITING

SECTION 1: PERSONAL INTRODUCTION

Read the prompt below. In 25 seconds, you must reply in your own words, as naturally and clearly as possible. You have 30 seconds to record your response. Your response will be sent together with your score report to the institutions selected by you.

Please introduce yourself. For example, you could talk about one or more of the following:

- Your interests
- Your plans for future study
- Why you want to study abroad
- Why you need to learn English
- Why you chose *this* test

SECTION 2: READ ALOUD

Look at the text below. In 40 seconds, you must read this text aloud as naturally and clearly as possible. You have 40 seconds to read aloud.

(Allow 40 seconds for each separate text.)

A The ritual of the state opening of parliament still illustrates the basis of the British constitution. The sovereignty of the Royal Family has passed to the sovereignty of parliament, leaving the monarchy with the trappings of power, while prime ministers are still denied the kind of status that is given to American and French presidents.

B Most peasants remained self-sufficient and sceptical about money – and with good reason: the triumph of capitalism probably made them worse off. They now had to deal with a centralized imperial state that was collecting tax more efficiently, giving more power to landlords, and slowly reducing customary peasant rights to land and produce.

C Another method governments use to try and influence the private sector is economic planning. For a long time now, socialist and communist states have used planning as an alternative to the price mechanism, organizing production and distributing their resources according to social and strategic needs, rather than based on purely economic considerations.

D Most succulent plants are found in regions where there is little rainfall, dry air, plenty of sunshine, porous soils and high temperatures during part of the year. These conditions have caused changes in plant structures, which have resulted in greatly increased thickness of stems, leaves and sometimes roots, enabling them to store moisture from the infrequent rains.

E Line engraving on metal, which, to a great extent, was a development of the goldsmith's craft of ornamenting armour and precious metals, did not emerge as a print-making technique until well into the 15th century. Copper, the metal mainly used for engraving, was expensive, and engraving itself was laborious and took a long time.

F For the first two or three years after the Second World War, a new title would often sell out within a few months of publication. However, unless public demand for the book was unusually high, they were rarely able to reprint it. With paper stocks strictly rationed, they could not afford to use up precious paper or tie up their limited capital with a reprint.

You can hear model answers on the CD1, track 30.

SECTION 2: REPEAT SENTENCE

You will hear some sentences. Please repeat each sentence exactly as you hear it. You will hear each sentence only once.

 1.31 Play the CD to listen to the recording that goes with this item.

For Further Guidance, see page 49.

REPEAT SENTENCE

WHAT'S TESTED

The purpose of this task is to assess your ability to repeat a sentence exactly as you hear it. Both speaking and listening skills are assessed. You will hear a sentence and must then repeat it. You will hear each sentence only once. You will have 15 seconds to record your response. You will hear 10 to 12 sentences.

TIPS

- Try to imagine who the speaker is and to whom he or she is speaking. What is the context in which the sentence might be spoken?

- Focus on the meaning of the sentence. What is the main point of the message? What are the important words?

- Listen for "chunks" of language, phrases or groups of words that commonly go together.

- If you cannot repeat the entire sentence, repeat as much of it as you can. It is better to repeat part of the sentence than to remain silent. If all you hear are isolated words, say those. Try to connect them grammatically as best you can.

A DETAILED STUDY

The exercises below will help you to practice listening carefully to and accurately repeating spoken sentences.

A You will hear eight sentences. First, cover all the answer options below with a piece of paper. Then, after hearing each sentence, uncover the two answer options and circle the sentence you heard.

 1.32 Play the CD to listen to the recording that goes with this item.

1

   a The courses you choose can also have a great effect on you.

   b Of course, you can also choose to have your grades e-mailed to you.

2

   a Does the professor keep them or are they ours?

   b Does the professor keep regular office hours?

3

   a I'll check again, but I'm pretty sure we were supposed to read that chapter, too.

   b I'll check again, but I'm pretty sure we're supposed to read Chapter Two.

4

   a I think the university's main campus is closed.

   b I think the university's main campus is close.

5

   a If your parents come to visit you this semester, where will they stay?

   b If your parents came to visit you this semester, where would they stay?

6

   a When I was in school, I had many of the same problems you do now.

   b When I was in school, I had many of the same professors you do now.

7

   a I thought the mid-term exam would cover only the first half of the course.

   b I thought the mid-term exam was worth only half our course grade.

8

   a Many of the most popular courses are available online.

   b Many of the most popular courses aren't available online.

Now check your answers.

B Now listen to the sentences again. Repeat each sentence exactly as you hear it. Concentrate on imitating the speed, rhythm, and stress of the speaker.

SECTION 2: DESCRIBE IMAGE

A Look at the pie chart below. Describe in detail what the pie chart is showing. You will have 40 seconds to give your response.

Amount of time on average spent in consultation with local doctor (GP) (hrs / year)

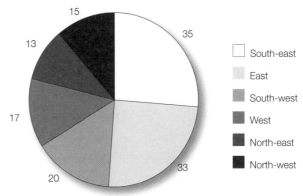

- □ South-east
- ▒ East
- ▒ South-west
- ▓ West
- ▓ North-east
- ■ North-west

B Look at the graph below. Describe in detail what the graph is showing. You will have 40 seconds to give your response.

Average number of students late for college

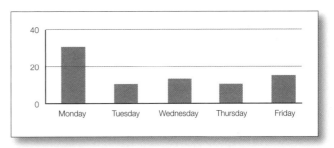

C Look at the table below. Describe in detail what the table is showing. You will have 40 seconds to give your response.

Time spent on main activities: by sex, 2005, GB

	Hours and minutes per day	
	Males	Females
Sleep	8.04	8.18
Resting	0.43	0.48
Personal care	0.40	0.48
Eating and drinking	1.25	1.19
Leisure		
Watching TV/DVD and listen to radio/music	2.50	2.25
Social life and entertainment/culture	1.22	1.32
Hobbies and games	0.37	0.23
Sport	0.13	0.07
Reading	0.23	0.26
All leisure	5.25	4.53
Employment and study	3.45	2.26
Housework	1.41	3.00
Childcare	0.15	0.32
Voluntary work and meetings	0.15	0.20
Travel	1.32	1.22
Other	0.13	0.15

Notes

People aged 16 and over

For Further Guidance, see page 53.

D Look at the graph below. Describe in detail what the graph is showing. You will have 40 seconds to give your response.

Internet access and broadband connections: by households and enterprises, 2006

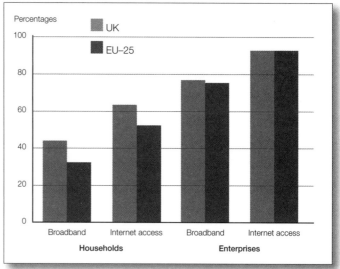

E Look at the graph below. Describe in detail what the graph is showing. You will have 40 seconds to give your response.

Components of population change, United Kingdom, mid-1998 to mid-2010

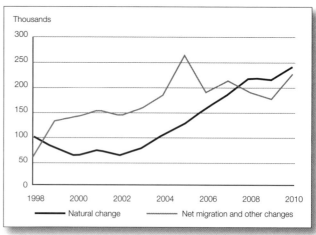

F Look at the pie chart below. Describe in detail what the pie chart is showing. You will have 40 seconds to give your response.

How much of their reading time do students spend on different forms of reading?

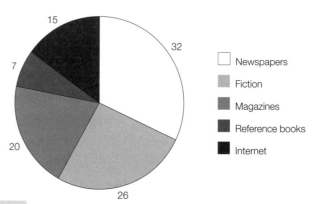

You can hear model answers on the CD1, track 33.

DESCRIBE IMAGE

A DETAILED STUDY

The exercises below will help you to practice describing a table.

A Look at Image C on page 51 again and answer the following questions.

1 What kind of image is it?

....

2 What is the image mainly showing?

....

3 What general trend does the image show?

....

4 Which category shows the largest difference, and how large is the difference?

....

B The following is a transcript of a summary describing what Image C on page 51 shows. Choose the correct word to fill each blank from the box below. There are more words than you need to complete the exercise. Refer to Image C if you need help.

The table **(1)** .... how males and females over age sixteen spend their time doing various activities each day. For **(2)** .... , it shows how much time they spend sleeping, eating, watching TV, and so **(3)** .... For most activities, men and women spend **(4)** .... the same amount of time. Men spend about 5.25 hours on leisure activities, while women spend 4.53. The biggest difference is **(5)** .... for housework. Women spend three hours a day doing housework on **(6)** .... , whereas men spend just 1.41 hours.

```
    explanation    average    compares    near    on    seen

       instance    does    provides    there    approximately
```

Now check your answers.

SECTION 2: RE-TELL LECTURE

A You will hear a lecture. After listening to the lecture, please retell what
you have just heard from the lecture in your own words. You will have
40 seconds to give your response.

Alexis de Tocqueville

 1.34 Play the CD to listen to the recording that goes with this item.

B You will hear a lecture. After listening to the lecture, please retell what
you have just heard from the lecture in your own words. You will have
40 seconds to give your response.

 1.35 Play the CD to listen to the recording that goes with this item.

C You will hear a lecture. After listening to the lecture, please retell what
you have just heard from the lecture in your own words. You will have
40 seconds to give your response.

 1.36 Play the CD to listen to the recording that goes with this item.

You can hear model answers on the CD1, track 37.

SECTION 2: ANSWER SHORT QUESTION

You will hear some questions. Please give a simple and short answer to each one. Often just one or a
few words is enough.

 1.38 Play the CD to listen to the recording that goes with this item.

For Further Guidance, see page 55.

ANSWER SHORT QUESTION

WHAT'S TESTED

The purpose of this task is to assess your ability to understand a spoken question and to give a brief response. Both listening and speaking skills are assessed. You will hear a brief question; some questions may also be accompanied by an image related to the question. After you hear the question, you will have 10 seconds to give your answer. There are 10 to 12 questions.

TIPS

- Listen carefully to identify the topic of the question.

- Keep your answer brief. Often, just one or a few words are required to answer correctly.

- Listen carefully for question words (e.g., *who, what, where, why, when, how*). These will give you clues as to what kind of answer is expected. For example, the answer to a *who* question will involve a person, a *when* question will involve a timeframe, a *why* question will need a reason, a *where* question will involve a location, and so on.

- Some questions ask you to make a choice from among options that are given in the question. For example, if you hear a list of items (e.g., *... X, Y, and Z ...*) you are probably being asked to choose one of them. Questions with *which* or *or* in them are also most likely asking you to make a choice from among the options mentioned.

- Some questions are posed as open-ended statements. For example: *There are two main types of sporting contest. One is for amateurs, the other is for ...* Your answer should complete the statement.

A DETAILED STUDY

The exercise below will help you to practice answering short questions. First read the answer options below. Then listen to ten questions. Write each question number (1–10) next to the correct answer. You will not use all of the answer options.

A the top of a volcano	☐	**K** a dry cleaner's	☐
B a clothing store	☐	**L** midday	☐
C chicken	☐	**M** a refrigerator	☐
D crooks	☐	**N** a tropical forest	☐
E in the ocean	☐	**O** farmers	☐
F sunrise	☐	**P** a microwave oven	☐
G the police	☐	**Q** a bridge	☐
H eggs	☐	**R** grocery stores	☐
I an iron	☐	**S** a needle and thread	☐
J an island	☐	**T** a stream	☐

🄯 **1.39 Play the CD to listen to the recording that goes with this item.**

Now check your answers.

SECTION 3: SUMMARIZE WRITTEN TEXT

Read the passage below and summarize it using one sentence. You have 10 minutes to finish this task. Your response will be judged on the quality of your writing and on how well your response presents the key points in the passage.

It wasn't until the 19th century that Britain had a police force as we know it today. In medieval times, the maintenance of law and order was in the hands of local nobles and lords who were expected to keep the peace in their own land, and they would often appoint "constables" to police it. For a long time policing remained an unpaid activity or was paid for privately, either by individuals or organizations. There were also people who made a living as "thief takers". They were not paid wages, but were rewarded by a proportion of the value of the stolen possessions they recovered. Later, in London, where the population was rapidly increasing and crime was rising, night-watchmen – the first paid law enforcement body – were created and worked alongside the unpaid, part-time constables.

Britain, then, was slower to create and develop a police force than the rest of Europe: France had one long before – indeed, the word *police* is taken from the French. This fact was not unimportant, as the very idea of a police force was seen as foreign – that is, French – and particularly undesirable, and was generally regarded as a form of oppression.

It was not until Robert Peel set up his "new police" as a separate force in 1829 that policemen began to replace the old part-time constables. Sir Robert "Bobby" Peel's own name provided two common nicknames for the new force: "Peelers" or "Bobbies". These names seem mild, if not affectionate, and are possibly an interesting gauge of how the police were viewed by people at the time, in contrast with the kind of names they get called these days.

....

....

....

SECTION 4: SUMMARIZE WRITTEN TEXT

Read the passage below and summarize it using one sentence. You have 10 minutes to finish this task. Your response will be judged on the quality of your writing and on how well your response presents the key points in the passage.

Many people have problems with irony, both in their everyday lives and as it is used or deployed in literature. We learn early on at school about "dramatic irony", that is, we are told, when the audience of a play is aware of some situation or circumstance, or has information that one or more characters in the play do not. If you like, you are sharing a secret with the writer – you are in the know. Perhaps, as you go about your daily business, irony is not so clear-cut.

Here's an example: your neighbour draws your attention to how lovely the dandelions and daisies growing in your lawn are. Now, to someone not familiar with the care and attention many English people give to their gardens, this might need a bit of explanation. Lawns are grass, and are cut and rolled regularly so that a professional golfer could practice his putting on it. Daisies and dandelions are weeds. For a moment – but just for a moment – you wonder how serious your neighbour is being. Does he really think the weeds are lovely or is he telling you – in a rather superior way – that you're a lousy gardener?

Irony, however, usually needs an audience; and not only does it need some people to get the point, it also very much needs there to be people who don't. There is, it has to be said, a rather undemocratic air of superiority about it.

Irony is slippery, sometimes difficult to get a firm hold on, and can easily backfire, like a joke that falls flat. Those who don't like irony – usually those who don't get the point – argue that, in a world that is already difficult enough to deal with, why should we want to complicate things further? Why throw everything you say into doubt? Besides, there's an unpleasant air of intellectual snobbery about it, and that sort of thing doesn't go down well any more.

....

....

....

SECTION 5: WRITE ESSAY

You will have 20 minutes to plan, write and revise an essay about the topic below. Your response will be judged on how well you develop a position, organize your ideas, present supporting details, and control the elements of standard written English. You should write 200–300 words.

It has recently been suggested that the classical, or "dead", languages Latin and Greek should be re-introduced into the school curriculum. Those that oppose the idea claim that the ancient languages are of no practical use and no help in getting a job. Those in favor of the idea say that education is more about training the mind than preparing for a career.

Which of these points of view do you most agree with? Support your argument, where possible, with reasons and/or examples from your own experience and observations.

....
....
....
....
....
....
....
....
....
....

SECTION 6: WRITE ESSAY

You will have 20 minutes to plan, write and revise an essay about the topic below. Your response will be judged on how well you develop a position, organize your ideas, present supporting details, and control the elements of standard written English. You should write 200–300 words.

More and more students are studying at universities abroad, either because it is cheaper, or because they feel they can receive a better education, or because it will provide them with greater professional opportunities.

Discuss the advantages and disadvantages of studying abroad. Support your arguments with reasons and/or examples from your own experience and observations.

....
....
....
....
....
....
....
....
....
....

For Further Guidance, see page 58.

WRITE ESSAY

WHAT'S TESTED

The purpose of this task is to assess your ability to write a persuasive or argumentative essay in response to a prompt. Only writing skills are assessed. You will read an on-screen prompt. You will have 20 minutes to write your response. You will have either one or two essays to write. Your essay must be between 200 and 300 words.

TIPS

- Read the essay prompt carefully. Be sure you understand what you are being asked to write about.

- Use the Erasable Noteboard Booklet and pen provided to make notes and help you plan the organization of your essay.

- Identify the type of essay you have been asked to write and plan accordingly. Common essay types on the PTE Academic include: agreeing or disagreeing with a statement; arguing for or against an opinion or position; describing a situation, occasion or experience; answering a question; and discussing the advantages or disadvantages of an issue.

- Use the on-screen timer to keep track of your remaining time. Remember that you have only 20 minutes to complete the task. Spend no more than 5 minutes planning your essay. Be sure to leave yourself a few minutes to check your essay when you have finished writing it.

- Your essay should be organized into paragraphs. Each paragraph will usually present one main idea which is supported with various arguments and evidence.

- Your first paragraph will typically be an introduction to the topic and will often include a brief description of what will be discussed in the rest of your essay. Your last paragraph will typically end with a conclusion.

- Each paragraph will usually have its own topic sentence. Typically, the topic sentence is the first sentence in the paragraph. The topic sentence usually expresses the paragraph's main idea. The rest of the paragraph generally supports the main idea by presenting a number of arguments, details and other evidence.

- Your essay must be between 200 and 300 words. The on-screen response box has a "Total Word Count" indicator that will tell you how many words you have written. If you are getting close to the word limit, but still need to write more, quickly re-read what you have written and edit out any unnecessary words or phrases.

- Use standard spelling and punctuation. Do not use Internet or texting abbreviations (e.g., **LOL**) or emoticons (**:)**) in your essay. Do not write everything in capital letters.

A DETAILED STUDY

The exercise below will help you to plan an essay. Read the prompt for the essay in Section 6 on page 57 again. Match each paragraph (1–4) to a summary of the possible content of that paragraph (a–g) to create an essay plan. You will not use all of the summaries.

Paragraph 1: ....

Paragraph 2: ....

Paragraph 3: ....

Paragraph 4: ....

a   Your own observations about why so many students are studying abroad these days.

b   A summary of the ways that students can receive a better education, with examples from your own experience.

c   The advantages of studying abroad, supported with reasons and/or examples.

d   Reasons and examples supporting the idea that education can provide students with greater professional opportunities.

e   The disadvantages of studying abroad, supported with reasons and/or examples.

f   A statement of the issue and an indication of what will be discussed in the next paragraph.

g   A summary of the advantages and disadvantages, as they have been described, and a conclusion indicating your own view.

Now check your answers.

PART 2: READING

MULTIPLE-CHOICE, CHOOSE SINGLE ANSWER

A Read the text and answer the multiple-choice question by selecting the correct response. Only one response is correct.

So far, we have been looking at the work of humanist historians in the Renaissance and the new way in which they approached their subject. Not only did they use close reading of ancient texts, as you would expect, but they also did a lot of research in the archives. That is, they didn't just read the historians that came before them, they looked for real documents. For example, they studied the records of cases that went to court, official letters that had survived, and so on to get a fuller picture of how people really lived and went about their business.

These same techniques of historical research were used in what we can call "legal humanism". The idea here was to get as accurate a picture as possible of the law and its practice in ancient, especially Roman, times. Legal historians did this with a view to refining the laws and applying them to the present historical situation. Legal scholarship's original desire to recover and purify the heritage of the ancient world later came to be distorted by political views, but even here, in the 16th century, such intense study could lead to unexpected conclusions. For example, in France, inquiries meant to uncover and apply the legal wisdom of the Romans ended by uncovering a Roman law so pure that it was totally alien. This law, in fact, belonged to the past and to a different society, and was therefore unusable.

What was the ultimate aim of legal scholarship?

1 To purify the ancient legal system.

2 To promote humanism in general.

3 To apply Roman law to their own society.

4 To perfect techniques of historical research.

B Read the text and answer the multiple-choice question by selecting the correct response. Only one response is correct.

When it comes to an organ of such complexity as the eye, it is not difficult to understand why some people cannot accept that such perfection was arrived at by the trial and error, or gradual development, of natural selection. Yet people thought the Earth stood still until Copernicus told them otherwise. In the same way, it shouldn't be hard to believe that a complex eye could be formed by natural selection if it can be shown that there were numerous stages from a simple and imperfect eye to a complex and perfect one, with each development being useful to its possessor and the variations being inherited.

However, the search for the stages through which an organ in any one species has come to perfection, which ideally would mean looking exclusively at its past generations, is rarely possible. Therefore, researchers are forced to examine species and genera of the same group to discover what stages or gradual developments are possible. Even the state of development of the same organ in a different class of creature may throw light on the steps taken towards perfection.

Some people object that in order for the eye to modify and still remain a useful instrument to its owner, many changes would have had to take place simultaneously. However, it is not necessary to suppose this if the modifications were extremely slight and gradual.

Why are researchers forced to look outside a specific species for clues to gradual development?

1 Because the eye is so complex and perfect already.

2 Because evidence of its ancestors is almost impossible to find.

3 Because the eye cannot change without losing its usefulness.

4 Because other species have more complex eyes.

MULTIPLE-CHOICE, CHOOSE MULTIPLE ANSWERS

A Read the text and answer the question by selecting all the correct responses.
More than one response is correct.

A Xhosa bride in southern Africa, in contrast to her western counterpart, is expected to show both reluctance and sadness during her wedding – any signs of joy are considered inappropriate. She may even cry, and not without reason, because she is leaving her own family and relatives to live among a group of strangers where she will have to be careful of what she says and does.

For example, a new bride is not allowed to walk across the central meeting place in the middle of the *kraal*, or village, nor the cattle pen. And when she wishes to go from house to house, she must take the back way. To show respect for her husband's senior relatives, she has to avoid using the names of senior male relatives or even words similar to them, which can lead to some complex paraphrases. Furthermore, she is not allowed to use the personal names of her mother-in-law, nor those of her husband's aunts and elder sisters. Her first priority is the care of her husband, which means doing most of the heavy domestic work. Further constraints are having to wear a handkerchief low over her forehead, never showing her bare head to her husband's relatives, not being allowed to drink milk from the homestead herd, and not touching the drinking utensils.

However, these rules become less strict as time passes. The handkerchief is eventually removed, gifts are exchanged, and family relationships become a bit more relaxed. Finally, there is a ritual killing of a cow and the bride is allowed to drink the milk of the homestead. However, once she has done this, she can no longer drink the milk of her father's house, symbolizing her final separation from her family.

According to the text, which of the following behaviors are expected of a new Xhosa bride?

1 She is not allowed to drink milk from her father's cows.

2 She cannot use the name of any of her husband's male relatives.

3 At her wedding she is meant to appear unwilling.

4 She is not allowed to enter her new home by the front entrance.

5 She must wear a head scarf when meeting her husband's relatives.

6 She is not allowed to touch plates in the family home.

7 She must avoid using the names of some of her husband's female relatives.

B Read the text and answer the question by selecting all the correct responses.
More than one response is correct.

There are perhaps three ways of looking at furniture: some people see it as purely functional and useful, and don't bother themselves with aesthetics; others see it as essential to civilized living and concern themselves with design and how the furniture will look in a room – in other words, function combined with aesthetics; and yet others see furniture as a form of art.

In the past, designers of furniture usually worked for royalty, the nobility, landowners and rich merchants and so were not constrained by the limits of space, economy, or even practicality that inhibit the contemporary designer. Indeed, function was not the first consideration and interiors did not always have to be practical. In the Renaissance, for example, fine furniture and interiors were designed to show off not only the riches of the owners, but their learning, wisdom and good taste as well. No doubt, this attitude still exists among a number of the wealthy.

Apart from a brief period in the 20th century when furniture designers mistook themselves for artists and sculptors, producing, say, chairs that were nice to look at, but impossible to sit on comfortably, modern designers have, for the most part, come to terms with the functional aspect of furniture. These days, a well-designed interior must be practical and exclude what is unnecessary. Limited space must be used imaginatively, and a sense of space and clarity is needed as a setting for efficient living. Therefore, in the modern home, furniture should fulfil a specific purpose, and need as little care and attention as possible. In addition to this, costs must be kept to a minimum because, these days, there are many luxuries competing for our attention. Function and economy, therefore, are of the utmost importance.

According to the text, how does modern furniture design differ from that of the past?

1 Practicality and economy are the most important considerations.

2 Designers are only employed by the wealthy.

3 Designers are primarily concerned with aesthetic appeal.

4 Modern furniture should need little looking after.

5 Making the best use of available space is important.

6 Furniture should be as decorative as possible.

For Further Guidance, see page 63.

MULTIPLE-CHOICE, CHOOSE MULTIPLE ANSWERS

WHAT'S TESTED

The purpose of this task is to assess your ability to read an academic text for a variety of purposes, including reading for the main idea, reading for specific details, reading for the writer's purpose, analyzing discourse, making inferences, assessing the quality and usefulness of the text, and assessing the writer's style. The texts are up to 300 words long and cover a variety of academic topics drawn from the humanities, natural sciences, and social sciences. Each text has one multiple-choice question; there will be between five and seven options to choose from, more than one of which will be correct. You will have either two or three items in this part. The individual questions are not timed; you will have a fixed time of between 32 and 41 minutes to complete the entire Reading part, depending on which form of the PTE Academic you receive.

TIPS

- Read the question before you read the text. This will tell you what information you will be reading for.

- Scan the answer options to further help you focus on the information you will be reading for.

- Skim the text to get an idea of its general content and the main idea. You should be able to answer the question "*What is the passage mainly about?*" in your own words.

- Read the entire text again carefully. Pay attention to details that support the main idea.

- Read the question and the answer options again. Select any correct answers if you know them – remember, there is more than one correct choice. If you are not sure about the answers, eliminate any options that are obviously incorrect and choose from those that remain.

- If you do not know the answers, and are unable to eliminate any choices, guess. Never leave the question unanswered. If you leave the question unanswered, it will be marked as incorrect. By guessing, you have the possibility of answering correctly.

A DETAILED STUDY

The exercise below will help you to practice answering multiple-answer multiple-choice questions. Read Text B on page 61 again and answer the following questions.

1 What does the writer say about economy and practicality in the second paragraph?

  a It constrains modern furniture designers.

  b It was more important for furniture designers in the past.

2 What is implied about the wealthy in the second paragraph?

  a They are willing to pay extra for custom-designed furniture.

  b In the past, only they could afford well-designed furniture.

3 In the third paragraph, what does the writer say is of utmost importance to modern furniture designers?

  a Function and economy.

  b Aesthetics and craftsmanship.

4 According to the writer, what should modern furniture need little of?

   a Function and practicality.

   b Care and attention.

5 What is suggested about space in modern homes?

   a It is limited.

   b It is greater than in the past.

6 What is implied about the decorative aspect of modern furniture?

   a It is less important than function.

   b It is more important than practicality.

Now check your answers.

RE-ORDER PARAGRAPHS

> **ON-SCREEN**
> Remember that in the exam, you will re-order the paragraphs
> by dragging and dropping them with your mouse.

A The paragraphs have been placed in a random order. Restore the original order.

Jumbled paragraphs	Correct paragraph order (1–4)
a *Habeas corpus*, a law by which a prisoner could demand to be brought before the courts and have his case heard, was a well-established right in England, but the authorities had found a number of ways of getting round its use where political prisoners were concerned.	
b The new act put a stop to such abuses and deprived the executive of powers it might have used to support oppressive and arbitrary government.	
c In 1679, what became known as the first Exclusionist Parliament passed at least one useful piece of legislation: on the day parliament was suspended, the King gave his assent to a *Habeas Corpus* Act.	
d James Harrington, the philosopher, is a good example. When his sisters applied for *habeas corpus*, he was taken from the Tower of London to a barren island where *habeas corpus* could not be imposed.	

B The paragraphs have been placed in a random order. Restore the original order.

Jumbled paragraphs	Correct paragraph order (1–4)
a However, the potential for crime is enormous. Some experts believe that American financial systems are losing up to $5 billion a year to computer fraud. Once a hacker has got into the bank's system, he or she can order it to transfer large sums of money to a foreign account.	
b Any computer network connected to the telephone system is vulnerable because the hacker needs only to discover the coded password in order to gain entry to the network. All it takes is intelligent guesswork, trial and error, and perseverance.	

c At first, this appeared to be a perfect example of electronic spying, but it turned out to be a bunch of talented computer buffs doing it for fun. If they had wanted to create real problems, they could have altered files or deleted them altogether.	
d A German student sitting at home at a computer terminal connected to the telephone system managed to hack into NASA's computers and read top secret files. He and a group of other students in Hamburg had also got into about thirty other restricted computer networks.	

C The paragraphs have been placed in a random order. Restore the original order.

Jumbled paragraphs	Correct paragraph order (1–4)
a At the turn of the 19th century, however, only a relatively small sector of the British economy had been directly affected by the Industrial Revolution.	
b For each of the three major countries of western Europe – Britain, France, and Germany – the closing decades of the 18th century were years of increasing economic prosperity, and the pace of economic development in Britain far outdid that of the others.	
c It would be a mistake to call the other two countries underdeveloped – in terms of cultural achievement, especially literature, art, and philosophy, they outstripped Britain – but they lagged behind in terms of economic development.	
d Even two decades later, the picture was little different, except that cotton had become the country's leading manufacturing industry. It was not until the middle of the century that it could be properly described as an industrial society.	

READING: FILL IN THE BLANKS

> **ON-SCREEN**
> Remember that in the exam, you will fill the blanks by
> dragging and dropping the words with your mouse.

A In the text below some words are missing. Choose the correct word to fill each blank from the box below. There are more words than you need to complete the exercise.

This MPhil **(1)** .... students from a wide variety of academic, business and political **(2)** .... to the traditions, methods, and state-of-the-art research that shape an advanced analysis of human society. The MPhil is an eleven-month course designed for those who wish to go on to do doctoral research or **(3)** .... for those who **(4)** .... want to improve their understanding of methodology and analysis, and attain an independent postgraduate degree in its own right.

backgrounds	plainly	equally	professions	introduces	presents	simply

B In the text below some words are missing. Choose the correct word to fill each blank from the box below. There are more words than you need to complete the exercise.

The main **(1)** .... of advertising is to sell **(2)** .... by getting them known and, here, brash, sensational ideas may often serve the **(3)** .... But by no means is all advertising aimed at promoting a new product or even a product at all. One of the most famous posters of the 20th century **(4)** .... Lord Kitchener early in the 1914–18 war pointing a finger, perhaps accusingly, at the entire male military-age population of Britain.

aim	illustrates	products	purpose	point	shows	produces

For Further Guidance, see page 69.

C In the text below some words are missing. Choose the correct word to fill each blank from the box below. There are more words than you need to complete the exercise.

Universities are, of course, the primary centers of intellectual life in modern society. Therefore, they are a **(1)** .... center of criticism: criticism of society and of the dominant **(2)** .... in it, especially its politics, by sections of both the **(3)** .... and the student bodies. This critical **(4)** .... of the university, as the place where ideas are born and where support for criticism is **(5)** .... among students, who form the mass base for many protest movements, has been true for a long time and in many countries.

semester	revealed	key	found	staff	trends	participation	role

D In the text below some words are missing. Choose the correct word to fill each blank from the box below. There are more words than you need to complete the exercise.

When it comes to low-cost housing, architects are hardly ever **(1)** .... About 98% of the market is built without architects and the result is usually rows of clones of a building, regardless of whether they are **(2)** .... for an area or not. Developers alone, without the **(3)** .... of an architect, do not see the big picture needed to make housing part of a safe, vibrant community. A little more thought could instantly improve community **(4)** .... as well as lead to building houses that are both comfortable and cheap.

useful   safety   relations   involved   input   practical   consultation

E In the text below some words are missing. Choose the correct word to fill each blank from the box below. There are more words than you need to complete the exercise.

During the 19th century, the enormous expansion of world production and trade was **(1)** .... mainly by gold. Even the **(2)** .... issued by the banks were fully convertible to gold on demand, and this was the basis of their acceptance. However, production and trade were expanding at a faster **(3)** .... than new **(4)** .... of gold were being discovered. If trade was to continue growing at this rate, some commodity other than gold also had to be used as a **(5)** .... of exchange.

cash   amounts   notes   supplies   way   means   rate   financed

FILL IN THE BLANKS

WHAT'S TESTED

The purpose of this task is to assess your ability to analyze lexical, contextual, and grammatical cues to correctly complete incomplete sentences in an academic reading text. The texts are up to 300 words long and cover a variety of academic topics. There are three to five blanks in each text. The options appear in a separate box; there are always three more options than the number of blanks in the text. There will be a minimum of six and a maximum of eight. The number of blanks and options depends on the nature of the text. For each blank, you have to choose the option that best completes the sentence and drag it to the text with your mouse. You will read either four or five texts. The individual texts are not timed; you will have a fixed time of between 32 and 41 minutes to complete the entire Reading part, depending on which form of the PTE Academic you receive.

TIPS

- Skim the text, skipping over the blanks, to get an idea of its general content and the main idea. You should be able to answer the question *"What is the passage mainly about?"* in your own words.

- Read the first sentence containing a blank carefully. Using vocabulary and grammatical cues provided by the words surrounding the blank, determine what kind of word is needed – that is, what part of speech is required (e.g., adjective, adverb, plural noun, preposition). Check the options and eliminate any that are clearly the wrong part of speech. Choose from among what remains.

- Look for any obvious clues to the logical order or chronology of events, such as *first, second, lastly, finally, next, then, after*, and so on, and eliminate any answer options that are illogical. Choose from among what remains.

- Some items test your knowledge of idioms and collocations. Check whether any of the options form a common expression, and if so, whether this makes sense in the given context.

- If you do not know the answer, and are unable to eliminate any options, guess. Never leave the question unanswered. If you leave the question unanswered, it will be marked as incorrect. By guessing, you have the possibility of answering correctly.

- Keep track of your time using the on-screen timer.

A DETAILED STUDY

The exercise below will help you to use contextual clues to eliminate answer options. Read Text B on page 67 again and answer the following questions.

1 What part of speech must the word in the first blank be?

....

2 Based on your answer to Question 1, which of the answer options cannot go in the first blank?

....

3 What part of speech must the word in the second blank be?

....

4 Based on your answer to Question 3, which of the answer options cannot go in the second blank?

....

5 What word collocates with *sell*?

....

6 What part of speech must the word in the third blank be?

....

7 Based on your answer to Question 6, which of the answer options cannot go in the third blank?

....

8 Is the word that goes in the third blank part of an idiomatic expression? If so, what is the expression?

....

9 What part of speech must the word in the fourth blank be?

....

10 Based on your answer to Question 9, which of the answer options cannot go in the fourth blank?

....

Now check your answers.

READING AND WRITING: FILL IN THE BLANKS

> **ON-SCREEN**
>
> Remember that in the exam, a drop-down menu will appear when you click on each blank with your mouse. You will select an answer from each menu.

A Below is a text with blanks. Select the appropriate answer choice for each blank.

The first printed books began to **(1)** .... during the second quarter of the 15ᵗʰ century. The earliest examples were put together in a number of different ways, sometimes leaving space for decorations and ornate capitals to be **(2)** .... by miniaturist painters, and sometimes containing handwritten text alongside printed illustrations. Most of them had texts and pictures printed **(3)** .... from woodblocks, which is how they got the name "block-books". Printing was normally done on separate leaves which were then bound together in book form.

The obvious advantage of having printed text and visual images together on one sheet was quickly grasped by monks, who saw its **(4)** .... as a means of spreading knowledge, and as an economic and effective way to get their message across to a wide audience. The monasteries, however, by no means had a monopoly on the production and sale of woodcut printing; in fact, probably the most profitable area of European printmaking was the production of playing cards.

Nonetheless, the content of most surviving block-books is essentially biblical. The purpose of the illustrations was functional: to make the meaning of the stories as clear and as understandable as possible to those who were unable to read the often difficult text. It was also a result of the need to **(5)** .... the stories that the characters were presented in contemporary clothes and the illustrations contained details of ordinary life in the late Middle Ages.

1	occur	publish	appear	seem
2	made	printed	copied	added
3	early	entirely	singly	only
4	potential	possibility	advantage	ability
5	simplify	popularize	modernize	improve

B Below is a text with blanks. Select the appropriate answer choice for each blank.

For copyright purposes, a literary, dramatic, musical or artistic work must be original and it must be set down in some **(1)** .... form, for example, on paper, computer disk, or on audio or video tape. It is not unusual for people to have the same idea at roughly the same time, but copyright applies in the way an idea is expressed, not in the idea itself. This is because ideas can encompass a wide range of concepts: for example, thousands of books and films have the same basic **(2)** .... – boy meets girl, loses girl, gets girl back, good triumphs over evil, and so on. So ideas, as opposed to the way in which they are expressed, cannot be protected under copyright law. Perhaps oddly, statistical lists and computer programs are also **(3)** .... as literary works and therefore come under copyright law.

You are breaking the law when you reproduce the whole or a significant part of someone else's creation without their permission. This would include, for example, recording a CD or a video, putting on a public **(4)** .... of a play, making photocopies, or copying onto a computer disk. It is also a breach of the law to key copyright material into a computer without consent, as is storing it on the computer memory. This can even apply to a small part of a work if the **(5)** .... is considered to be essential.

Infringement of copyright can be both a criminal act and a civil wrong. However, consumers who buy illegally copied materials, such as music CDs and films on DVD, for private use cannot be prosecuted, even if they know its origin.

1	solid	complete	actual	permanent
2	histories	plots	scenes	genres
3	thought	presented	regarded	given
4	acting	show	performance	display
5	content	substance	subtext	matter

C Below is a text with blanks. Select the appropriate answer choice for each blank.

In prehistoric times, Europe was **(1)** .... with vast primeval woods and forests, which must have deeply influenced the minds as well as the lives of our ancestors. In places where they had not made clearings, they must have lived in a constant half-light. As far as we know, the oak was the commonest and most **(2)** .... tree. We get our evidence partly from the statements of some classical writers, but more convincingly from the **(3)** .... of ancient villages built on wooden piles in lakes and from the oak forests which have been found embedded in peat bogs.

These bogs, which are most evident in northern Europe, but which are also found in some central and southern parts of the continent, have **(4)** .... the plants and trees which flourished after the end of the Ice Age. The great peat bogs of Ireland reveal that there was a time when vast woods of oak and yew covered the country, the oak growing on hills that were up to a height of four hundred feet or so above the sea, while the yew grew at higher **(5)**........................ . Ancient roadways made of oak have been found, as have, more famously, human relics.

1	smothered	covered	overgrown	flourishing
2	useful	productive	practical	varied
3	rest	remains	leftovers	lack
4	kept	maintained	conserved	preserved
5	levels	piles	degrees	points

D Below is a text with blanks. Select the appropriate answer choice for each blank.

A rule of thumb for distinguishing butterflies from moths in this country is to examine the antennae or feelers, although, when comparing Lepidoptera worldwide, this technique is not to be relied on. Generally, especially among those native to the UK, butterflies have clubbed feelers, **(1)** .... moths can have feelers of various kinds other than clubbed. There are moths that fly by day and the more brightly colored of them are sometimes **(2)** .... for butterflies, but their feelers will distinguish them.

Variations within a single species of butterfly often occur, and all kinds are **(3)** .... to vary in their tint or markings, or sometimes both. These variations may at times be so **(4)** .... as to be hardly noticeable, but in a fair proportion, the variation is quite striking. In such cases, unless the difference is extreme, it is possible to track all the intermediate stages between the ordinary form of a species and its most extreme variety. The coloring on the underside of a butterfly differs from that of the upper side and matches, or **(5)** .... in with, its natural habitat to a remarkable degree. This is why, when they settle, you can see them with their wings positioned together upright over their back.

The number of known species of butterflies throughout the world has been put at about thirteen thousand or more, but some believe there are several thousand more species as yet undiscovered.

1	nevertheless	however	whereas	nonetheless
2	mistaken	misplaced	misled	misunderstood
3	bound	probable	liable	susceptible
4	invisible	slight	marginal	unimportant
5	colors	shades	blends	moves

E Below is a text with blanks. Select the appropriate answer choice for each blank.

Every day, on television, on the radio, and in the newspapers, we see, hear, and read about leaders and politicians making decisions that are clearly wrong-headed and that seem to us, the horrified watchers, listeners, and readers, counter-productive. To be reasonably impartial about such blunders, we must try to put **(1)** .... for the moment how the decision might affect us as individuals; what we are looking for are decisions that are contrary to the interests of their makers. A glaring historical example of such stupidity would be the respective attempts of Charles XII, Napoleon Bonaparte, and Hitler to invade Russia **(2)** .... the disasters it brought each of their predecessors.

Now, when investigating these matters we must tread carefully and remember that it is wrong to judge the past by the ideas of the present. Therefore, the disastrous **(3)** .... made in the past must have been seen at the time by contemporaries to be counterproductive, not just with the **(4)** .... of experience. Again, we must check to see if there were any other **(5)** .... of action that could have been taken and, if so, why they were not.

1 away	aback	aside	behind
2 although	despite	regardless	whatever
3 actions	decisions	practices	effects
4 benefit	aim	interest	clarity
5 ways	means	possibilities	courses

F Below is a text with blanks. Select the appropriate answer choice for each blank.

Light is usually **(1)** .... as a form of energy and it is indeed a kind of electromagnetic energy, not much different from radio waves, television signals, heat, and X-rays. All of these are made up of waves that spread, bend, interfere with one another, and **(2)** .... with obstacles in their path, rather like waves in water. A physicist might tell you that light, along with all its electromagnetic relatives, is really a form of matter, little different from more substantial matter such as houses and, like them, it is made up of individual particles. Light particles, called photons, **(3)** .... in streams, similar to the way in which water pours through a hose.

To most people, this might sound paradoxical or illogical, as many things to do with physics seem to these days. How can light be both energy and matter, wave and particle? The reason it can be is, in fact, not at all **(4)** .... : all energy is a form of matter. Almost everybody recognizes – even if they do not understand – Einstein's famous equation, $E = mc^2$, which spells it out: E refers to energy and m to the mass of matter. Furthermore, all matter has some of the **(5)** .... of waves and some of particles, but the waves of such solid-seeming things as houses are not discernable and can generally be ignored because ordinary matter acts as if it were made up of particles.

1 illustrated	pictured	described	referred
2 crash	encounter	collide	react
3 journey	travel	pour	voyage
4 complicated	sophisticated	unknowable	incomprehensible
5 particulars	characteristics	character	actions

PART 3: LISTENING

SECTION 1: SUMMARIZE SPOKEN TEXT

A You will hear a short lecture. Write a summary for a fellow student who was not present at the lecture. You should write 50–70 words.

You will have 10 minutes to finish this task. Your response will be judged on the quality of your writing and on how well your response presents the key points presented in the lecture.

2.1 Play the CD to listen to the recording that goes with this item.

....

....

....

....

....

....

B You will hear a short lecture. Write a summary for a fellow student who was not present at the lecture. You should write 50–70 words.

You will have 10 minutes to finish this task. Your response will be judged on the quality of your writing and on how well your response presents the key points presented in the lecture.

2.2 Play the CD to listen to the recording that goes with this item.

....

....

....

....

....

....

C You will hear a short lecture. Write a summary for a fellow student who was not present at the lecture. You should write 50–70 words.

You will have 10 minutes to finish this task. Your response will be judged on the quality of your writing and on how well your response presents the key points presented in the lecture.

2.3 Play the CD to listen to the recording that goes with this item.

....

....

....

....

....

....

SECTION 2: MULTIPLE-CHOICE, CHOOSE MULTIPLE ANSWERS

A Listen to the recording and answer the question by selecting all the correct responses. You will need to select more than one response.

Which of the following were the presses adapted for printing originally used for?

1 crushing beans

2 flattening out boards

3 pressing clothes

4 crushing seeds and herbs

5 pressing grapes

6 pressing olives for their oil

 2.4 Play the CD to listen to the recording that goes with this item.

For Further Guidance, see page 76.

B Listen to the recording and answer the question by selecting all the correct responses. You will need to select more than one response.

Which of the following technological advances have had an effect on the economics and distribution of music?

1 piano sales

2 electronic recording systems

3 the Internet

4 the introduction of the valve trumpet

5 the popularity of pianolas

6 the ability to download music

 2.5 Play the CD to listen to the recording that goes with this item.

C Listen to the recording and answer the question by selecting all the correct responses. You will need to select more than one response.

Which of the following statements is true of Rousseau's beliefs in *The Social Contract*?

1 Men form societies to better cope with the dangers in life.

2 Society has a corrupting influence on people.

3 People were far happier in a "state of nature" before civilization.

4 By forming societies, law and morality come into force.

5 Children's emotions should be educated before their intellect.

 2.6 Play the CD to listen to the recording that goes with this item.

MULTIPLE-CHOICE, CHOOSE MULTIPLE ANSWERS

WHAT'S TESTED

The purpose of this task is to assess your ability to listen to an academic text for a variety of purposes, including listening for the main idea, listening for specific details, listening for the speaker's purpose, making connections among pieces of information, analyzing discourse, making inferences, making generalizations, drawing conclusions, and gauging the speaker's attitude or feelings. You will hear a recording, which may be accompanied by video or an image on-screen in the actual PTE Academic. Each recording is between 40 and 90 seconds long and will be played only once. Each recording has one multiple-choice question. There will be between five and seven answer options to choose from, more than one of which will be correct. You will have either two or three recordings in this part. The individual tasks in Section 2 of the Listening part are not timed; you will have between 23 and 28 minutes to complete all of Section 2 of the Listening part, depending on which form of the PTE Academic you receive.

TIPS

- There is a seven-second pause before the recording begins to play. Use this time to read the prompt carefully. This will help you identify what the topic of the recording will be and what you need to focus on listening for. Skim the answer options to get a further idea about the topic and the information you will be listening for.

- Take notes. Use the Erasable Noteboard Booklet and pen provided. Do not try to write down every word you hear. Instead, focus on key words.

- Use abbreviations whenever possible. Ignore articles (e.g., *a, an, the*) unless they are necessary.

- Key words include names, numbers, dates, times, and words and phrases that are stressed. Words and phrases that are repeated are usually central to the main idea.

- Focus on understanding the main idea of the lecture and on the key points that support it. If the speaker draws a conclusion, be sure you have identified it. Try to identify the overall purpose of the lecture.

- Listen for clues to the speaker's attitude or opinion. Be aware of the speaker's tone of voice and delivery, and notice whatever emotions are being conveyed.

- After the recording has finished, re-read the prompts and the answer options carefully. Eliminate any answer options that contain incorrect information or that contain information that was not mentioned in the recording.

- Do not choose an option simply because it uses words or phrases taken directly from the recording. Often, correct answers will be paraphrases of what was said – that is, they will say the same thing as the recording, but using different words.

- If you do not know the answer, and are unable to eliminate any choices, guess. Never leave the question unanswered. If you leave the question unanswered, it will be marked as incorrect. By guessing, you have the possibility of guessing correctly.

A DETAILED STUDY

The exercise below will help you to practice listening to identify key information. Listen to Recording A on page 75 again and answer the following questions in your own words.

1 What is the talk mainly about?

....

2 What were the early screw presses used for?

....

3 What were large presses used for?

....

4 What were beam presses made out of?

....

5 Why were beam presses unsuitable for printing?

....

6 What were *platens* originally?

....

7 What were the older printing presses eventually replaced with?

....

Now check your answers.

SECTION 2: FILL IN THE BLANKS

A You will hear a recording. Write the missing words in each blank.

Paper was first manufactured in Europe by the Spanish in the 12th century, although it had been
(1) .... since the 10th century. Around the year 1276, a **(2)** .... was established
at Fabriano in Italy. The town became a major center for paper making and throughout the 14th century
(3) .... most of Europe with fine quality paper, which it has continued to produce ever
since. By the 15th century, paper was also being manufactured in Germany and France, and it was not
long before both countries became almost completely independent of material bought overseas. With the
increasing **(4)** .... of paper in Europe, the **(5)** .... of identical printed pictures
became almost inevitable.

2.7 Play the CD to listen to the recording that goes with this item.

B You will hear a recording. Write the missing words in each blank.

The spinal cord – the link between the brain and the body – is a band of **(1)** .... tissue
about the thickness of your little finger that runs through the backbone. Nerve cells called motor neurons
(2) .... electric impulses that travel from the brain to the spinal cord, branching off at the
appropriate point and passing to the various parts of the body. Similarly, **(3)** .... neurons
transmit messages from organs and tissues via the spinal cord to the brain. But the spinal cord also
(4) .... without the brain having to intervene; it alone controls those actions called spinal
(5) .... that need to be carried out very fast in response to danger.

2.8 Play the CD to listen to the recording that goes with this item.

C You will hear a recording. Write the missing words in each blank.

The growth of the modern **(1)** .... brought with it the development of mass political parties
and the emergence of professional politicians. A man whose occupation is the **(2)** .... for
political power may go about it in two ways. First, a person who relies on their political activities to
supply their main **(3)** .... of income is said to *live off* politics, while a person who
(4) .... in full-time political activities, but who doesn't receive an income from it, is said
to *live for* politics. Now, a political system in which **(5)** .... to positions of power is filled
by those who *live for* politics is necessarily drawn from a property-owning elite, who are not usually
entrepreneurs. However, this is not to imply that such politicians will necessarily pursue policies which
are wholly **(6)** .... towards the interests of the class they **(7)** .... from.

2.9 Play the CD to listen to the recording that goes with this item.

SECTION 2: HIGHLIGHT CORRECT SUMMARY

A You will hear a recording. Choose the paragraph that best relates to the recording.

1

The speaker talks about the use of memory in Proust's novel *In Search of Lost Time* and how memories are usually brought about by the taste or smell of something, in this case, a biscuit dipped in tea. So, it is the senses that provoke memories that can take us back to our childhood.

2

Using the writer Proust as an example, the speaker tells us how long-term memory works before going on to talk about short-term memory. Distant memories are usually involuntary and are brought to mind by something that stimulates one of the senses. Short-term memory also requires sensory input, but it lasts only a fraction of a second.

3

What we experience is processed by the brain into memories in three stages. First, there is the sensory input, which is momentary. This is then stored in the short-term memory. If this experience is important or meaningful to us, we will reinforce the memory, possibly by repetition, and it will then be stored in the long-term memory.

 2.10 Play the CD to listen to the recording that goes with this item.

B You will hear a recording. Choose the paragraph that best relates to the recording.

1

There are three main interpretations of the English Revolution. The longest lasting interpretation was that the Revolution was the almost inevitable outcome of an age-old power struggle between parliament and crown. The second sees it as a class struggle, and a lead-up to the French and other revolutions. Finally, the third interpretation sees the other two as too fixed, not allowing for unpredictability, and that the outcome could have gone either way.

2

The speaker reminisces about his views of the English Revolution when he was a student and how it seemed quite clear which side he was on – the aristocrats', not the puritans'. Later he realised there was more to it than that and there were several ways of interpreting the Revolution: as a struggle between the king and parliament, as a class war or as an unpredictable situation without clear sides.

3

The English Revolution has been interpreted in several ways by historians: as a fight between the aristocratic Cavaliers, who were open to life, and the serious Puritans; as a battle for power between parliament and the monarchy over the rights of Englishmen that had been going on for centuries; and as a class war similar to the French Revolution, of which it was a forerunner.

 2.11 Play the CD to listen to the recording that goes with this item.

SECTION 2: MULTIPLE-CHOICE, CHOOSE SINGLE ANSWER

A Listen to the recording and answer the multiple-choice question by selecting the correct response. Only one response is correct.

Which of the following is true according to the speaker?

1 The concept of reasonable force is very clearly defined.

2 Your use of force may be judged on how strong you are compared to the other person.

3 If you hit someone first, you cannot then claim self-defence.

4 Courts do not expect ordinary people to react rationally.

 2.12 Play the CD to listen to the recording that goes with this item.

B Listen to the recording and answer the multiple-choice question by selecting the correct response. Only one response is correct.

In the speaker's opinion, which of the following is true of editors who are also novelists?

1 They are always able to see the novel from the author's point of view.

2 They are sympathetic to the difficult lives authors lead.

3 They may try to re-shape the novelist's work in their own way.

4 They find it difficult to see the author's real intentions.

 2.13 Play the CD to listen to the recording that goes with this item.

C Listen to the recording and answer the multiple-choice question by selecting the correct response. Only one response is correct.

According to the speaker, which of the following is true of people who speak two or more languages?

1 They are more intelligent than people who speak only one language.

2 They find it difficult to express their emotions.

3 They tend to lead healthier lives than other people.

4 They develop a more attractive personality than other people.

5 They are generally regarded as being clever.

 2.14 Play the CD to listen to the recording that goes with this item.

SECTION 2: SELECT MISSING WORD

A You will hear a recording about photography. *At the end of the recording, the last word or group of words has been replaced by a beep.* Select the correct option to complete the recording.

1 asking to take pictures

2 as they shot films

3 by taking holiday snaps

4 as they took pictures

5 as they take pictures

 2.15 Play the CD to listen to the recording that goes with this item.

B You will hear a recording about career aspirations. *At the end of the recording, the last word or group of words has been replaced by a beep.* Select the correct option to complete the recording.

1 hopeful

2 realistic

3 successful

4 fulfilling

5 obtained

 2.16 Play the CD to listen to the recording that goes with this item.

For Further Guidance, see page 82.

SELECT MISSING WORD

WHAT'S TESTED

The purpose of this task is to assess your ability to use context to correctly predict how a speaker will finish a talk. Only listening skills are assessed. You will hear a short talk; the last word or group of words will be replaced with a "beep" tone. From a set of options, you must choose the one that best completes the talk. Each recording is between 20 and 70 seconds long. There will be between three and five options to choose from, depending on the nature of the recording. You will hear either two or three recordings. The individual tasks in Section 2 of the Listening part are not timed; you will have between 23 and 28 minutes to complete all of Section 2 of the Listening part, depending on which form of the PTE Academic you receive.

TIPS

- There is a seven-second pause before the recording begins to play. Use this time to read the instructions carefully. The topic is identified for you in the instructions. This will help you to focus on what you will be listening to.

- Skim the answer options to get a further idea about the topic and the information you will be listening for.

- Watch the on-screen progress indicator carefully. This will let you know when the end of each recording is near.

- Listen very carefully to the last few words that are spoken. These will be connected to one of the answer options in some way.

- If you do not know the answer, and are unable to eliminate any options, guess. Never leave the question unanswered. If you leave the question unanswered, it will be marked as incorrect. By guessing, you have the possibility of guessing correctly.

A DETAILED STUDY

The exercise below will help you to practice completing spoken sentences. You will listen to five speakers saying a sentence. For each speaker, choose the option that best completes their sentence.

A The speaker is talking about tours of a museum.

   1 about an hour.

   2 without charge.

   3 the whole museum.

B The speaker is talking about natural disasters.

   1 especially droughts.

   2 parts of the world.

   3 kinds of farmers.

C The speaker is talking about making presentations.

   1 are appreciated.

   2 a short break.

   3 from the audience.

D The speaker is talking about funding a building project.

   1 to the lender.

   2 at low interest rates.

   3 is in the budget.

E The speaker is talking about taking courses on the Internet.

   1 much cheaper.

   2 travel further.

   3 less enjoyable.

2.17 Play the CD to listen to the recording that goes with this item.

Now check your answers.

SECTION 2: HIGHLIGHT INCORRECT WORDS

> **ON-SCREEN**
> Remember that in the exam, you will click on the words that are different with your mouse in order to highlight them in yellow.

A You will hear a recording. Below is a transcription of the recording. Some words in the transcription differ from what the speaker(s) said. As you listen, circle the words that are different.

In the 19th century, few people could afford to travel abroad; it was expensive and there weren't the massive transport systems that we have today. So curiosity about foreign lands had to be satisfied through books and drawings. With the advent of photography, a whole new version of "reality" became available. Publishers were not slow to realize that here was a large new market of people eager for travel photography and they soon had photographers out shooting the best known European cities, as well as more exotic places further afield. People bought the pictures by the millions, and magic lantern shows were presented in schools and leisure halls. Most popular of all, however, was the stereoscopic picture which pretended three-dimensional views and was considered a marvel of Victorian technology.

 2.18 Play the CD to listen to the recording that goes with this item.

B You will hear a recording. Below is a transcription of the recording. Some words in the transcription differ from what the speaker(s) said. As you listen, circle the words that are different.

Classified advertisements placed by individuals in newsprint and magazines are not covered by the Advertising Standards Authority's "court of practice". If you happen to buy goods that have been wrongly described in such an advertisement, and have lost money as a result, the only thing you can do is bring a case against the person who placed the advertisement for misrepresentation or for breach of contrast. In this case, you would use the small claims procedure, which is a relatively cheap way to sue for the recovery of a debt. If you want to pursue a claim, you should take into account whether the person you are suing will be able to pay damages, should any be rewarded. Dishonest traders are wary of this and often pose as private sellers to expose the legal loopholes that exist: that is, they may claim they are not in a position to pay damages.

 2.19 Play the CD to listen to the recording that goes with this item.

SECTION 2: WRITE FROM DICTATION

You will hear some sentences. Write each sentence exactly as you hear it. Write as much of each sentence as you can. You will hear each sentence only once.

 2.20 Play the CD to listen to the recording that goes with this item.

1 ....

2 ....

3 ....

4 ....

For Further Guidance, see page 85.

WRITE FROM DICTATION

WHAT'S TESTED

The purpose of this task is to assess your ability to write down a sentence that you hear. Both listening and writing skills are assessed. You will hear a sentence spoken only once. You must type exactly what the speaker said. The recordings are between three and five seconds long. You will hear either three or four sentences.

TIPS

- There is a seven-second pause before the recording begins. Use this time to place the cursor at the beginning (i.e. top left) of the box where you will type, so that you are ready to begin typing as soon as the recording ends.
- Watch the on-screen progress indicator so that you will know when you can begin typing.
- Type the sentence as fast as you can so that you do not forget it.
- Once you have typed it, go back and check for any mistakes. Make sure you have not omitted any words, and that your grammar, spelling, and punctuation are all correct.
- If you hear unfamiliar words, and are unsure how to spell them, guess.
- If you are able to write by hand faster than you can type, take notes using the Erasable Noteboard Booklet and pen provided.

A DETAILED STUDY

The exercise below will help you to practice listening carefully and to write from dictation. Each sentence below has some words missing. You will hear the complete sentences. Listen and write the missing words.

1 The course .... non-science majors.

2 Many of the world's lakes are ....

3 Repetitive stress injuries .... nearly two-thirds

....

4 .... that the human brain ....

.... the way it is used.

(◉) **2.21 Play the CD to listen to the recording that goes with this item.**

Now check your answers.

TEST 3

PART 1: SPEAKING AND WRITING

SECTION 1: PERSONAL INTRODUCTION

Read the prompt below. In 25 seconds, you must reply in your own words, as naturally and clearly as possible. You have 30 seconds to record your response. Your response will be sent together with your score report to the institutions selected by you.

Please introduce yourself. For example, you could talk about one or more of the following:

- Your interests
- Your plans for future study
- Why you want to study abroad
- Why you need to learn English
- Why you chose *this* test

SECTION 2: READ ALOUD

Look at the text below. In 40 seconds, you must read this text aloud as naturally and clearly as possible. You have 40 seconds to read aloud.

(Allow 40 seconds for each separate text.)

A The Atlantic coast of the peninsula can be thought of as the cold side, and the sea on this coast tends to be clear and cold, with a variety of seaweeds growing along the rocky shoreline. On a hot day, however, this cold water can be very refreshing and is said to be less hospitable to sharks, which prefer warmer waters.

B All the works of art shown in this exhibition were purchased on a shoestring budget. The criteria that the curators had to follow were that works must be acquired cheaply, appeal to a broad range of tastes, and fit with unusual environments. Thus, many of our better known modern artists are not represented.

C Foam-filled furniture is very dangerous if it catches fire, and foam quickly produces a high temperature, thick smoke and poisonous gases – including carbon monoxide. Therefore, set levels of fire resistance have been established for new and second-hand upholstered furniture and other similar products.

D The starting point of Bergson's theory is the experience of time and motion. Time is the reality we experience most directly, but this doesn't mean that we can capture this experience mentally. The past is gone and the future is yet to come. The only reality is the present, which is real through our experience.

For Further Guidance, see page 87.

E It is important to note that saving is not the same as investment. Saving is about cash, while investment is about real product. The difference is important because money, being liquid, can leak out of the economic system – which it does when someone who is putting aside unspent income keeps it under the mattress.

F Historically, the low level of political autonomy of the cities in China is partly a result of the early development of the state bureaucracy. The bureaucrats played a major role in the growth of urbanization, but were also able to control its subsequent development and they never completely gave up this control.

You can hear model answers on the CD2, track 22.

SECTION 2: REPEAT SENTENCE

You will hear some sentences. Please repeat each sentence exactly as you hear it. You will hear each sentence only once.

 2.23 Play the CD to listen to the recording that goes with this item.

READ ALOUD

WHAT'S TESTED

The purpose of this task is to assess your ability to read a short text aloud. Both speaking and reading skills are assessed. The texts you will read aloud are up to 60 words long. You will have either six or seven texts to read. You will be presented with a text on your screen, which you will then read aloud. The amount of time you have for each text will depend on how long the text is, but will vary from 30 to 40 seconds. The on-screen instructions for each task will tell you how much time you have.

TIPS

- You will have from 30 to 40 seconds to read the text before the recording begins. Use this time to read the text. Read the text aloud softly to yourself. Be sure to sound out the words the way you will say them when you read. Quickly work out how you will pronounce any unknown words.

- You are being assessed, in part, on your ability to read naturally, which means reading with the correct pronunciation, rhythm, stress, and intonation.

- Pay special attention to the content words – nouns, verbs, adjectives, and adverbs. These are words that carry the content or the main meaning in a sentence. These words are usually stressed. Function (grammatical) words, such as articles, prepositions, auxiliary verbs, and pronouns are not usually stressed.

- Pay attention to punctuation. Make a slight pause when you see a comma. Take a slightly longer pause at the end of each sentence.

- While you are speaking, remember that the microphone turns off automatically if there is no sound for three seconds. Do not pause in the middle of the text for that long, because once the microphone turns off, you cannot turn it on again.

A DETAILED STUDY

The exercise below will help you to practice reading aloud with correct rhythm, stress, and intonation.

A The sentences that follow are from Text D on page 86. Listen to the sentences being read aloud. As you listen, underline the words that the speaker stresses.

2.24 Play the CD to listen to the recording that goes with this item.

1 The starting point of Bergson's theory is the experience of time and motion.

2 Time is the reality we experience most directly, but this doesn't mean that we can capture this experience mentally.

3 The past is gone and the future is yet to come.

4 The only reality is the present, which is real to us through our experience of it.

Now check your answers.

B Now listen to each sentence again. Read each sentence aloud and try to match the speaker's rhythm, stress, and intonation.

SECTION 2: DESCRIBE IMAGE

A Look at the graph below. Describe in detail what the graph is showing. You will have 40 seconds to give your response.

Holiday destinations that have shown the largest percentage growth, 2003 to 2007, UK residents

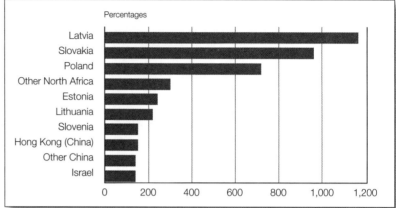

B Look at the graph below. Describe in detail what the graph is showing. You will have 40 seconds to give your response.

Daily newspaper readership

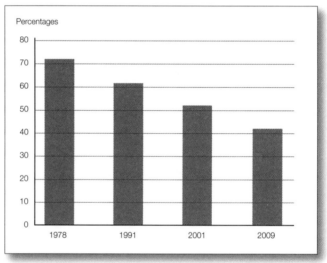

C Look at the graph below. Describe in detail what the graph is showing. You will have 40 seconds to give your response.

Public and private sector sickness rates, 2000–2010, UK

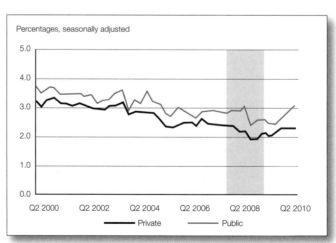

D Look at the graph below. Describe in detail what the graph is showing. You will have 40 seconds to give your response.

Businesses suffering malicious e-security incident: by type of incident, UK

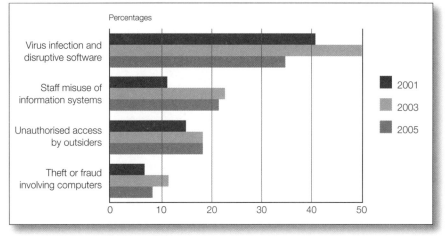

E Look at the graph below. Describe in detail what the graph is showing. You will have 40 seconds to give your response.

Average weekly household expenditure in relation to the UK average, 2003/04 to 2005/06

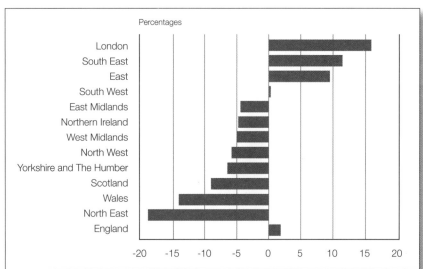

F Look at the picture below. Describe in detail what the picture is showing. You will have 40 seconds to give your response.

For Further Guidance, see page 90.

You can hear model answers on the CD2, track 25.

DESCRIBE IMAGE

A DETAILED STUDY

The exercises below will help you to practice describing a picture.

A Look at Image F on page 89 again and answer the following questions.

1 What is this a picture of?

This is a picture of ....

2 What can you see in the foreground?

....

3 What can you see in the background?

....

4 Where do you think the picture may have been taken?

....

B The following is a transcript of a summary describing what Image F on page 89 shows. Choose the correct words to complete the summary. Refer to Image F if you need help.

This is a picture **(1) from / of** part of a city with different kinds of building. **(2) In / On** the foreground, **(3) here / there** is an area of poor housing. The buildings are badly built and it **(4) looks / seems** like a slum. **(5) In / For** contrast, in the background are modern skyscrapers and office buildings. Judging **(6) by / with** the style of the buildings, the picture may have been taken **(7) to / in** a large South American city, such as São Paulo.

Now check your answers.

SECTION 2: RE-TELL LECTURE

A You will hear a lecture. After listening to the lecture, please retell what you have just heard from the lecture in your own words. You will have 40 seconds to give your response.

2.26 Play the CD to listen to the recording that goes with this item.

B You will hear a lecture. After listening to the lecture, please retell what you have just heard from the lecture in your own words. You will have 40 seconds to give your response.

2.27 Play the CD to listen to the recording that goes with this item.

C You will hear a lecture. After listening to the lecture, please retell what you have just heard from the lecture in your own words. You will have 40 seconds to give your response.

2.28 Play the CD to listen to the recording that goes with this item.

You can hear model answers on the CD2, track 29.

SECTION 2: ANSWER SHORT QUESTION

You will hear some questions. Please give a simple and short answer to each one. Often just one or a few words is enough.

 2.30 Play the CD to listen to the recording that goes with this item.

SECTION 3: SUMMARIZE WRITTEN TEXT

Read the passage below and summarize it using one sentence. You have 10 minutes to finish this task. Your response will be judged on the quality of your writing and on how well your response presents the key points in the passage.

A country's standard of living generally depends on the size of its national income. Standards of living are measured by such things as the number of cars, televisions, telephones, computers, washing machines, and so on, for every one thousand people. There is, however, no standard international index, which is why national income figures are used as a substitute. But the use of these figures to compare the standard of living between countries needs to be done carefully, because they are, at best, only a rough guide which can be misleading. The main problem here is that it is necessary to have a common unit of measurement if any sort of comparison is to be made at all. It has become the custom to use the dollar, and each country's currency is converted at its official exchange rate into a national income figure in dollars. Now, since the exchange rate is often set at an artificial level in relation to dollars, you are likely to end up with a figure that is useless for your purposes.

....
....
....
....

For Further Guidance, see page 93.

SECTION 4: SUMMARIZE WRITTEN TEXT

Read the passage below and summarize it using one sentence. You have 10 minutes to finish this task. Your response will be judged on the quality of your writing and on how well your response presents the key points in the passage.

The saying "The camera never lies." has been with us almost since the beginning of photography – yet we all now know that it can, and does lie, and very convincingly. Yet most of us still seem to trust the truth of a photographic image – especially in our newspapers or on TV news reports – even though we may question its message. We think of photographs as an accurate reflection of unaltered reality. We're convinced of this when we take unposed snaps on our family holidays or of colleagues the worse for wear at the office party. It is this property of photography that makes it hard to question the evidence before our eyes.

Our holiday snaps, though, like photographs showing life ten, fifty, a hundred years ago, tend only to bring about at most a feeling of nostalgia – not always a negative emotion. Many people keep albums to relive the better moments of their lives – and their impact is reduced by the fact that what they show is over, part of history. News photos, on the other hand, in presenting moments of an event that is probably still going on somewhere, must provoke a more vivid, emotional response.

....
....
....
....

SUMMARIZE WRITTEN TEXT

A DETAILED STUDY

The exercise below will help you to practice identifying correct summary sentences for a reading passage. Read the text in Section 3 on page 92. Then read the summaries below. Match each summary (1–4) to a statement (a–e). You will not use all of the statements.

1 To compare standards of living using national income, each country's currency is converted to dollars at an official exchange rate, but because the exchange rate is often set at an artificial level, you can end up with a figure that is useless.

....

2 A country's standard of living is often expressed as the number of cars, televisions, computers, and washing machines per 1,000 people; however, income in dollars is a better measure.

....

3 Comparing the standard of living among countries using national income in dollars as a measure can be misleading, because official exchange rates are often set artificially.

....

4 Because there is no standard international index, national income figures are used to measure the standard of living, as expressed in each nation's own currency.

....

This summary

a correctly summarizes the text.

b omits important information.

c focuses on irrelevant details.

d misstates information in the text.

e exceeds the allowable word count.

Now check your answers.

SECTION 5: SUMMARIZE WRITTEN TEXT

Read the passage below and summarize it using one sentence. You have 10 minutes to finish this task. Your response will be judged on the quality of your writing and on how well your response presents the key points in the passage.

We know that Shakespeare took whole chunks of Plutarch word for word to use in his Roman plays – though, of course, in doing so he turned them into great poetry. Does this make Shakespeare a plagiarist? Was he a word thief?

In its legal definition, plagiarism includes "both the theft or misrepresentation of intellectual property and the substantial textual copying of another's work". But it is also considered to be a factor of a particular culture or time – that is, in some cultures and in some periods the idea was undefined – which makes it harder to identify precisely. However, the main problem these days is plagiarism in academic writing, which is becoming increasingly common, due to the vast amount of material that has been published which can be accessed via the Internet. This easy access, coupled with the increasing pressure put on students, has led to a rapid rise in incidents of plagiarism. It comes down to who owns the intellectual property in question, and with the advent of the Internet this has become less clearly defined.

....

....

....

....

SECTION 6: WRITE ESSAY

You will have 20 minutes to plan, write and revise an essay about the topic below. Your response will be judged on how well you develop a position, organize your ideas, present supporting details, and control the elements of standard written English. You should write 200–300 words.

Some people prefer to spend their holidays in resorts where everything is organized for them and they take little interest in the country they are visiting. Others prefer to travel around the country and to see how the people live, to get to know their customs and traditions and cuisine.

Write an essay on which type of foreign travel you think is best for both the tourist and the local community.

....

....

....

....

....

....

....

....

....

....

....

....

....

....

PART 2: READING

MULTIPLE-CHOICE, CHOOSE SINGLE ANSWER

A Read the text and answer the multiple-choice question by selecting the correct response.
Only one response is correct.

By the 15th century, the various Zulu chiefdoms had reached the south-eastern part of Southern Africa. They were largely cattle farmers and cultivators who lived in scattered villages across the land. Like other African peoples at this time, they lived within a system of clans and tribes under independent chiefs until, in the latter part of the 18th century, the system changed, possibly due to land shortage, and a number of larger political groupings were formed. The most powerful among these were the Mthethwa under the leadership of Dingiswayo, who radically changed some aspects of traditional life during his reign.

Formerly, military activity was based on local recruitment; men from a district would fight together under their chief. So, in order to create a large unified fighting force and control the fierce rivalry between supporters of different groups, Dingiswayo reorganized his army along the lines of age rather than old local allegiances. Thus, men of a particular age group, regardless of clan or residence, formed a regiment whose loyalty was to the king alone. Fathers and sons fought in different regiments and men from the same district found themselves in completely different groups, and as a result local rivalry was prevented. This was the basic military system that Shaka, the most famous Zulu chief, inherited and built on.

Which of the following is mentioned as one of the changes made to the Zulus' traditional life?

1 They no longer farmed or cultivated the land.

2 Fathers and sons fought against each other.

3 The army was arranged in a new way.

4 Rivalry between villages was encouraged.

For Further Guidance, see page 96.

B Read the text and answer the multiple-choice question by selecting the correct response.
Only one response is correct.

The Second World War brought a period of austerity and tough rationing in Britain, especially for food: before the war Britain had imported about 55 million tons of food, but, only a month after the war began, this had dropped to 12 million. Strangely enough, this period also saw a general improvement in health standards across the country. Rationing began at the beginning of 1940 and lasted until July 1954 when the last restrictions on meat were lifted.

Everyone was issued with an identity card and each household had a ration book. Then they had to register with a local supplier of food whose name was stamped in the ration book so that you could only buy your ration from that supplier, and only the amount you were allowed. The books contained coupons which the shopkeepers cut out every time you made a purchase, and the amount you were allowed depended, to a certain extent, on the color of your ration book. The majority of adults had a buff or brownish book. Then there was the green book for pregnant women, nursing mothers and children under five, and this allowed them first choice of fruit, a daily pint of milk and a double supply of eggs. Children between the ages of 5 and 16 had a blue book, which allowed them fruit, a full meat ration and half a pint of milk a day.

The idea was to make as sure as possible that everybody got a fair share of the food available, the worry being that as food and other consumer goods became scarcer, prices would rise and the less well-off might not be able to pay. However, some thought it unfair, as people living in rural areas could get hold of eggs, butter and milk fairly easily without coupons.

According to the text, which of the following statements is true?

1 Teenagers were allotted more milk than other age groups.

2 People who lived in the country didn't have to pay for eggs and butter.

3 People had a healthier diet under rationing.

4 Pregnant women were allowed twice as many eggs as other adults.

MULTIPLE-CHOICE, CHOOSE SINGLE ANSWER

A DETAILED STUDY

The exercise below will help you practice answering single-answer multiple-choice items. Read each extract from Text A on page 95 and the statement that follows. Write T if the statement is true or F if the statement is false.

1 By the 15th century, the various Zulu chiefdoms had reached the south-eastern part of Southern Africa. They were largely cattle farmers and cultivators who lived in scattered villages across the land.

Zulus are described as farmers and cultivators. ....

2 Like other African peoples at this time, they lived within a system of clans and tribes under independent chiefs until, in the latter part of the 18th century, the system changed, possibly due to land shortage, and a number of larger political groupings were formed.

The Zulus stopped being farmers. ....

3 The most powerful among these were the Mthethwa under the leadership of Dingiswayo, who radically changed some aspects of traditional life during his reign. Formerly, military activity was based on local recruitment; men from a district would fight together under their chief.

Men from the same area were part of the same unit in the army. ....

4 So, in order to create a large unified fighting force and control the fierce rivalry between supporters of different groups, Dingiswayo reorganized his army along the lines of age rather than old local allegiances.

Dingiswayo wanted to encourage rivalry between villages. ....

5 Thus, men of a particular age group, regardless of clan or residence, formed a regiment whose loyalty was to the king alone. Fathers and sons fought in different regiments and men from the same district found themselves in completely different groups, and as a result local rivalry was prevented.

Fathers and sons fought against each other. ....

6 This was the basic military system that Shaka, the most famous Zulu chief, inherited and built on.

Shaka developed the army structure created by Disingwayo. ....

Now check your answers.

MULTIPLE-CHOICE, CHOOSE MULTIPLE ANSWERS

A Read the text and answer the question by selecting all the correct responses.
More than one response is correct.

Why do some countries drive on the left, while others – the majority – drive on the right? In fact, those that drive on the left make up about twenty-five per cent of the world's countries and are, apart from the UK itself, mostly countries that were British colonies: India, South Africa, Singapore, Jamaica, and so on. Japan does too, although it wasn't a colony, and as late as 2009, Samoa switched from driving on the right largely because they wanted to buy right-hand drive cars made in Japan and New Zealand.

The Romans introduced the custom of keeping to the left, a habit that was reinforced in medieval times when riders throughout Europe passed oncoming strangers sword arm to sword arm – this idea is based on the fact that the majority of people are right-handed. An increase in horse traffic towards the end of the 18th century meant that the convention gained strength, but it was not put into law until 1835. Legend has it that Napoleon is responsible for making the European countries which he conquered keep to the right, for the simple reason either that he was left-handed himself, or that he wanted to be different from his enemy, England. This is most probably nonsense, but an Emperor's whims can go a long way. So France, obviously, and Spain, the Netherlands and other countries Napoleon overran used this system, and over the years other countries adopted the practice to make crossing borders easier and safer. The latest European country to convert was Sweden, in 1967.

According to the text, which of the countries listed below drive on the left?

1 Japan

2 Scotland

3 Spain

4 Samoa

5 South Africa

6 Germany

B Read the text and answer the question by selecting all the correct responses.
More than one response is correct.

In 1861, Matthew Brady, a well-known portrait photographer, approached President Lincoln requesting permission to move freely about the country photographing the Civil War. Lincoln granted him permission to travel anywhere with the Union armies, and his record of this conflict brought home to millions the horrors of war.

Brady wasn't the first official war photographer. Six years earlier, Roger Fenton, a lawyer and amateur photographer, had returned from the Crimea, having been personally chosen by Queen Victoria and Prince Albert. However, his instructions were more likely to have been to send back work that boosted morale back home rather than the terrible realities of war.

Brady's coverage of the war made him a household name, but he had hundreds of assistants, and it's even possible that he didn't take any of the 7,000 pictures that were marketed under his name. But no one else could have organized the large army of photographers needed to cover the broad sweep of the war and provided access to many leading generals and politicians.

Which of the following statements are true of Matthew Brady?

1 He was given permission to travel anywhere in the US.

2 He was able to give his photographers introductions to politicians.

3 He took as many as seven thousand pictures of the war.

4 He was responsible for organizing a large number of photographers.

5 Before the war he had been an amateur photographer.

RE-ORDER PARAGRAPHS

> **ON-SCREEN**
> Remember that in the exam, you will re-order the paragraphs
> by dragging and dropping them with your mouse.

A The paragraphs have been placed in a random order. Restore the original order.

Jumbled paragraphs	Correct paragraph order (1–4)
a Now, Polybius, if we forget Aristotle for the moment, was to become the main authority on the three types of constitution and the cycles through which they pass, becoming more corrupt as they do so: kingship turns into tyranny, aristocracy to oligarchy, and democracy into mob rule.	
b The constitution was then at its healthiest, while that of the Carthaginians was already in decline because, in Polybius' opinion it was becoming more democratic.	
c Polybius believed that this progression could be halted at least temporarily by keeping the three elements held in some kind of balance, and the Romans achieved this not by abstract reasoning but by trial and error.	
d The Roman state was tested almost to destruction by the defeat at Cannae by the Carthaginians led by Hannibal – and according to the historian Polybius it was only what he called the "peculiar virtues" of the Roman constitution that allowed it to survive this crisis.	

B The paragraphs have been placed in a random order. Restore the original order.

Jumbled paragraphs	Correct paragraph order (1–4)
a In the late 18th century, groups of skilled workers began to control the hiring of apprentices, and bargained with employers for better working conditions, but, as the movement grew, these trade unions tried to find ways of creating an alliance among themselves.	
b The first meeting of the Trades Union Congress took place in Manchester, at which thirty-four delegates represented well over a hundred thousand trade union members.	

c Trade unions were legalized in an Act of 1871, and by the end of the century more than one and a half million workers were members. Conditions for workers slowly improved over the years, but it wasn't until 1974 that legislation covering the health and safety of all employees was introduced.	
d Until the 19th century, workers were given little or no protection. Child labor was common, as were long hours worked in unsafe conditions for minimal pay.	

For Further Guidance, see page 100.

C The paragraphs have been placed in a random order. Restore the original order.

Jumbled paragraphs	Correct paragraph order (1–4)
a It is not as easy to estimate the influence of German literature on English as it is French, because it didn't begin to have any measureable impact until quite recent times. That is, not much before the Romantic Movement.	
b It was perhaps the "storm and stress" movement of the late 18th century that had the first and most widespread effect on the rest of Europe, and chief among those who were affiliated with this movement was Goethe.	
c Goethe was a polymath, a man whose interests ranged across the whole spectrum of human knowledge. As well as writing enduring plays and fiction, he was involved in politics, and made important contributions to scientific thought.	
d It was the epistolary novel *The Sorrows of Young Werther* that had the greatest impact, which, despite upsetting many people, was the first German novel to gain recognition throughout Europe and was translated into many languages.	

RE-ORDER PARAGRAPHS

A DETAILED STUDY

The exercise below will help you focus on how to place pieces of text in their correct order. Look at Text B on page 98 again and answer the following questions.

1   Which of these best describes the topic of the whole text?

   a   the history of trade unions

   b   the history of Manchester

   c   the dangers of working life

2   Which paragraph (a–d) describes the background situation before trade unions developed?

....

3   Which paragraph (a–d) describes the beginning of the trade union movement?

....

4   Which paragraph (a–d) describes the formation of a large association of trade unions?

....

5   Which paragraph (a–d) describes development of the trade union movement up to modern times?

....

Now check your answers.

READING: FILL IN THE BLANKS

> **ON-SCREEN**
> Remember that in the exam, you will fill the blanks by
> dragging and dropping the words with your mouse.

A In the text below some words are missing. Choose the correct word to fill each blank from the box below. There are more words than you need to complete the exercise.

Today we **(1)** .... Aesop's fables with childhood, and the Victorians are largely **(2)** .... for that. There were at least seven separate **(3)** .... or retellings in the 19th century, all targeted at children. Rewritten as parables, they were seen as an effective way of communicating Victorian morality. Yet, in antiquity, Aesop wasn't read by children: **(4)** .... the talking animals and the sometimes childlike atmosphere of the tales, the setting was perceived at the time as being political.

relate	translations	stories	blamed	responsible	associate	despite	though

B In the text below some words are missing. Choose the correct word to fill each blank from the box below. There are more words than you need to complete the exercise.

Very intelligent people often make the **(1)** .... of assuming that other people's minds work in the same way as theirs do. Economists, for example, create mathematically-based models on the **(2)** .... that people act rationally as far as their own economic **(3)** .... are concerned. You don't have to look much further than family and friends to see how off the **(4)** .... this idea is. The problem with a lot of such scientifically-based theories is that they are not friendly to facts that don't **(5)** .... the case.

make	fit	mistake	fact	interests	business	mark	notion

C In the text below some words are missing. Choose the correct word to fill each blank from the box below. There are more words than you need to complete the exercise.

With today's incredible **(1)** .... of technological change a lot of age-old human skills may be getting left behind or **(2)** .... out. It's not just that if you buy a laptop today it's obsolete within **(3)** .... than a year and the rest of the world has moved on; it's more that, as workers get more expensive and equipment gets cheaper, companies are spending more on machines rather than people. Fewer people, therefore, are being **(4)** .... in necessary skills.

losing	trained	under	less	rate	taught	dying	speed

D In the text below some words are missing. Choose the correct word to fill each blank from the box below. There are more words than you need to complete the exercise.

Twelve hundred miles east of Australia **(1)** .... the islands of New Zealand. Long before they were **(2)** .... by Europeans, a Polynesian race of warriors, the Maoris, had sailed across the Pacific from the northeast and established a civilization **(3)** .... for the brilliance of its art and the strength of its military **(4)** .... When Captain Cook visited these islands towards the end of the 18ᵗʰ century, he **(5)** .... that the population numbered about a hundred thousand.

discovered   counted   notable   lie   estimated   found   army   system

E In the text below some words are missing. Choose the correct word to fill each blank from the box below. There are more words than you need to complete the exercise.

The most common **(1)** .... for carrying out a detailed medical examination of a dead person – a post-mortem or autopsy – is when it is necessary to **(2)** .... the cause of death.
In some circumstances, a doctor may be allowed to perform a post-mortem in pursuit of medical **(3)** .... The examination is usually performed by a pathologist, and **(4)** .... dissection of the body, and tests done on blood, tissues and internal organs, but sometimes it is performed by a doctor.

purpose   reason   means   establish   specimens   knowledge   involves

READING AND WRITING: FILL IN THE BLANKS

> **ON-SCREEN**
> Remember that in the exam, a drop-down menu will appear when you click on each blank with your mouse. You will select an answer from each menu.

A Below is a text with blanks. Select the appropriate answer choice for each blank.

Of all those whose names are associated with the **(1)** .... of photography, Louis Daguerre is perhaps the most famous. He started out as a student of architecture, but by the age of sixteen was working as a stage designer and his work in this field, especially his handling of lighting effects, **(2)** .... him to fame. His **(3)** .... in photography grew out of his use of the *camera obscura* to help with perspective in painting and his desire to freeze the image. To this end, he formed a partnership with the photographer Nicephore Niepce – but this was short-lived as Niepce died not long after.

Daguerre continued to experiment and made, it seems by **(4)** .... , an important discovery: he had put an exposed photographic plate – this was, of course, before the age of film – in his chemical cupboard and some days later found that the latent image had developed. There was also a broken thermometer in the cupboard, and he assumed that the vapour from the mercury had caused it. This meant it was now possible to reduce the time the plate was exposed from eight hours to thirty minutes.

This produced an image. The next step was to fix it, which he managed to do in 1837. He called this new process the Daguerreotype, then advertised and looked for sponsors, but initially very few people were interested. The discovery was made **(5)** .... in January 1839, but details of the process were not given until August the same year, the French government in the meantime having bought the rights to the process.

1	creation	discovery	invention	manufacture
2	gave	won	brought	gained
3	interest	curiosity	desire	concern
4	mistake	accident	default	purpose
5	open	general	official	public

B Below is a text with blanks. Select the appropriate answer choice for each blank.

The term "trencherman" means a good hearty eater. It could be assumed, therefore, that a "trencher" was something people used to eat off, such as a wooden **(1)** .... , or the like, which **(2)** .... as a plate – as the dictionary confirms. In fact, it was originally a large chunk or slice of stale bread used to soak up the juices, which would later be fed to the domestic animals or the poor. **(3)** .... , those who had a very strong stomach or large appetite could eat it themselves.

Before the invention of cutlery, our ancestors usually ate with their hands. It is quite surprising to realize how **(4)** .... in the day it was before cutlery – knives, forks and spoons, even drinking cups – became commonly used for eating. It is not a question of being slow to **(5)** .... the concept of such tools and their possible uses – they had been around for ages, though it was usually only the wealthier people who had them at the dinner table. So the reason for this late development or fashion must be looked for elsewhere.

1	plank	table	board	box
2	tried	used	worked	served
3	Also	Furthermore	Whereas	Alternatively
4	long	late	far	early
5	grab	grasp	grip	hold

C Below is a text with blanks. Select the appropriate answer choice for each blank.

Woodcuts, as printed illustrations, went well with type, which is why this form of printing was the only
(1) .... used to print pictures together with moveable type until late in the 16th century.
Woodblocks and type are both relief surfaces – that is, raised from the flat surface of the block – and are
(2) .... the same height on the bed of the printing press; furthermore, the same oil-based ink
can be used on both surfaces so that they can be printed simultaneously. As with cutting the woodblocks
and setting the type, the ink was applied by hand, using what was **(3)** .... an "ink ball" – a
pad made of leather stuffed with wool or hair and tied around a wooden handle. The ink was like a thick
black oil paint and it usually **(4)** .... of a mixture of linseed oil that had been boiled until it
was free of fats, and various pigments. Varnishes were then added to get the ink to the right consistency
or thickness, and also as an aid to drying.

Book illustration, then, was to be one of the major factors in the development of the woodcut, and its
influence lasted until the 19th century. The aesthetic side of book making – the arrangement of the text,
ornamentation and pictures together on the page – required an inventive and subtle **(5)** ....
to the problems of pictorial composition.

1 form	means	method	system
2 roughly	hardly	closely	evenly
3 known	called	said	told
4 combined	composed	consisted	comprised
5 approach	mixture	manner	technique

D Below is a text with blanks. Select the appropriate answer choice for each blank.

Whenever you see a film set in ancient Greece or Rome – or anywhere for that matter – the men are all
wearing togas or kilts or are **(1)** .... in a cloak. How much closer to our own age do we
have to come to see men wearing trousers? In fact they, or something very much like them, were worn
in ancient times: the Chinese dressed in trousers tied at the waist and often at the ankles to protect them
against the cold, while Asian nomads wore something similar for riding. In Persia too, they were
(2) .... for both men and women. This was a form of dress that found its
(3) .... to central Europe by 400 BC. In the following century, Celtic people began wearing
similar garments, while the English wore ankle-length britches until about the 1100s, when they
(4) .... knee-length britches – whether as a matter of fashion or practicality it's difficult to say.

What became known as bell-bottoms, which were fashionable in the late 1960s and early 1970s, and
(5) .... a comeback in the 21st century, were worn by English sailors from about the 1730s,
but trousers only really became fashionable in the first quarter of the 19th century, and usually only for
informal day wear.

1 layered	wrapped	surrounded	fitted
2 convenient	traditional	conventional	commonplace
3 way	path	route	acceptance
4 adapted	altered	changed	adopted
5 took	made	had	showed

E Below is a text with blanks. Select the appropriate answer choice for each blank.

It is thought that around 12,000 years ago the Earth's climate became relatively **(1)** .... or more temperate, allowing for a greater variety of plant life. Those early humans leading a nomadic life, who hunted and gathered food where they happened to find it, began to supplement their diet with wild grasses such as wheat and barley.

Noticing how discarded seeds and roots later germinated and sprouted may have been what **(2)** .... the first farmers to settle down and cultivate crops. We know that farmers in the Stone Age had discovered pulses – beans, peas, lentils, and so on – which they **(3)** .... up and ate as a kind of porridge. Later they learnt to domesticate sheep and goats, developing tamer and manageable **(4)** .... of these and other animals. In addition to that, they also discovered how to use the process of fermentation for brewing and making bread.

It was some time later that farmers noticed that the amount of crops produced declined if they were always grown in the same ground and, by the 1ˢᵗ century, the Romans were **(5)** .... crops with pasture for grazing animals to restore the soil's fertility. This practice was followed in medieval England where the fields were divided into strips, planting cereals and vegetables, and the land left uncultivated one year in three.

1	harsher	easier	milder	colder
2	made	forced	convinced	decided
3	mashed	squashed	squeezed	broke
4	types	breeds	species	sorts
5	changing	alternating	swapping	revolving

F Below is a text with blanks. Select the appropriate answer choice for each blank.

In the late 1700s, Franz Joseph Gall founded what came to be known **(1)** .... phrenology – though it was originally called 'organology' – that 'science' of the size and shape of a person's cranium being a way to estimate character and mental abilities. It was a curious mixture of early psychology and neuroscience and as such **(2)** .... towards later research into those fields of human enquiry. Most people, however, think of it as simply a question of feeling the bumps on a person's head and have seen one of those **(3)** .... of the head that map out the various mental faculties, and consider it no more a valid science than astrology. Yet it was intended as a science of the mental faculties in general, and was on to something with its theory that each mental faculty is **(4)** .... by an organ in a particular part of the brain. That is to say he correctly guessed that there were many parts to the brain and that there was specialization in terms of the functions by those parts. Brain specialization is now a well-established fact. What Gall did not **(5)** .... , though – and he couldn't reasonably be expected to – was that the function of each separate brain part is not independent but contributes to the workings of larger systems composed of those separate parts.

1	as	to	for	about
2	directed	signaled	gestured	pointed
3	models	sculptures	shapes	impressions
4	acted	controlled	radiated	chosen
5	discover	find	realize	show

PART 3: LISTENING

SECTION 1: SUMMARIZE SPOKEN TEXT

A You will hear a short lecture. Write a summary for a fellow student who was not present at the lecture. You should write 50–70 words.

You will have 10 minutes to finish this task. Your response will be judged on the quality of your writing and on how well your response presents the key points presented in the lecture.

2.31 Play the CD to listen to the recording that goes with this item.

....
....
....
....
....
....

B You will hear a short lecture. Write a summary for a fellow student who was not present at the lecture. You should write 50–70 words.

You will have 10 minutes to finish this task. Your response will be judged on the quality of your writing and on how well your response presents the key points presented in the lecture.

2.32 Play the CD to listen to the recording that goes with this item.

....
....
....
....
....
....

C You will hear a short lecture. Write a summary for a fellow student who was not present at the lecture. You should write 50–70 words.

You will have 10 minutes to finish this task. Your response will be judged on the quality of your writing and on how well your response presents the key points presented in the lecture.

2.33 Play the CD to listen to the recording that goes with this item.

....
....
....
....
....
....

SECTION 2: MULTIPLE-CHOICE, CHOOSE MULTIPLE ANSWERS

A Listen to the recording and answer the question by selecting all the correct responses. You will need to select more than one response.

Which of the following conditions need to be met by parents who want to have their children educated at home?

1 They must provide lesson plans.

2 They must ensure their child plays a sport.

3 They must provide regular assessments.

4 They must provide book lists.

5 They must keep a record of attendance.

 2.34 Play the CD to listen to the recording that goes with this item.

B Listen to the recording and answer the question by selecting all the correct responses. You will need to select more than one response.

According to the text, who were originally responsible for popularizing rice in Europe?

1 the Chinese

2 the Greeks

3 the Spanish

4 the Indians

5 the Italians

6 the Arabs

 2.35 Play the CD to listen to the recording that goes with this item.

C Listen to the recording and answer the question by selecting all the correct responses. You will need to select more than one response.

Which of the following are suggested as reasons why contemporary writers on politics are less readable and relevant than the ancient writers?

1 They only write about institutions.

2 They tend to focus on only one aspect of political systems.

3 Being university-based forces them to specialize.

4 They ask largely irrelevant questions.

5 They follow the example of 19th century writers.

 2.36 Play the CD to listen to the recording that goes with this item.

SECTION 2: FILL IN THE BLANKS

A   You will hear a recording. Write the missing words in each blank.

There have been many studies in America of the **(1)** .... and behavior of university lecturers and professors, and of well-known "free" or public thinkers who are not **(2)** .... to a university or other **(3)** .... , which show that those who are recognized as being more successful or productive as scholars in their field, or are at the best universities, are much more likely to have critical opinions. That is to say that they are more likely to hold liberal views – in the American use of that word – than those of their **(4)** .... who are less creative or who have less of a **(5)** .... The better a university is, as measured by the test results of its students or by the prestige of its **(6)** .... , the more likely it has been that there will be student unrest and a relatively left-of-center faculty.

 2.37 Play the CD to listen to the recording that goes with this item.

For Further Guidance, see page 109.

B   You will hear a recording. Write the missing words in each blank.

However simple or complex the chain of events in any given situation, when looked into it usually reveals a train of **(1)** .... relationships – they are seen to be **(2)** .... in some way. The methods of analysis aim to establish these relationships and provide a solid background for useful **(3)** .... based on what at first appear to be separate events. The first step in this process is to collect facts and then see if any particular **(4)** .... emerge. If they do, it then becomes possible to form theories related to the facts, and this type of empirical theory forms a useful basis for **(5)** .... and prediction. However, on its own this theory is not enough; the essential second step is to test it by collecting more facts and by checking predictions against events. These new facts may mean you have to **(6)** .... the theory, bearing in mind that new facts can only either disprove or **(7)** .... a theory – they cannot prove it to be right.

 2.38 Play the CD to listen to the recording that goes with this item.

C   You will hear a recording. Write the missing words in each blank.

It is difficult to know how to place Montesquieu – if you're the kind of person who likes to **(1)** .... Historian, political philosopher, **(2)** .... , jurist or, if you think the *Persian Letters* a novel, a novelist – he was all these things. Perhaps, as some have, he could be placed among that almost extinct species, the man of **(3)** .... The books that make up *The Spirit of the Laws* have had the most **(4)** .... on later thinkers, and in them, as in his equally great *Considerations on the Causes of the Grandeur and Decadence of the Romans*, he makes his underlying purpose clear. It is to make the random, apparently meaningless variety of events understandable; he wanted to find out what the historical truth was. His starting point then was this almost endless variety of morals, **(5)** .... , ideas, laws and institutions and to make some sense out of them. He believed it was not chance that ruled the world, and that, beyond the chaos of accidents, there must be underlying causes that **(6)** .... for the apparent madness of things.

 2.39 Play the CD to listen to the recording that goes with this item.

FILL IN THE BLANKS

WHAT'S TESTED

The purpose of this task is to assess your ability to identify missing words in a transcript as you listen to a recording. Only listening skills are assessed. You will hear a recording, and read a transcript that has up to seven blanks in it where words are missing. You have to type in the missing words that you hear. Each recording will be played only once. The recordings are from 30 to 60 seconds long. You will hear either two or three fill in the blanks items. The individual tasks in Listening Part 3 are not timed. You will have between 45 and 57 minutes to complete all of Listening Part 3, depending on which form of the PTE Academic you receive.

TIPS

- There is a seven-second pause before the recording begins. Use this time to skim the transcript. You will not have enough time to read it in detail, but by skimming it, you will have a better idea of what the recording will be about.

- Before the recording begins, place the cursor on the first word of the transcript so that you are ready to type when the speaker gets to the missing word.

- Watch the timer in the status box so that you will be ready to follow the text as soon as the recording begins. When the recording begins, follow the text with the cursor or your finger on the screen.

- It is important to read along at the same speed as the recording. If you fall behind do your best to find where the speaker is in the transcript. If you hear a slight pause, this often – but not always – signals that the speaker has finished one sentence and is about to start the next. In English, sentences always begin with capital letters. Scan the text for capitals during the pause.

- You can use the "tab" key to advance to the next blank after you have finished typing. This is quicker and more accurate than using the mouse.

- You will need to be able to read at the same speed that the recording is playing. If you are a naturally slow reader, you will need to practice reading more quickly.

- Be sure to check your answers when you have finished. Check that there are no typing errors or spelling mistakes. Quickly read the complete transcript with your words in it. Does it make sense? Only change words that you are sure are wrong.

A DETAILED STUDY

The exercise below will help you to practice listening for missing words.Listen to Recording A on page 108 again and read the transcript. The transcript has some words missing. The first syllable of each missing word has been provided. Listen to the recording and fill in the missing words.

There have been many studies in America of the opinions and **(1)** be........................ of university lecturers and professors, and of well-known "free" or public thinkers who are not attached to a **(2)** un........................ or other institution, which show that those who are **(3)** re........................ as being more successful or **(4)** pro........................ as scholars in their field, or are at the best universities, are much more likely to have **(5)** cri........................ opinions. That is to say that they are more likely to hold liberal views – in the American use of that word – than those of their **(6)** col........................ who are less creative or who have less of a reputation. The better a university is, as measured by the test results of its students or by the prestige of its staff, the more likely it has been that there will be student unrest and a **(7)** rel........................ left-of-center faculty.

Now check your answers.

SECTION 2: HIGHLIGHT CORRECT SUMMARY

A You will hear a recording. Choose the paragraph that best relates to the recording.

1

The speaker is a trained marine biologist who became an anthropologist after hearing about an ancient people who lived on beaches and got their food from the sea. Because he was a keen fisherman, he identified with these people and began to study anthropology. They lived in a very simple way, catching fish with their hands and gathering shells, such as oysters.

2

The speaker is a marine biologist who became interested in the Strandlopers, an ancient people who lived on the coastline, because of their and his connection to the sea. Their way of life intrigued him – as a child he had spent a lot of time by the sea, exploring and collecting things – so he began to study them, and discovered some interesting information about their way of life, how they hunted, what tools they used, and so on.

3

The speaker is a marine biologist who became an archaeologist when he heard about a mythical people called the Strandlopers, or beach-walkers. He was interested in them because as a child he had lived by the sea and so he identified with them. His aim was to prove they were not a myth and set about finding evidence to prove they really existed, and in this he was successful.

 2.40 Play the CD to listen to the recording that goes with this item.

B You will hear a recording. Choose the paragraph that best relates to the recording.

1

To understand the past you have to be able, as far as possible, to think as the people in the period you are studying thought. The example of what it must have been like to be a peasant in the Middle Ages is used. However, sensibilities change over time and we can't completely throw off the mentality of the present. Therefore, every age will have a slightly different perspective on the same period of the past, no matter what the facts are.

2

The text explains how, in order to understand people in the historical period they are studying, a historian must have the same ability the novelist has to get into the minds of characters. This is due to the fact that the world was different then, and the ways of thinking have changed, for example, between the Middle Ages and the 21st century. He explains this by saying historian's sensibilities change over time.

3

As a historian, if you really want to understand the sensibilities of those who lived in the past, you must be like a novelist and get into the skins of your characters and think and feel as they do. You are asked to imagine what it's like to be a peasant in medieval times, asking the sort of questions a peasant might ask. What the writer is saying is that a historian needs imaginative sympathy with ordinary people in the past.

 2.41 Play the CD to listen to the recording that goes with this item.

For Further Guidance, see page 111.

HIGHLIGHT CORRECT SUMMARY

A DETAILED STUDY

The exercise below will help you to identify the correct summary by focusing on information presented in the recording. Listen to Lecture B from page 110 again and answer the following multiple-choice questions.

1 The speaker says that to understand the past we must understand how people in that age

....

   a thought and acted

   b related to the natural environment

2 The Middle Ages are mentioned as an example of ....

   a a time of political troubles

   b a historical period

3 The peasant the speaker mentions is ....

   a a character in a novel

   b an ordinary person

4 The speaker emphasizes the need to ....

   a learn to see the world in a new way

   b have a strong, creative imagination

5 The speaker makes the point that ....

   a every age has a different view of history

   b history is a fascinating subject to study

Now read the paragraphs on page 110 again and choose the one that best summarizes the recording.

Now check your answers.

SECTION 2: MULTIPLE-CHOICE, CHOOSE SINGLE ANSWER

A Listen to the recording and answer the multiple-choice question by selecting the correct response. Only one response is correct.

Which of the following statements is true about the use of contour lines in map-making?

1 They were first used on Ordnance Survey maps.

2 Before the 16th century they were used to show hills, valleys and rivers.

3 Land contour lines were first used on a map of France.

4 Contour lines originally had a military purpose.

 3.1 Play the CD to listen to the recording that goes with this item.

B Listen to the recording and answer the multiple-choice question by selecting the correct response. Only one response is correct.

According to the text, when did signs advertising businesses become compulsory?

1 In the Middle Ages

2 During the Roman occupation of Britain

3 In the 17th century

4 In the 14th century

 3.2 Play the CD to listen to the recording that goes with this item.

C Listen to the recording and answer the multiple-choice question by selecting the correct response. Only one response is correct.

Which of the following statements is true, according to the text?

1 There were no root crops in medieval times.

2 Potatoes and tomatoes were extremely popular.

3 In the 16th century people had a wider choice of food.

4 Spices were too expensive for the average person.

 3.3 Play the CD to listen to the recording that goes with this item.

SECTION 2: SELECT MISSING WORD

A You will hear a recording about climate change. *At the end of the recording, the last word or group of words has been replaced by a beep.* Select the correct option to complete the recording.

1 good production and wealth

2 food production and health

3 full production and wealth

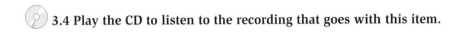 **3.4 Play the CD to listen to the recording that goes with this item.**

B You will hear a recording about parental discipline. *At the end of the recording, the last word or group of words has been replaced by a beep.* Select the correct option to complete the recording.

1 partners

2 parents

3 peers

4 punishment

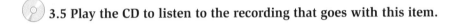 **3.5 Play the CD to listen to the recording that goes with this item.**

SECTION 2: HIGHLIGHT INCORRECT WORDS

> **ON-SCREEN**
> Remember that in the exam, you will click on the words that are different with your mouse in order to highlight them in yellow.

A   You will hear a recording. Below is a transcription of the recording. Some words in the transcription differ from what the speaker(s) said. As you listen, circle the words that are different.

"No news is good news" may be true for most of us most of the time – after all, we don't look forward to unpleasant things happening to us – but "Bad news is good news" is true for those who work in the news media, and, I suspect, for the rest of us, at least some of the time. It is tied up with stories and our seemingly unsatisfied need for stories. Have you ever been grasped by a story where nothing goes wrong for the characters? There's an accident in a Kingsley Amis novel that nicely illuminates this: the main character Jake comes home to find his wife chatting to a friend about a hairdresser both women know who has moved with his family to somewhere in Africa. Jake listens in, expecting tales of cannibalism and such like, but no, the friend has just received a letter saying they love the place and are settling in nicely. Jake leaves the room in disgrace.

We demand to be entertained, and while we don't object to a happy ending, the characters have to have experienced loss, pain and hardship in one form or another along the way to have earned it.

 3.6 Play the CD to listen to the recording that goes with this item.

B   You will hear a recording. Below is a transcription of the recording. Some words in the transcription differ from what the speaker(s) said. As you listen, circle the words that are different.

Leisure travel was, in a sense, a British invention. This was mostly due to economic and social factors; Britain was the first country to become fully industrialized, and industrial society offered greater numbers of people time for leisure. This, coupled with improvements in transport, especially the railways, meant that large numbers of people could get to holiday resorts in a very short time.

Modern mass tourism of a sort we can easily recognize today began in 1841 when Thomas Cook organized the first packet tour, in which everything was included in the price – travel, hotel and entertainment. To cater for the large numbers of new holiday-makers, holiday camps were established, both on the coast and in the countryside, and they became immensely popular. Their popularity declined, however, with the rise of cheap overseas tours, which gave many people their first opportunity to travel about.

 3.7 Play the CD to listen to the recording that goes with this item.

For Further Guidance, see page 115.

SECTION 2: WRITE FROM DICTATION

You will hear some sentences. Write each sentence exactly as you hear it. Write as much of each sentence as you can. You will hear each sentence only once.

 3.8 Play the CD to listen to the recording that goes with this item.

1 ....

2 ....

3 ....

4 ....

HIGHLIGHT INCORRECT WORDS

A DETAILED STUDY

The exercise below will help you to practice matching a recording with a transcript. Listen to the recordings while reading the transcripts. Circle the words in the transcript that do not match the recording.

1   A team of marine biologists studying whale carcasses – the dead bodies of whales – has found that they create a unique environment, one that is rich in animals and bacteria, including several new species.

2   When a whale dies, its body slowly sinks to the ocean floor, where it becomes food for a vast ecosystem.

3   One whale carcass contains more nutrients than would normally filter down through the water column in 2,000 years.

4   Using a submersible robot, the team collected collarbones of whales from the seafloor and raised them to the surface.

5   Back in the lab, the team found the bones were covered in bacteria and other organisms, more than 10 of which had never been catalogued before.

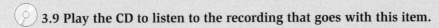 **3.9 Play the CD to listen to the recording that goes with this item.**

Now check your answers.

TEST 4

PART 1: SPEAKING AND WRITING

SECTION 1: PERSONAL INTRODUCTION

Read the prompt below. In 25 seconds, you must reply in your own words, as naturally and clearly as possible. You have 30 seconds to record your response. Your response will be sent together with your score report to the institutions selected by you.

Please introduce yourself. For example, you could talk about one or more of the following:

- Your interests
- Your plans for future study
- Why you want to study abroad
- Why you need to learn English
- Why you chose *this* test

SECTION 2: READ ALOUD

Look at the text below. In 40 seconds, you must read this text aloud as naturally and clearly as possible. You have 40 seconds to read aloud.

(Allow 40 seconds for each separate text.)

A Writers may make the mistake of making all their sentences too compact. Some have made this accusation against the prose of Gibbon. An occasional loose sentence prevents the style from becoming too formal and allows the reader to relax slightly. Loose sentences are common in easy, unforced writing, but it is a fault when there are too many of them.

B There is a long history of rulers and governments trying to legislate on men's hair – both the length of the hair on their heads and the style of facial hair. For practical reasons, Alexander the Great insisted his soldiers be clean-shaven, but Peter the Great of Russia went further, insisting no Russians had beards.

C Early in the 19th century, Wordsworth opposed the coming of the steam train to the Lake District, saying it would destroy its natural character. Meanwhile, Blake denounced the "dark satanic mills" of the Industrial Revolution. The conservation of the natural environment, however, did not become a major theme in politics until quite recently.

D In the distribution of wealth, America is more unequal than most European countries. The richest tenth of the population earns nearly six times more than the poorest tenth. In Germany and France, the ratio is just over three to one. The United States also has the largest proportion of its people in long-term poverty.

E Chaucer was probably the first English writer to see the English nation as a unity. This is the reason for his great appeal to his contemporaries. A long war with France had produced a wave of patriotism, with people no longer seeing each other as Saxon or Norman but as English.

F What can history tell us about contemporary society? Generally, in the past, even in Europe until the 18th century, it was assumed that it could tell how any society should work. The past was the model for the present and the future. It represented the key to the genetic code by which each generation produced its successors and ordered their relationships.

You can hear model answers on the CD3, track 10.

SECTION 2: REPEAT SENTENCE

You will hear some sentences. Please repeat each sentence exactly as you hear it. You will hear each sentence only once.

 3.11 Play the CD to listen to the recording that goes with this item.

For Further Guidance, see page 117.

REPEAT SENTENCE

A DETAILED STUDY

The exercises below will help you to practice listening carefully to and accurately repeating spoken sentences.

A You will hear eight sentences. First, cover all the answer options below with a piece of paper. Then, after hearing each sentence, uncover the two answer options and circle the sentence you heard.

 3.12 Play the CD to listen to the recording that goes with this item.

1

   a We're warming the climate, and the rate is increasing.

   b We're warning the client that the rates are increasing.

2

   a Much of his research objectives are driven by his natural curiosity and instincts.

   b Much of his research is objective and driven by his natural curiosity about insects.

3

   a They left the area almost immediately to avoid the devastation.

   b The fire left the area almost completely devoid of vegetation.

4

   a I'll now demonstrate how the reaction can be arrested by adding a dilute acid.

   b Now the demonstrators' reactions to the arrests are adding to the dilemma.

5

   a The initial results are intriguing; however, statistically speaking, they are insignificant.

   b The initial results are intriguing; however, statistically speaking, they're not significant.

6

   a The opposition has so far not responded to our proposal.

   b The opposition has so far been unresponsive to our proposal.

7

   a I believe the children should be allowed to read more.

   b I believe that children should read aloud more.

8

   a The majority of the hardware we're using was built for a customer.

   b The majority of the hardware we're using was billed to a customer.

Now check your answers.

B Now listen to the sentences again. Repeat each sentence exactly as you hear it. Concentrate on imitating the speed, rhythm, and stress of the speaker.

SECTION 2: DESCRIBE IMAGE

A Look at the chart below. Describe in detail what the chart is showing. You will have 40 seconds to give your response.

Measures taken in households to, or receipt of, offensive Internet material, 2003/04, England & Wales

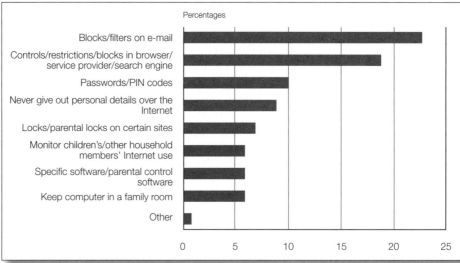

B Look at the graph below. Describe in detail what the graph is showing. You will have 40 seconds to give your response.

Premium unleaded petrol and diesel pump prices, UK

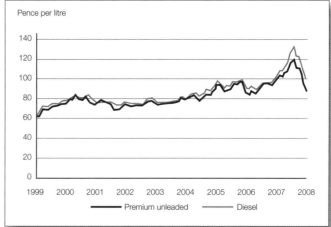

For Further Guidance, see page 120.

C Look at the picture below. Describe in detail what the picture is showing. You will have 40 seconds to give your response.

D Look at the pie chart below. Describe in detail what the pie chart is showing. You will have 40 seconds to give your response.

Survey of means of transport used by commuters living outside the city

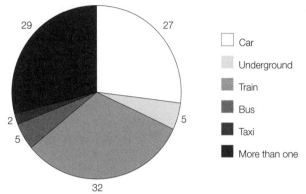

E Look at the graph below. Describe in detail what the graph is showing. You will have 40 seconds to give your response.

Morgan Drinks Company, projected sales of soft drinks

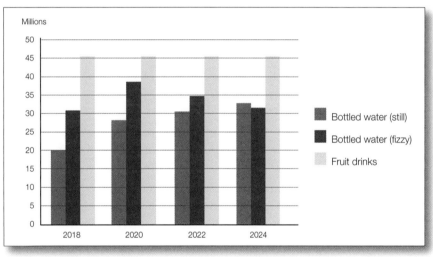

F Look at the map below. Describe in detail what the map is showing. You will have 40 seconds to give your response.

World forest distribution

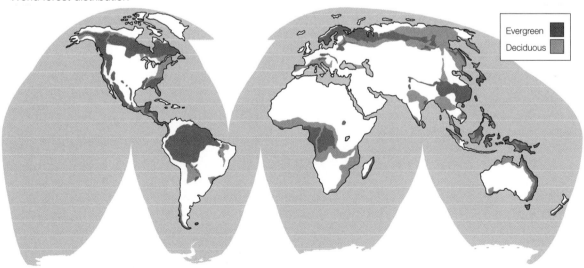

You can hear model answers on the CD3, track 13.

DESCRIBE IMAGE

A DETAILED STUDY

The exercise below will help you to practice describing a graph. Look at Graph B on page 118. Read the sentences below, which have been taken from a model answer. Each sentence contains a mistake. Underline each mistake and write what it should say.

1 This graph shows the pump price for unleaded petrol and diesel in Europe from 1999 until 2008.

    ....

2 The first thing to notice is that the line for diesel is always lower than for premium unleaded, which means it's generally more expensive.

    ....

3 The other thing to notice is that the price for both fuels roughly doubled from 1999 to 2008, going from about 62 or 63 pence a litre to more than 120 pence a litre in the case of petrol.

    ....

4 Prices for both seemed to peak in 2008, but fell dramatically later that same year, diesel ending on a price of 100 pence per litre and petrol on a price of about 80 pence per litre.

    ....

Now check your answers.

SECTION 2: RE-TELL LECTURE

A You will hear a lecture. After listening to the lecture, please retell what you have just heard from the lecture in your own words. You will have 40 seconds to give your response.

Niccolò Machiavelli (1469–1527)

 3.14 Play the CD to listen to the recording that goes with this item.

B You will hear a lecture. After listening to the lecture, please retell what you have just heard from the lecture in your own words. You will have 40 seconds to give your response.

3.15 Play the CD to listen to the recording that goes with this item.

C You will hear a lecture. After listening to the lecture, please retell what you have just heard from the lecture in your own words. You will have 40 seconds to give your response.

3.16 Play the CD to listen to the recording that goes with this item.

You can hear model answers on the CD3, track 17.

SECTION 2: ANSWER SHORT QUESTION

You will hear some questions. Please give a simple and short answer to each one. Often just one or a few words is enough.

3.18 Play the CD to listen to the recording that goes with this item.

SECTION 3: SUMMARIZE WRITTEN TEXT

Read the passage below and summarize it using one sentence. You have 10 minutes to finish this task. Your response will be judged on the quality of your writing and on how well your response presents the key points in the passage.

For those political analysts whose main interest remains class divisions in society the biggest split these days is that between those who control and work with informational technology (IT) and those we might still call blue-collar workers. The old divisions of class have become a lot more difficult to apply, if not completely outdated. There's no escaping the enormous impact of information technology in the late 20th and, even more, the early 21st centuries, both economically and socially.

During the scientific revolution of the 17th and 18th centuries, the spirit of experiment was in the air, and those involved were practical people working to practical ends – often on their own or with a small group of trusted friends. Secrecy was important as there was money to be made in new inventions. What interested them were results, not theories. Most modern technological advances, however, were developed as theories first, and then made reality by large teams of scientists and experts in the field. What we have now is that more and more of this type of expertise is being used to analyse and find solutions to all kinds of business and social problems, thus creating – in the eyes of the political analysts mentioned above – a whole large new economic and social class.

....

....

....

....

SECTION 4: SUMMARIZE WRITTEN TEXT

Read the passage below and summarize it using one sentence. You have 10 minutes to finish this task. Your response will be judged on the quality of your writing and on how well your response presents the key points in the passage.

The English have the reputation of being a nation of tea drinkers, but this wasn't always the case. By the end of the 17th century, the English were the biggest coffee drinkers in the Western world, and coffee houses became the places to be seen. As well as gossip, you could pick up talk of the latest intellectual developments in science, politics, and so on, in this age of scientific discovery and progress. At first coffee houses were very basic; a room with a bar at one end and a few plain tables and chairs. Customers paid a penny for a bowl – not a cup – of coffee. A polite young woman was usually in charge of the bar because it was thought her presence would ensure that the customers didn't use bad language or cause any trouble. An added attraction was that coffee houses provided free newspapers and journals.

But people didn't go to the coffee houses just to drink coffee. They went to talk. They soon developed from simple cafés, where anyone with a penny could go for a drink and a chat, into clubs. People started to go to coffee houses where they would find other people who had the same jobs or who shared their interests and ideas, to talk and conduct business.

The great popularity of coffee houses lasted about a hundred years. In the later 18th century, increased trade with other countries made such luxuries as coffee cheaper and more easily available to the ordinary person. As a result people started to drink it at home. Also at this time more tea was imported from abroad, and the century of the coffee house was replaced by the domestic tea-party as the typical English social occasion.

....

....

....

....

SECTION 5: WRITE ESSAY

You will have 20 minutes to plan, write and revise an essay about the topic below. Your response will be judged on how well you develop a position, organize your ideas, present supporting details, and control the elements of standard written English. You should write 200–300 words.

Most people in what are known as the developed nations have homes full of gadgets and labor-saving devices, from vacuum cleaners and dishwashers to the latest in computer technology. Some people claim that despite all these labor-saving devices, we seem to have less free time.

In your opinion, has technology improved the quality of life or made it more complicated? Support your arguments with reasons and/or examples from your own experience and observations.

....
....
....
....
....
....
....
....
....

SECTION 6: WRITE ESSAY

You will have 20 minutes to plan, write and revise an essay about the topic below. Your response will be judged on how well you develop a position, organize your ideas, present supporting details, and control the elements of standard written English. You should write 200–300 words.

A recent trend in the entertainment world is to adapt classic works of literature for either TV or the movies. One argument is that this is to everyone's benefit, as it introduces people to works they might otherwise never have experienced, while others say that turning books into movies not only cheapens the original, but is rarely done successfully.

In your opinion, do works of literature translate effectively to the screen? Support your arguments with reasons and/or examples from your own experience and observations.

....
....
....
....
....
....
....
....
....

For Further Guidance, see page 124.

WRITE ESSAY

A DETAILED STUDY

The exercise below will help you to plan an essay. Read the essay prompt for Section 6 on page 123. Below are parts of a response to the prompt. Decide which extract (A–G) is most suitable for each paragraph (1–4). You will not use all the extracts.

Paragraph 1: ....

Paragraph 2: ....

Paragraph 3: ....

Paragraph 4: ....

A

With so many books now available electronically, either as so-called e-books, or as digital files available for download on the Internet, it should surprise no one that traditional books are becoming increasingly irrelevant to young audiences. Adaptations for the movies and TV are clearly the best way to reach youngsters.

B

Some people feel that adapting classic works for the movies or TV brings these works to a wider audience, introducing people to works they might not otherwise have experienced. Adaptation, they claim, broadens our horizons and gives us access to higher culture. This is true, as long as the adaptation retains the key elements of the original work.

C

A recent trend in the entertainment world has been to adapt classic works of literature for the movies or TV. Although the results of this are often very popular, not everyone agrees that this is a good thing. I'd like to argue that it depends on the quality of the adaptation.

D

Other people feel that adapting classic works detracts from the originals, and that, in fact, the movie or TV version of a classic work may become better known than the original. Adaptation, they claim, lowers our cultural standards. This view, however, assumes that written works are necessarily of better quality than works produced for the screen, which is not necessarily the case.

E

Because so many of our shared cultural references come from classic literature, it is important that these works be introduced in schools – and the earlier the better. Increasingly, young people today are more likely to know these classic references through the movies and TV, rather than from original sources, and this is to the detriment of our collective culture.

F

Most of the works adapted for the movies and TV have been novels written recently, especially those in the fantasy or science fiction genres, because these lend themselves more easily to animation and digital special effects.

G

In my opinion, neither view is correct on its own. The truth is somewhere in the middle. One can point to cases that support both points. Some adaptations have been highly successful in faithfully presenting the original work, while other adaptations have failed miserably, and should probably have never been attempted.

Now check your answers.

PART 2: READING

MULTIPLE-CHOICE, CHOOSE SINGLE ANSWER

A Read the text and answer the multiple-choice question by selecting the correct response. Only one response is correct.

On meeting a person for the first time, our first question is often "What do you do?" That is, we ask what they do for a living, what their job is, because we feel this will help us place them. It helps us to define their status. We can judge where they stand socially, we can make a guess at how much they earn, and through that what kind of a standard of living they can afford. In addition, it can give us a fairly good idea of their educational background.

The problem is that people often choose a career for the wrong reasons. For instance, some people follow in the footsteps of a parent, either entering the same trade or profession, or inheriting the family business. Others make exactly the opposite decision, either out of a fierce desire for independence, or to spite a parent, or simply to get away from family. They decide that whatever else they might do, they will certainly not do what their mother or father did. People may also persuade themselves to pursue a career for which they are unsuited out of hero-worship, or as a result of meeting people they admire. It is a pity that we have to make such an important decision about our future career at a stage in our lives when we are so easily influenced by factors which have little or nothing to do with the central issue, namely, that we should do those things for which we have a natural talent.

Which of the following is not given as an example of a wrong reason for choosing a career?

1 Doing the same job as one's parents.

2 Doing a job that suits your abilities.

3 Deliberately not joining the family business.

4 Following the career path of someone you admire.

B Read the text and answer the multiple-choice question by selecting the correct response. Only one response is correct.

Politically, the Roman Empire laid the foundations on which modern Europe was built. Culturally, partly through native genius and partly through absorbing the achievements of the older and richer culture of Greece, its literature became the basis of European values, in particular those values that arise out of the individual's relationship to their society. Rome began to produce literature between 300 and 100 BC at about the same time as it was conquering the rich Greek colonies in the south of Italy.

Roman writers and orators began to expand their imaginative and intellectual horizons and refine the Latin language through the study of Greek literature. Early Roman literature had been basically of two kinds: the recording and examination of public life and behavior through life stories of famous men, and the particularly Roman art of satirical comedy and drama.

There were those, however, who objected to the Greek influence, most notably Cato the Censor, who did his best to uphold the virtues of no-nonsense Latin prose against Greek luxury. More typical, and in the end more successful, was the poet Ennius, who managed to keep a balance between Greek and Latin values by writing a Homeric epic poem in Latin idiom, but using Greek poetic metre.

According to the text, which of the following statements is true of ancient Roman literature?

1 It was mainly the biographies of famous men.

2 It was deeply influenced by Greek writing.

3 It was mostly satirical.

4 It was subject to heavy censorship.

MULTIPLE-CHOICE, CHOOSE MULTIPLE ANSWERS

A   Read the text and answer the question by selecting all the correct responses.
More than one response is correct.

Before Luke Howard invented his system for classifying clouds, they had simply been described by their shape and color as each person saw them: they were too changeable and moved too quickly for anyone to think they could be classified in any useful way. Howard had been interested in clouds – and meteorology in general – ever since he was a small boy, and for thirty years kept a record of his meteorological observations. In 1802–1803, he produced a paper in which he named the clouds, or, to be more precise, classified them, claiming that it was possible to identify several simple categories within the various and complex cloud forms. As was standard practice for the classification of plant and animal species, they were given Latin names, which meant that the system could be understood throughout Europe.

Howard believed that all clouds belonged to three distinct groups; *cumulus*, *stratus* and *cirrus*. He added a fourth category, *nimbus*, to describe a cloud "in the act of condensation into rain, hail or snow". It is by observing how clouds change color and shape that weather can be predicted, and as long as the first three types of cloud keep their normal shape there won't be any rain.

This system came to be used across the European continent, and in the 20th century his cloud classification system was adopted, with some additions, as the international standard, but that was not his only contribution to meteorology. He wrote papers on barometers and theories of rain, and what is probably the first textbook on weather. He can also be considered to be the father of what is now called "urban climatology". Howard had realized that cities could significantly alter meteorological elements. One of these he called "city fog". Nowadays we call it "smog", a combination of smoke and fog.

Which of the following achievements can be attributed to Luke Howard?

1   He wrote a book about barometers.

2   He was the first to notice the different shapes and colors of clouds.

3   He was the first to identify and classify different cloud forms.

4   His classification system became used all over the world.

5   He was the first to use the word "smog".

6   He realized that cities could have an effect on the weather.

For Further Guidance, see page 128.

B   Read the text and answer the question by selecting all the correct responses.
More than one response is correct.

When does a hobby or pastime, or whatever you want to call what you do in your leisure time for rest and relaxation, cease to be a hobby or a pastime and become something a bit more serious, such as something you realize can be turned into financial gain, or an obsession that can mess up your life as much as any other addiction? The whole point of them, of course, is that they are done out of personal interest and for pleasure and enjoyment, not for financial gain.

Most people's hobbies turn out to be easy and stress-free pastimes such as collecting things, making things, sports, playing a musical instrument, reading, and so on. And – so it is claimed – they are good for you, too. Pursuing a hobby can have calming and helpful beneficial effects. For a start, it can take your mind off your problems, and the more interests you have, the more you enjoy life.

One way in which the subject becomes a little bit serious is when you are applying for a job and writing out your curriculum vitae, or résumé. There's invariably a section which asks what your outside interests are, and because getting a job is a serious business, and you want to impress your prospective employers, you might find yourself claiming that you like nothing better at weekends than being flown by helicopter to the top of the Alps and then making your way home by snowboard and hang-glider. Perhaps people find themselves doing this because they feel that applying for a job and coming across well at interview is a test of character and being an aficionado of extreme sports is a lot cooler than stamp collecting. But why turn what is supposed to be calming and relaxing into a cause for anxiety?

Which of the following statements are true about hobbies and pastimes, according to the text?

1 They are often used as therapy.

2 They are not pursued for economic profit.

3 Your leisure time activities reveal your true character.

4 Many people do extreme sports because it's cool.

5 Most people's hobbies are simple and undemanding.

MULTIPLE-CHOICE, CHOOSE MULTIPLE ANSWERS

A DETAILED STUDY

The exercise below will help you to practice answering multiple-answer multiple-choice items. Read Text A on page 126 and answer the following questions.

1 What did Howard write about barometers?

   a papers

   b textbooks

2 How were clouds described before Howard's classification system?

   a by their height in the atmosphere

   b by their shape and color

3 What is mentioned about Howard's system?

   a It was the first to organize cloud forms in groups.

   b It was based on an earlier system.

4 What cloud identification system is used internationally?

   a One based on Howard's ideas.

   b One based on theories of rain.

5 What term did Howard coin?

   a smog

   b city fog

6 What is Howard considered the father of?

   a rain theory

   b urban climatology

Now check your answers.

RE-ORDER PARAGRAPHS

> **ON-SCREEN**
> Remember that in the exam, you will re-order the paragraphs
> by dragging and dropping them with your mouse.

A The paragraphs have been placed in a random order. Restore the original order.

Jumbled paragraphs	Correct paragraph order (1–4)
a By 1817, trousers were shoe-length. Popular with the king, they became accepted as standard daywear by 1825, and were worn with a waistcoat and, by day, a frock coat, but with a tailcoat in the evening.	
b Jackets didn't become fashionable for casual wear until the 1850s. The jacket was derived from the short jacket worn by boys and working men, and in the age of mass-production and ready-made suits, its simple style was easier to produce than the tailored coat.	
c It was George "Beau" Brummell, the champion of simple English style, who started a trend for wearing tight black trousers in the early 1800s.	
d The favorite patterns for trousers were strong plaids, stripes and checks. The loose straight cut came in about the 1860s, and front creases in the 1880s. By the turn of the century, they had become the common way to dress.	

B The paragraphs have been placed in a random order. Restore the original order.

Jumbled paragraphs	Correct paragraph order (1–5)
a Between May and August 1783, two volcanic eruptions had occurred, one in Iceland and one in Japan. The northern hemisphere had been covered in a "great fog".	
b A year earlier, a volcano had erupted in Indonesia, sending up vast quantities of fine volcanic dust into the atmosphere. Circling the Earth, the dust reflected sunlight back into space.	
c This, of course, was an extraordinary event. In fact, it is considered one of the most catastrophic global events in recorded history. But something like it had happened before, and within living memory.	

d	
The Earth literally darkened, temperatures dropped. Throughout western Europe and North America crops failed, and cattle died. A large portion of the world lay under a huge volcanic cloud.	
e	
In the spring of 1816, the weather suddenly changed. The unseasonably warm spring turned cold and people were forced indoors by continual rain. The skies darkened and there was no summer.	

C The paragraphs have been placed in a random order. Restore the original order.

Jumbled paragraphs	Correct paragraph order (1–5)
a Only four years later did football become an official competition at the Games. At this stage it was, of course, for amateurs only.	
b Ironically, the first tournament was won by an amateur team from the north-east of England, who had been especially invited after the British Football Association refused to be associated with the competition.	
c The first international football match was played in 1872 between England and Scotland, when football was rarely played anywhere outside Great Britain.	
d As an alternative, Sir Thomas Lipton decided to organize an event for professionals. Often described as The First World Cup, it took place in Turin in 1909 and featured the most prestigious professional clubs from Italy, Germany and Switzerland.	
e However, as football increased in popularity, it was admitted to the Olympics™ in 1900 and 1904, but only as a sideshow and not in the competition for medals.	

READING: FILL IN THE BLANKS

> **ON-SCREEN**
> Remember that in the exam, you will fill the blanks by
> dragging and dropping the words with your mouse.

A In the text below some words are missing. Choose the correct word to fill each blank from the box below. There are more words than you need to complete the exercise.

You may think that the World Cup, like the Olympic Games™, only occurs once every four years. It is the **(1)** .... rounds that take **(2)** .... every four years, but the competition as a whole is an ongoing **(3)** .... , since the qualifying rounds take place over the preceding three years. The final phase of the tournament now involves thirty-two teams competing over a four-week **(4)** .... in a previously nominated **(5)** .... nation. It has become the most widely-viewed sporting event in the world.

event	final	home	host	last	period	place	time

B In the text below some words are missing. Choose the correct word to fill each blank from the box below. There are more words than you need to complete the exercise.

Ideas as well as people can take **(1)** .... stage at the right time and the right place. If new ideas are to have a wide-ranging **(2)** .... , they had better occur at the right time – usually when old theories are worn out or have reached a dead **(3)** .... Then they make people think along new lines and in ways that may **(4)** .... in unexpected directions. These ideas needn't be new in themselves. They can be older, half-forgotten ideas brought back to life, or new combinations of **(5)** .... ones presented in a new light.

center	effect	end	familiar	front	known	lead	stop

C In the text below some words are missing. Choose the correct word to fill each blank from the box below. There are more words than you need to complete the exercise.

Most of us believe that when we are making decisions about money we are being clear-headed and sensible, and assume that any rational person would **(1)** .... in the same way and make the same decisions. But our **(2)** .... are always based on the private logic of our own **(3)** .... mind-set, our deep beliefs about money and what it's for, and no two people are the same. Even when two people come to the same **(4)** .... , they have probably used quite different logical paths.

answer	behave	choices	conclusion	economical	financial	ideas

For Further Guidance, see page 133.

D In the text below some words are missing. Choose the correct word to fill each blank from the box below. There are more words than you need to complete the exercise.

There are, I have been **(1)** .... , some languages that don't have a word for rubbish, garbage, or whatever you call it. For their speakers, nothing is useless or goes to **(2)** .... – just as our ancestors used to hoard, patch up, reuse and hand things **(3)** .... to the next generation rather than throw them **(4)** .... These days, however, rubbish and how to **(5)** .... of it has become a major problem: we are running out of places to put it.

away	dispose	waste	over	said	down	rid	told

E In the text below some words are missing. Choose the correct word to fill each blank from the box below. There are more words than you need to complete the exercise.

A "duel of honour" was a way of settling disputes between gentlemen over some injury or insult. The **(1)** .... had to be arranged privately because duelling was never **(2)** .... , but it became common in the 17th century. A social code governed the duel of honour and, as long as the rules were **(3)** .... to, the survivor could usually escape without being punished by the law. Duels were fought with either pistols or swords, but pistols became the more usual **(4)** .... after swords went out of fashion at the end of the 18th century.

battle	fight	gun	kept	legal	obeyed	weapon

FILL IN THE BLANKS

A DETAILED STUDY

The exercise below will help you to use context clues to eliminate answer choices. Look at Text C on page 131 and answer the following questions.

1 What part of speech must the word in the first blank be?

....

2 Based on your answer to the previous question, which of the answer choices cannot go in the first blank?

....

3 What part of speech must the word in the second blank be?

....

4 Based on your answer to the previous question, which of the answer choices cannot go in the second blank?

....

5 What part of speech must the word in the third blank be?

....

6 Based on your answer to the previous question, which of the answer choices cannot go in the third blank?

....

7 What part of speech must the word in the last blank be?

....

8 Based on your answer to the previous question, which of the answer choices cannot go in the last blank?

....

9 Is the blank part of an idiomatic expression?

....

Now check your answers.

READING AND WRITING: FILL IN THE BLANKS

A Below is a text with blanks. Select the appropriate answer choice for each blank.

The human body is designed to (1) .... physically rather than mentally to stressful situations. This instinctive reaction to a situation is (2) .... as the "fight or flight" response. The body is prepared to either stand and deal with the problem by fighting it, or to escape to safety. Even if the problem or threat is emotional and not physical, the body behaves in the same way: the heart beats faster, the muscles tense, and the skin sweats more. If someone finds themselves in a situation where there is no (3) .... to escape or overcome the (4) .... of the threat, then stress and anxiety will occur.

Some of the first signs that the pressure is getting to you are loss of concentration, inability to sleep, loss of temper for minor reasons, headaches, aching limbs and a general feeling of uneasiness. These (5) .... can lead on to more serious problems, such as high blood pressure which increases the risk of a heart attack. Stress weakens the body's defence system, so you are more likely to get minor ailments like colds. It can also lead to baldness. Mentally, it becomes harder and harder to perform your normal day-to-day activities, and can lead to a nervous breakdown. Recognizing all this is the first step (6) .... getting back to health and being able to cope with the causes of stress.

1	deal	respond	cope	act
2	called	named	known	referred
3	chance	occasion	hope	likelihood
4	reason	cause	manner	purpose
5	symptoms	infections	moods	pains
6	away	back	towards	forward

B Below is a text with blanks. Select the appropriate answer choice for each blank.

Most of the rubbish we produce – about two-thirds of it – goes into landfills. Now, it is (1) .... that the average UK household produces about one and a half tons of rubbish a year. These figures may not sound alarming, but the UK is geographically small and it all adds up, and there aren't many places (2) .... where we can dig huge holes and fill them with our rubbish, which is why ever-increasing amounts of waste from western countries are being exported to the developing world. Furthermore, (3) .... European recycling laws and higher landfill taxes mean that the days of dumping waste into landfill sites are almost at an end.

Landfill is cheap but wasteful and, as we have seen, unsustainable in the long run, whereas burning or incineration is expensive and wasteful. Besides, local communities don't want huge incineration plants in their back yards.

Recycling is considered by many to be the best solution, but it isn't nearly as good as most people think. The recycling process degrades most materials, so that they can only be used in limited ways. Also, many of the products we buy that are (4) .... as recyclable can only be recycled with great difficulty and at great (5) .... Perhaps the best idea is to have reusable packaging, such as returnable bottles and refillable packets.

1	researched	estimated	surveyed	assumed
2	still	over	around	left
3	harder	stricter	austere	extreme
4	labelled	marked	produced	branded
5	effort	cost	price	hardship

C Below is a text with blanks. Select the appropriate answer choice for each blank.

We all have our own ideas about what constitutes anti-social behavior, some of us being more tolerant than others, but the **(1)** .... definition allows for a fairly broad interpretation. To quote the Crime and Disorder Act of 1998, it is behavior which "causes or is likely to cause harassment, alarm or distress to one or more people who are not in the same household as the perpetrator". Such behavior **(2)** .... writing graffiti, which can make even the cleanest urban space look squalid, making excessive noise, especially at night, and throwing litter onto the streets. Such behavior, however, affects everyone in the community, and requires the community to work together to find ways of dealing with it.

Just as the problems are many and varied, the solution too must work effectively on many levels. Anti-social behavior is not confined to any particular **(3)** .... group, and it affects the quality of life of young and old **(4)** .... This in turn means that it needs an active partnership between all of the various social groups that make up society. More than an efficient police force is required. Schools, for example, need to have effective rules to deal with truancy and bullying. Landlords should take **(5)** .... for anti-social behavior by or against their tenants. The same also goes for local authorities and social services when taking decisions that affect the community. Furthermore, they need to share information as openly as possible.

1	real	actual	legal	proper
2	concerns	includes	means	involves
3	generation	child	community	age
4	both	alike	together	separately
5	blame	responsibility	action	measures

D Below is a text with blanks. Select the appropriate answer choice for each blank.

Is altruism, the state of acting unselfishly on behalf of others, a particularly human trait, or is it a behavior other species practice too? What's more to the point, is it in fact a trait we have at all, or can all our actions be finally attributed to self-interest, however selfless they might at first **(1)** .... ? For example, if you rush into your neighbour's burning house and save him and his family, this is naturally seen as a good and noble deed, but some would argue that it wasn't a natural human instinct that **(2)** .... you to put your life at **(3)** .... , but that your true motive was that you would expect you neighbour to do the same for you under **(4)** .... circumstances. Other species do co-operate and work together for the mutual benefit of the group, mainly in terms of hunting for food and defence and is for the collective good. But altruism proper suggests that little or no advantage attaches to the altruistic act – you might even lose your life in the process. Cynics will say that at bottom all our actions are **(5)** .... in some way or another, while those who take a rosier view believe that altruism, and goodness, are a part of human nature. Aristotle himself was a bit of an optimist in this matter, believing that all people were basically good, but that this quality could only be brought out within society and that, therefore, we are, in the original sense of the word, political animals.

1	be	claim	occur	appear
2	made	caused	took	provoked
3	danger	trouble	risk	peril
4	other	same	different	similar
5	motivated	selfish	bad	deceitful

E Below is a text with blanks. Select the appropriate answer choice for each blank.

In the past people traveled, if they had to, for particular and practical reasons, for example, to trade in other countries, to find better land to **(1)** .... , to get away from an unpleasant political regime or situation, or to go on a pilgrimage. But at what point did travel become tourism? Certainly, pilgrimages had a sort of holiday air about them, as any reader of Chaucer's *Canterbury Tales* will know. And people on pilgrimages to other countries did touristy things like bringing back **(2)** .... "Travel," however, as Skeat's etymological dictionary points out, was the same word as "travail," meaning effort or labor, because of "the toil of traveling in olden times." Over time, the pilgrimage became the Grand Tour which was fashionable in the 16th century and after. This was a **(3)** .... around Europe made by the sons of the wealthy with the supposed purpose of **(4)** .... them in the great cultures of the past, the architecture and works of art, especially in Italy. So it could be said that the Grand Tour had **(5)** .... of the pilgrimage about it. It is therefore possible, at a pinch, to date the origins of tourism to the medieval pilgrimage. But the word itself was only officially used for the first time in 1937, and referred to people traveling abroad for periods of over twenty-four hours.

1	grow	harvest	cultivate	pick
2	postcards	visas	photos	souvenirs
3	trip	travel	voyage	ride
4	educating	teaching	involving	filling
5	something	aspects	attitudes	similarities

F Below is a text with blanks. Select the appropriate answer choice for each blank.

The words "garden" and "paradise" are related by more than just having similar definitions. Both mean a piece of ground, often enclosed or walled, where fruit, flowers, herbs or vegetables can be grown. The word paradise has its root in the ancient Persian *pairi-daeza*, meaning "a place walled in, a park, a pleasure ground". Formal gardens have a long **(1)** .... , from the gardens of the pharaohs in Egypt to today's neat suburban gardens and urban allotments and rooftop gardens. They are places of refuge, where one can go for solitude, peace and quiet, for thought. Nature, which in its wild **(2)** .... is unpredictable and dangerous, is tamed and domesticated and made to serve man. Trade and military conquest carried the cultural development of the Egyptian garden to Persia, where emperors built private pleasure gardens full of shade and water, large enclosed game reserves and terraced parks **(3)** .... with trees and shrubs. In Egypt, to begin with, gardens in private homes and villas were mostly used for growing vegetables and located close to a canal or the river, later, however, they were often surrounded by walls and their purpose incorporated pleasure and beauty besides utility. This, of course, was for the rich. The poor, meanwhile, kept a patch for growing vegetables, rather like today's allotments. But central Persia is largely hot and dry and it is water that makes such gardens possible. Therefore they came up with a brilliantly **(4)** .... system of aqueducts which brought melted snow down to the central plains from the mountains in the north-east for irrigation. In fact, water became the essence of the Persian garden. A rich variety of species thrived while thin channels delivered water throughout the garden, feeding fountains and pools and **(5)** .... the atmosphere.

1	past	history	record	story
2	state	situation	places	areas
3	full	bedded	planted	covered
4	built	manufactured	engineered	formed
5	wetting	spraying	soothing	cooling

PART 3: LISTENING

SECTION 1: SUMMARIZE SPOKEN TEXT

A You will hear a short lecture. Write a summary for a fellow student who was not present at the lecture. You should write 50–70 words.

You will have 10 minutes to finish this task. Your response will be judged on the quality of your writing and on how well your response presents the key points presented in the lecture.

🔘 **3.19 Play the CD to listen to the recording that goes with this item.**

....

....

....

....

....

....

B You will hear a short lecture. Write a summary for a fellow student who was not present at the lecture. You should write 50–70 words.

You will have 10 minutes to finish this task. Your response will be judged on the quality of your writing and on how well your response presents the key points presented in the lecture.

🔘 **3.20 Play the CD to listen to the recording that goes with this item.**

....

....

....

....

....

....

C You will hear a short lecture. Write a summary for a fellow student who was not present at the lecture. You should write 50–70 words.

You will have 10 minutes to finish this task. Your response will be judged on the quality of your writing and on how well your response presents the key points presented in the lecture.

🔘 **3.21 Play the CD to listen to the recording that goes with this item.**

....

....

....

....

....

....

SECTION 2: MULTIPLE-CHOICE, CHOOSE MULTIPLE ANSWERS

A Listen to the recording and answer the question by selecting all the correct responses. You will need to select more than one response.

Which of the following are mentioned as health problems caused by noise?

1 Extreme irritation

2 A certain degree of hearing loss

3 Problems with speech

4 Mental problems

5 Behavioral and anger problems

 3.22 Play the CD to listen to the recording that goes with this item.

B Listen to the recording and answer the question by selecting all the correct responses. You will need to select more than one response.

According to the text, which of the following countries has a Poet Laureate?

1 the Caribbean

2 Ireland

3 Saint Lucia

4 the USA

5 Germany

6 France

 3.23 Play the CD to listen to the recording that goes with this item.

C Listen to the recording and answer the question by selecting all the correct responses. You will need to select more than one response.

Which of the following are mentioned as being difficult to re-adapt to when returning to your native country after a long absence?

1 Technological change

2 More than nine years' absence

3 The difference in time zones

4 The way people go about their daily lives

5 People's terms of reference in conversation

6 Changes in government

 3.24 Play the CD to listen to the recording that goes with this item.

SECTION 2: FILL IN THE BLANKS

A You will hear a recording. Write the missing words in each blank.

Privacy and the right to privacy are increasingly becoming hot **(1)** .... in the media, which is a touch **(2)** .... , given that it is often the media that is responsible for invasion of privacy. This is not just about those whose careers put them in the public eye, but ordinary people who through no fault of their own have come to public notice because of some event that has attracted the attention of the media. It might be that a member of their family has been **(3)** .... for some crime, **(4)** .... or wrongfully, or perhaps they are the **(5)** .... of some natural disaster. Some people argue that those who have chosen to be in the public sphere, and have teams of public **(6)** .... people to make sure they get as much public attention as possible – actors, rock stars, politicians and the like – have given up their right to privacy and get everything they deserve.

 3.25 Play the CD to listen to the recording that goes with this item.

B You will hear a recording. Write the missing words in each blank.

There is such a thing as information **(1)** .... There is just so much information out there now that we can't **(2)** .... with it or fully absorb it, or even decide which bits of it we want to keep in our minds, or which to **(3)** .... There is a similar thing going on with the range of choices we have as **(4)** .... There is so much stuff out there, so much to choose from, that, according to some experts, this situation is making us **(5)** .... Most of us believe that the more we have to choose from the better, yet apparently our dissatisfaction with this wealth of choice, or rather the anxiety it produces, is part of a larger **(6)** .... It seems that, as society grows more **(7)** .... and people become freer to do what they want, the unhappier they become.

 3.26 Play the CD to listen to the recording that goes with this item.

C You will hear a recording. Write the missing words in each blank.

Post-modernism is broadly speaking a **(1)** .... against the movement or the period, or perhaps simply the values and beliefs of, modernism. Most people, even those who seem to know what it is or was about, tend to define it in **(2)** .... terms by telling us what it isn't, or doesn't do. **(3)** .... the term had a fairly limited application and referred to a new anti-modernist style of architecture. But it spread like a virus to include almost all aspects of **(4)** .... culture. One thing we can be sure about is that it wanted to get rid of what were called the grand narratives by which we explained how the world – and history – got us from the past to the present. Another feature of post-modernism is its belief that truth and reality are human-centered and **(5)** .... That is, the primary **(6)** .... of truth in the present age is the self. This, I believe, has now all passed and been thrown in the rubbish bin of history. Yet it is difficult to know whether the age of information technology confirms the passing of post-modernism or is a consequence of it.

 3.27 Play the CD to listen to the recording that goes with this item.

SECTION 2: HIGHLIGHT CORRECT SUMMARY

A You will hear a recording. Choose the paragraph that best relates to the recording.

1

The subject is culture and the two kinds of it – material, which is to do with technology and science, such as genetics, and non-material, which is basically what we think about it, our beliefs and so forth. The speaker's main point is how our beliefs and attitudes resist developments in the material culture even when they know they are beneficial.

2

In comparing material with non-material culture – the first being the objects and technologies we create, and the second our customs, beliefs and attitudes – the speaker gives greater emphasis to the material culture. He gives the example of the development of genetic science and the benefits it has brought to mankind, despite a fair amount of opposition.

3

For the purposes of argument, culture is divided into material and non-material, and the speaker's aim is to show how they both affect each other. Material developments in tools and technology can affect non-material culture, our customs and beliefs, and the other way around. Genetics is used as an example as it has changed the way we think about life, but also our beliefs have affected its rate of development.

 3.28 Play the CD to listen to the recording that goes with this item.

B You will hear a recording. Choose the paragraph that best relates to the recording.

1

The main point is to question whether the biographical facts of a writer's life are of any importance in evaluating his work. Hemingway is the example used here, and there does seem to be a direct connection between the events of his life and those in his books, but knowing this should not get in the way of a true critical judgement of the works.

2

The writer Ernest Hemingway had a particularly eventful and exciting life and a lot of his real-life experiences got into his books. The speaker thinks this is irrelevant and doesn't believe that having lived such a full life makes the books any better, but he regrets that people now would prefer to read the biographies of writers rather than the books they wrote.

3

It is difficult to tell whether the speaker approves of Hemingway's lifestyle or not. He was famously *macho* and spent a lot of time hunting wild animals, going to wars and getting into fights. All these things got into his books, and the speaker thinks that this is not necessarily a good thing as it means that too many people prefer to read about his life than read his books.

 3.29 Play the CD to listen to the recording that goes with this item.

SECTION 2: MULTIPLE-CHOICE, CHOOSE SINGLE ANSWER

A Listen to the recording and answer the multiple-choice question by selecting the correct response. Only one response is correct.

Which of the following is not mentioned as being a type of genre fiction?

1 mainstream

2 gothic

3 fantasy

4 romance

5 crime

 3.30 Play the CD to listen to the recording that goes with this item.

B Listen to the recording and answer the multiple-choice question by selecting the correct response. Only one response is correct.

According to the text, which of the following statements is true about stress?

1 Most people with stress-related problems do not consult their doctor.

2 A tolerance for stress is easily acquired.

3 Stress levels depend on the kind of job you have.

4 Working long hours can also contribute to stress.

 3.31 Play the CD to listen to the recording that goes with this item.

C Listen to the recording and answer the multiple-choice question by selecting the correct response. Only one response is correct.

According to the text, which of the following statements is true?

1 Our genetic inheritance plays a greater role than the environment in making us who we are.

2 Our temperaments are determined by our environment.

3 Some scientists now believe intelligence is genetically determined.

4 All non-physical traits are inherited.

 3.32 Play the CD to listen to the recording that goes with this item.

SECTION 2: SELECT MISSING WORD

A You will hear a recording about using the library. *At the end of the recording, the last word or group of words has been replaced by a beep.* Select the correct option to complete the recording.

1 out where books are kept

2 yourself in the reference section

3 the article you're looking for

4 time to go to the library

 3.33 Play the CD to listen to the recording that goes with this item.

B You will hear a recording about the sense of touch. *At the end of the recording, the last word or group of words has been replaced by a beep.* Select the correct option to complete the recording.

1 is surely misunderstood

2 still poorly understood

3 will surely be understood

4 is rarely understood

 3.34 Play the CD to listen to the recording that goes with this item.

SECTION 2: HIGHLIGHT INCORRECT WORDS

> **ON-SCREEN**
> Remember that in the exam, you will click on the words that are different with your mouse in order to highlight them in yellow.

A You will hear a recording. Below is a transcription of the recording. Some words in the transcription differ from what the speaker(s) said. As you listen, circle the words that are different.

When societies were still mostly rural and agricultural, waste dispersal was hardly an issue, partly because people tended to make use of everything and partly because there was plenty of space to bury rubbish. It was when societies became predominantly urban and industrious that problems arose – mainly to do with wealth. City authorities had a hard time trying to find effective ways of getting rid of all the rubbish. One of these was to get people to set out their rubbish into different types, just as these days we are encouraged to separate our rubbish into different categories for easier removal and recycling. So, for example, kitchen rubbish was set aside and used for feeding animals. However, fears of disease put an end to that. In fact, it wasn't until the 20th century that all waste was simply thrown together and put into landfills.

 3.35 Play the CD to listen to the recording that goes with this item.

B You will hear a recording. Below is a transcription of the recording. Some words in the transcription differ from what the speaker(s) said. As you listen, circle the words that are different.

Archery, the practice or art of shooting with a bow and arrow, has played an important part in English history, being the major weapon of the foot-soldier and instrumental in winning many battles in wars with the French – with whom we seemed to be continuously at war during the Middle Ages. The English featured the longbow over the short bow and the crossbow, the latter being the main firearm of militias on the European continent. The crossbow fired a metal bolt released by a trigger, rather like a gun, and had the farthest range of any of the bows, but the main advantage of the longbow was its accuracy. The importance placed on archery is illustrated by the fact that medieval kings in England encouraged the practice and one of them, Edward III, went so far as to bar all sports on Sundays and holidays except archery. Because there were no standing armies in those days, and in the event of war rulers had to call on the populace, everything was done to make sure there were large numbers of competent, if not expert archers, to recruit.

 3.36 Play the CD to listen to the recording that goes with this item.

SECTION 2: WRITE FROM DICTATION

You will hear some sentences. Write each sentence exactly as you hear it. Write as much of each sentence as you can. You will hear each sentence only once.

3.37 Play the CD to listen to the recording that goes with this item.

1 ....

2 ....

3 ....

4 ....

For Further Guidance, see page 144.

WRITE FROM DICTATION

A DETAILED STUDY

The exercise below will help you to practice listening carefully and to write from dictation. Each sentence below has some words missing. You will hear the complete sentences. Listen and write the missing words.

1 The airline .... the recent round of airfare
   .... on higher costs for aviation fuel.

2 Because deep-drilling is .... , most
   geothermal energy exploration is limited to reservoirs of steam or hot water located ....
   ....

3 A bank .... all its customers' money on
   hand, which means that if a majority .... their
   funds at the same time, the bank would be unable to pay them.

4 Although there are some .... the two
   countries, the United States and Canada are very different in terms of ....
   .... climates, resources, and population sizes.

3.37 Play the CD to listen to the recording that goes with this item.

Now check your answers.

KEY AND EXPLANATION

TEST 1

PART 1: SPEAKING AND WRITING

Page 8

SECTION 2: REPEAT SENTENCE

1 Please come to the next seminar properly prepared.
2 You'll find the economics section on the second floor of the library.
3 Next time, we'll discuss the influence of the media on public policy.
4 There is plenty of cheap accommodation off-campus.
5 The lecture on child psychology has been postponed until Friday.
6 The meeting will take place in the main auditorium.
7 You must establish a day and a time with your tutor.
8 There will be no extensions given for this project.
9 New timetables will be posted on the student noticeboard.
10 All students are encouraged to vote in the forthcoming elections.

Pages 10–11

SECTION 2: DESCRIBE IMAGE

(Model answers)

A

This pie chart shows where people get the news from. The largest number, forty percent, get the news from the television, but this is closely followed by newspapers, which are used by thirty six percent. It seems surprising that the Internet comes third with only fifteen percent of people getting the news from there. Finally, only nine percent get the news from other sources.

B

This graph shows the unemployment rate amongst people of different ages from 1992 to 2010. The rates for people aged 16–17 were the highest over the whole period, reaching 45% in 2009 and 2010. Between 1992 and 1995 the unemployment level for those aged 18–20 was about 25%, then dropped below 20% until 2008 when they continued to rise, reaching 27 to 28% in 2010. The levels of unemployment for those aged between 21–24 both with and without a degree followed a similar pattern, beginning at about 15% in 1992 and ending at about 12% and 14% respectively in 2010. But apart from a period from about 1993–6 the level of unemployment was higher for those without a degree.

C

This bar graph shows how many tonnes of carbon dioxide were emitted by residents in various places. The lowest figure is for London, where only about six tonnes were emitted by each resident. The North East was by far the worst, with about twelve tonnes of CO_2 emissions per resident. It was followed by Yorkshire and The Humber with approximately 9.5 tonnes per resident. Residents of all other regions emitted between about seven and eight tonnes of CO_2 in 2008.

D

This bar graph shows the growth in the number of households with Internet access over the four year period from 2006 to 2009. Growth has been fairly steady over the period shown at around four or five percent each year. According to the graph, about seventy percent of households had Internet access by 2009. This compares to only about 57 percent in 2006.

E

Two things are illustrated by this graph which covers a twenty-year period running from 1989 until 2009: the number of overseas visitors to the UK and the number of UK residents going abroad. Both show steady growth until about 2008, although there was a slight dip in the number of overseas visitors to the UK between 2001 and 2002. In 2008, both types of travel dropped, with a particularly sharp decrease in the number of UK residents going abroad. Generally, throughout this period, more people from the UK went abroad than there were visitors to the UK.

F

This demographic graph breaks down the estimated population of the UK in 2010 by age and gender. The largest age group consists of men and women in their early 40s. Other large age groups in both sexes are the 20 to 30 age group, and the early 60s. Up until the 70s, the numbers of men and women remain fairly equal, but then in old age, women outnumber men. It seems surprising that there are not more children and young people in the UK population today.

Page 12

FURTHER PRACTICE AND GUIDANCE: *PART 1, SECTION 2: DESCRIBE IMAGE*

(Suggested answers)

1 A line graph.
2 A comparison between the unemployment rates for different groups of young people.
3 The rates were significantly lower for the 16–17-year-old group but the rates for the other three groups a slight but erratic decline.
4 The rates rose quite significantly for all groups, the most significant increase being amongst young people aged under 21.
5 Although there have been dips, the overall general trend has been one of increasing unemployment, with the rates in 2010 being more than 10% higher than in 1992.

Page 14

SECTION 2: RE-TELL LECTURE

(Model answers)

A

The general topic of the lecture is modernism and architecture, but the speaker focuses on the work of modernist architect, Frank Gehry, in particular the Guggenheim Museum in Bilbao. Gehry wanted to break away from the usual straight line designs of other architects and experiment with other shapes – especially curves. He thought of architecture as an art like sculpture, and the museum is a brilliant example of his art.

B

The main point of the lecture is how various sciences can come together to enrich each other, in particular here mathematics and biology. The speaker talks first about their personal experience of school and choosing to study biology to avoid doing maths or subjects like it, but explains that maths has a lot to contribute to biology. The speaker then gives two examples. The first is the use of knot theory to analyse DNA. The second is using abstract geometry to study viruses.

C

The lecture is about daily life in ancient Rome. The speaker says that what we know is mostly about the aristocracy, but we know much less about the lives of ordinary people and how much say they had politically and socially. Most people lived very difficult lives. The speaker points out that it was the duty of the emperor to take care of ordinary people. He gives the examples of Claudius and Hadrian, both of whom had to be reminded of their duty.

**SECTION 2:
ANSWER SHORT QUESTION**

1 editorial
2 microscope
3 a virus
4 mammals
5 democracy
6 a receipt
7 CV, curriculum vitae, résumé
8 agricultural, rural
9 astronomy
10 public relations

Page 15

FURTHER PRACTICE AND GUIDANCE: *PART 1, SECTION 2: RE-TELL LECTURE*

1 The work of Frank O. Gehry.
2 An architect associated with Modernism – a modernist architect.
3 They use basic shapes, such as rectangles and straight lines.
4 Use other kinds of shapes, such as curves.
5 It allowed him to experiment with complex shapes and to work on the whole design as one piece.

6 He felt is was like sculpture.
7 The Guggenheim Museum in Bilbao.
8 He was a talented architect.

Page 17

**SECTION 3:
SUMMARIZE WRITTEN TEXT**

(Model answer)

Closure or privatization of inefficient national services may have short-term economic benefits, but can cause long-term damage both socially and culturally because some services are social provisions, not businesses.

**SECTION 4:
SUMMARIZE WRITTEN TEXT**

(Model answer)

History should not be used to promote national myths by glorifying a country's great victories and figures, but rather it should be approached in an analytical and critical way.

Page 18

**SECTION 5:
SUMMARIZE WRITTEN TEXT**

(Model answer)

In Trinidad, traditionalists think their Carnival is being destroyed by commerce, while others believe that opening the event up to foreign business will bring tourists and income to the country.

SECTION 6: WRITE ESSAY

(Model answer)

An important point to remember here is that these opinions were voiced when computers were in their infancy, and now, with the passage of time, we should have a clearer picture.

It is not simply a case of either/or. These days most of us find computers indispensable, whether at work or at home, and they do speed up certain daily routines – for example, doing your shopping on-line. On the other hand, a lot of time is wasted on such things as playing games and unnecessary personal communications – this time could be better spent. On a larger scale, in terms of big business and industry, computerized manufacturing and automated assembly lines have greatly increased production.

However, this too has its downside, as many jobs are lost as a result.

Whether computers make us smarter or happier is, again, not easy to answer definitively. It is claimed that playing computer games improves certain skills: this may be so, but there is no doubt that spending excessive amounts of time alone at the computer can damage your health and relationships, as well as take time away from other beneficial activities such as reading, socializing, playing sports, and so on. However, there is no denying that using computers does make at least some people happy.

While I find it hard to give a definite opinion on whether or not computers make us more productive, smarter and happier, I agree entirely with the opinion that information is not knowledge. Given that it is so easy to turn to the computer when we want to find something out, we no longer feel the need to learn things. This does seem to me a loss, both at an individual level and for society as a whole.

Page 19

FURTHER PRACTICE AND GUIDANCE: *PART 1, SECTIONS 3–5: SUMMARIZE WRITTEN TEXT*

Topic sentences underlined

How do we measure efficiency? <u>To economists – or to a certain type of economist – it is simply a question of profitability, even when it concerns what most people consider a social provision such as public transport.</u> What is lost when railway lines and bus routes to small, out-of-the-way communities are cut in the name of efficiency? After all, if a line or a route is only used occasionally by a few people, it would be much cheaper to rip up the lines and let everyone use their cars.

<u>For many governments, the way to turn inefficient national services into profitable businesses has been to sell off these services – and their responsibilities – to private enterprises.</u> Cost, in terms of profit and loss, is of course an important factor, but other factors need to be considered when dealing with the livelihoods of whole communities, however small. Among these are the social, environmental, human and

cultural costs incurred by cutting off more remote communities from greater opportunities, including economic activities that benefit society as a whole.

Taking away such links – the usual result of privatization – may well lead to economic benefits in the short term, but, as the last twenty to thirty years have shown, also leads to long-term social and cultural damage. Of course, no business with its eye on profits is going to "waste" money supporting underused services. Only large collective bodies such as national and local governments can do that. These services are, after all, a social provision, not businesses.

(Model answers)

Paragraph 1

Summary sentence: To economists, efficiency is a question of profitability.

Paragraph 2

Summary sentence: Many governments have turned their inefficient national services into profitable businesses by selling them.

Paragraph 3

Summary sentence: Privatization may have short-term economic benefits, but it can cause long-term social and cultural damage.

Single-sentence summary

Privatization of inefficient national services may have short-term economic benefits, but it can cause long-term social and cultural damage because certain services are social provisions, not businesses.

PART 2: READING

Page 21

MULTIPLE-CHOICE, CHOOSE SINGLE ANSWER

A: 2

1 is incorrect because although Rowley is a farm laborer, that's not the main reason he is mentioned. **3** is incorrect because Rowley does not support that view. **4** is incorrect because although Rowley speaks in a slightly humorous way, that's not the main reason he is mentioned.

2 is correct because the writer says: *"Rightly is they called pigs," said Rowley, a farm laborer looking at the*

wallowing animals before passing on to the cow sheds … This raises all sorts of questions about language and how we perceive the world …

B: 1

2 is incorrect because the writer says publishing companies must adapt, not that they have been unable to. **3** is incorrect because the writer raises this as a possibility in the first paragraph, rather than stating it will definitely happen. **4** is incorrect because the writer says that e-books provide opportunities to many writers, but does not say that most e-books are not by conventionally published writers. **5** is incorrect because the writer does not mention the number of sales of e-books and traditional books.

1 is correct because the writer says: *… For many writers, however, e-publishing provides new freedoms and opportunities.*

Page 23

FURTHER PRACTICE AND GUIDANCE: *PART 2: MULTIPLE-CHOICE, CHOOSE SINGLE ANSWER*

1c

The writer says: *For many writers, however, e-publishing provides new freedoms and opportunities.*

2b

The writer says: *Such companies must adapt … .*

3a

The writer says: *… a drastic change in how we read.*

4c

The writer says: *Many e-books are published by writers who do not have a readership through mainstream publishers … .*

5d

The writer says: *… there is no reason why the e-book and the traditional printed book should not exist happily side by side.*

Page 25

MULTIPLE-CHOICE, CHOOSE MULTIPLE ANSWERS

A: 2, 3, 5, 6

1 is incorrect because *leisurely pace* in the text means "slow speed".

4 is incorrect because *bustle* in the text means "excited activity". **7** is incorrect because *loiter* in the text means "wait idly".

2, 3, 5 and **6** are correct because they all mean "walk" in different ways.

B: 3, 4

1 is incorrect because the writer mentions the example of John Maynard Keynes, who worked for the Treasury. **2** is incorrect because the writer says that most people in England would think of France and be able to name a French intellectual. **5** is incorrect because in the first paragraph the writer describes English peoples' idea of what a typical intellectual is and does.

3 is correct because the writer says: *Our aversion to intellectuals, or to the term, may go back to when we were at school where nobody likes a "swot". In fact, almost any kind of braininess is disparaged: scientists are mad-haired "boffins", tech-savvy kids are "nerds", and people can be "too clever by half".* **4** is correct because the writer says: *… a situation not helped by many of the people who we consider to be intellectuals denying the fact.*

Page 26

RE-ORDER PARAGRAPHS

A

Correct order: 1c 2b 3a 4d

B

Correct order: 1d 2c 3a 4b

C

Correct order: 1d 2b 3a 4c

Page 28

FURTHER PRACTICE AND GUIDANCE: *PART 2: RE-ORDER PARAGRAPHS*

1 Paragraph d cannot go first because *This* must refer to something that came before it.

2 Paragraph c probably goes first because it refers to the *First World War* specifically. All the other Paragraphs refer simply to *"the war"* or *"wartime,"* which implies that the specific war must have been defined earlier.

3 Paragraph b goes second because it builds on the information presented in the first Paragraph. Paragraph c indicates that before the war people did not have very much money and needed to rent houses. Paragraph b says that this led to the building of houses that people could afford to rent.

4 Paragraph a goes third because it describes how home construction during the war declined. That is, it draws a contrast with the sentences coming before it.

5 Paragraph d goes last because *This* refers to the *shortage of close to a million houses* referred to in Paragraph a.

Pages 29–30

READING: FILL IN THE BLANKS

A

1 individual (We need an adjective to describe *tutorials*.)

2 offers (We need a verb to describe what the course does.)

3 understanding (We need a gerund to add to the list of what the course offers.)

4 necessary (The word *necessary* here means "which are necessary".)

5 field (The phrase *related field* means "a similar area of work".)

B

1 comes (This forms the phrasal verb *comes up to*, which means "reaches".)

2 force (We need a noun for what knocks a person down.)

3 objects (We need a plural noun.)

4 debris (The noun *debris* refers to the material picked up by the tsunami.)

C

1 grains (*Grains of sand* is a collocation.)

2 fertile (We need an adjective to describe *land* and to contrast with *desert*.)

3 planting (We need a gerund to refer to putting plants in the ground.)

4 nourishment (We need a noun to refer to what this plant gets from sand.)

5 surface (This refers to where the grass is, in contrast to the roots under the surface.)

D

1 scheme (*Health insurance scheme* and *pension scheme* are collocations.)

2 ensure (We need a verb that means "make sure".)

3 avoid (*Discrimination* is a negative thing, so we need to avoid it.)

4 includes (*Includes* collocates with *in* later in the sentence.)

5 treatment (We need a noun to describe what the employer does.)

E

1 thought (*Thought* here means "idea".)

2 mention (*Not to mention* is a collocation.)

3 ashamed (We need an adjective that means something similar to *guilty*.)

4 others (*Others* here refers to "other events".)

5 information (Names, numbers and dates are examples of information.)

Pages 31–33

READING AND WRITING: FILL IN THE BLANKS

A

1 claim (If you *claim to have* something, you say that you have it.)

2 caused (We need a verb to describe the fact that people and circumstances *cause* annoyance and frustration.)

3 fun (If you *make fun of someone*, you laugh at them.)

4 forward (*Put forward* is a phrasal verb which means "suggest, propose".)

5 effective (We need an adjective that means "working well, producing the desired results".)

B

1 global (The text is about the whole world, and *global* means "of the whole world".)

2 Indicators (This means "things that show the size of an effect", and it is followed by a list of such things.)

3 growth (*Population growth* is a collocation.)

4 crucial (This means "vitally important" and it collocates with *to*.)

5 rare (This refers to the fact that the habitats are becoming less common.)

C

1 stable (This means "unchanging".)

2 runs (*Runs in families* is a collocation.)

3 function (*Brain function* is a collocation.)

4 significant (*Significant number* is a collocation.)

5 searching (This means "looking for" and collocates with *for*.)

D

1 fact (*Fact of life* is a collocation.)

2 distinct (This means "separate", and *distinct types* is a collocation.)

3 speaking (*Strictly speaking* is a collocation.)

4 unsuspecting (This means "unaware, not knowing about a problem".)

5 skill (*Considerable skill* is a collocation.)

E

1 envisioned (This means "imagined".)

2 essentials (*The essentials of life* is a collocation.)

3 reconstruction (This means "rebuilding, recreation".)

4 harmony (*In harmony with* is a collocation.)

5 exploit (This means "use for your own benefit".)

F

1 admit (This collocates with *to* + *-ing*.)

2 persuade (If you persuade yourself that something is true, you believe it.)

3 deal (This means "bargain".)

4 getting (*There's no getting away from* is an idiom that means "you can't avoid".)

Page 34

FURTHER PRACTICE AND GUIDANCE: *PART 2: READING AND WRITING: FILL IN THE BLANKS*

1 threat	**11** saying
2 reality	**12** talking
3 theory	**13** unsuspecting
4 fact	**14** incredulous
5 isolated	**15** ignorant
6 distinguished	**16** sceptical
7 precise	**17** courage
8 distinct	**18** skill

9 speaking	**19** gift
10 telling	**20** qualifications

PART 3: LISTENING

Page 36

SUMMARIZE SPOKEN TEXT

(Model answers)

A

The speaker says modern economic circumstances have changed the nature of loyalty. People no longer work for the same company for life, and companies today must adapt to a large employee turnover as workers take up new opportunities elsewhere. People will be loyal while they are in a given job, but may move on. However, companies do function better socially and economically when they have a core group of long-term employees.

B

The speaker explains why Latin writing was so outstanding, especially as compared to the other arts. The main reason was the nature of the language itself, which is capable of great compression. Another factor was the Roman educational system, which concentrated on language and literature. One drawback was that, as education was only available to the rich, the subject matter of Latin literature is fairly limited.

C

The two main types of aid for developing countries are mentioned. One is long-term aid for countries with problems that money alone cannot fix (drought, poor agriculture), and the other is emergency aid, which includes the basic things needed immediately following a natural disaster. For long-term problems, it is more important to teach the skills needed to develop the economy, and to organize and run social services than to give cash aid.

Page 37

FURTHER PRACTICE AND GUIDANCE: *PART 3, SECTION 1: SUMMARIZE SPOKEN TEXT*

(Model answers)

Extract 1

Some say that giving money to developing countries isn't the best way to help them in the long term. There are two main types of aid for developing countries, the first of which is long-term aid to countries with problems that money can't fix, like drought or poor agriculture.

Extract 2

The second type of aid is emergency aid following natural disasters like earthquakes or tsunamis. This includes food, clothing, shelter, and medical aid.

Extract 3

Countries with long-term problems need more than just money. A lot of the money doesn't go where it should. It's more important to teach the skills needed to develop the economy and social services, and to build the bureaucracy to organize and run these services.

Page 39

MULTIPLE-CHOICE, CHOOSE MULTIPLE ANSWERS

A: 1, 2, 4

3 is incorrect because the writer says that individual gardens expressed their owners' political affiliations, but this was not an influence on the English landscape garden. **5** is incorrect because no mention is made of *gardens* from classical Greece and Rome, only of classical Greek and Roman temples and statues.

1 is correct because the speaker says: *There then came a backlash against this rigid formality, led by, among others, the poet Alexander Pope. Pope and his allies argued for a more natural nature.* **2** is correct because the speaker says: *Until the picturesque style emerged as part and parcel of the Romantic Movement, gardens had been strictly formal … There then came a backlash against this rigid formality … .* **4** is correct because the speaker says: *Lord Burlington was a major figure in the landscape garden movement, and he was famously influenced by … the picturesque or romanticized landscapes of Italian classical painting.*

B: 2, 3, 6

1 is incorrect because the technique was used in Japan in the past. **4** is incorrect for the same reason. **5** is incorrect for the same reason.

2, 3 and **6** are correct because the speaker says: *At the same time, the craft seems to have been widely established, even commonplace, elsewhere: for example, in India, Mexico and Peru, where the same techniques continue to be practised today.*

C: 2, 4, 5

1 is incorrect because France is mentioned as a country where people who don't vote are punished, not by law, but by having a government they didn't elect raise their taxes. **3** is incorrect for the same reason. **6** is incorrect because the law is no longer acted on in Greece.

2 is correct because the speaker says: *… in Bolivia, non-voters may be banned from using banks or schools for up to three months.* **4** and **5** are correct because the speaker says: *In Austria, for example, failure to vote results in an automatic fine, as it does in Australia.*

Page 40

FILL IN THE BLANKS

A	**B**
1 relatively	**1** specialized
2 influence	**2** impact
3 manufacture	**3** familiar
4 quantities	**4** composition
5 financial	**5** hearing

C

1 gathering
2 permanently
3 tools
4 erosion
5 colonists

Page 41

HIGHLIGHT CORRECT SUMMARY

A: 2

The speaker says: *A cliché, as you know, is an overused and worn out phrase … there is no greater danger to either education or thinking than the popular phrase … Now, if you think of graphic design as a language with its own vocabulary, grammar, and so on, it too must have its clichés. … the visual cliché is essential in the world of graphic communication. This is certainly true when it comes to advertising and propaganda. The visual cliché can give immediate life to an idea and a clear meaning to what could be a mere abstraction.*

B: 1

The speaker says: *All whales, dolphins and porpoises are social animals, although the degree of sociability varies greatly from one species to another. ... we can expect the group size adopted by a species to be the most suitable for its environment and lifestyle. ... Some of the reasons for living in groups include greater efficiency in searching for and catching food, benefits for mating, learning, defence, and sensory integration. ... . For example, if one animal discovers a shoal of fish or a hungry shark, it can immediately pass on this information to the others in the group so that all may benefit.*

Page 42

FURTHER PRACTICE AND GUIDANCE: *PART 3, SECTION 2: HIGHLIGHT CORRECT SUMMARY*

1a 2b 3b 4a 5a 6b 7a 8b

Page 44

MULTIPLE-CHOICE, CHOOSE SINGLE ANSWER

A: 3

1 is incorrect because, although the speaker mentions this aspect, he does not say it influenced him in his choice of career. **2** is incorrect for the same reason. **4** is incorrect for the same reason.

3 is correct because the speaker says: *I suppose the reason I got into geology was, well, as a kid I was fascinated by fossils – the fact that they went back countless years, long before there were any people on the planet. That was exciting and, um, they were beautiful too. And one thing led to another.*

B: 2

1 is incorrect because the speaker says classes will improve someone's writing, but you can't teach someone to write extremely well. **3** is incorrect because the speaker says that close reading is part of his writing classes. **4** is incorrect because there is no mention of developing a love of language in writing classes.

2 is correct because the speaker says: *Obviously, you can't teach someone to have a talent for storytelling, or a love of language: but there are important lessons to be gotten across that will improve their writing and, at the very least, make it publishable.*

C: 4

1 is incorrect because the speaker does not mention being amused nor does he mock the report. **2** is incorrect because he says that he is not at all sure about the report, not that he doesn't believe any of it. **3** is incorrect because he doesn't say that he is angered by it.

4 is correct because he says: *I must say at the outset that I'm not at all sure about the findings of a recent survey I've been studying ... .*

Page 45

SELECT MISSING WORD

A: 3

The text is about how the brain works and, in particular, how different areas of the brain perform different functions. It describes a patient who had damage to one part of the brain. This affected his ability to talk, but not his ability to understand. So, the missing words are: *understood spoken language.*

B: 1

The text is about the development of paper money. The Chinese used paper money, and bankers in Spain and Italy used bills of exchange. The Swedes are thought to be the first to use paper money in Europe. So, the missing word is: *notes.*

Page 46

HIGHLIGHT INCORRECT WORDS

A

When the European Economic Community was established in 1957, its aim was, in broad terms, to move towards closer political and economic co-operation. Today, the much <u>bigger</u> (*larger*) European Union has a far-reaching <u>importance</u> (*influence*) on many aspects of our lives, from the conditions we work under, to the safety standards we must adhere to, and the environment in which we live.

In order to achieve the free flow of goods and services, <u>work</u> (*workers*) and capital between the member countries, they needed to establish mutual <u>politics</u> (*policies*) in areas as diverse as agriculture, transport, and working conditions. When they had agreed on these policies, they became <u>legal</u> (*law*). Now, though, the EU is concerned with a far wider range of issues.

B

Stem cells are the body's master cells, the <u>rare</u> (*raw*) material from which we are built. Unlike normal body cells, they can reproduce an indefinite number of times and, when manipulated in the right way, can turn themselves into any <u>sort</u> (*type*) of cell in the body. The most versatile stem cells are those found in the embryo at just a few days old. This ball of a few dozen stem cells eventually goes on to form everything that makes up a <u>human</u> (*person*).

In 1998, James Thompson <u>pronounced</u> (*announced*) that he had isolated human embryonic stem cells in the laboratory. At last, these powerful cells were within the <u>grip</u> (*grasp*) of scientists to experiment with, understand, and develop into fixes for the things that go wrong.

WRITE FROM DICTATION

1 Hundreds of scientific papers have been published on global warming.

2 Political power only disappears when this stage has been completed.

3 Social networks are changing the way we communicate.

4 The cotton industry purchased all its raw cotton from abroad.

Page 47

FURTHER PRACTICE AND GUIDANCE: *PART 3, SECTION 2: HIGHLIGHT INCORRECT WORDS*

1 One way to think about voltage is to <u>imaginary</u> (*imagine*) it as the pressure that pushes charges along a conductor.

2 The electrical resistance of a conductor would then <u>become</u> (*be*) a measure of the difficulty of pushing those charges along.

3 Now, if we use an analogy of water flowing in a pipe, a long narrow pipe resists flow more than a short fat one does – a long narrow one has more <u>resisting</u> *(resistance)*.

4 Currents work in the <u>similar</u> *(same)* way: long thin wires have more resistance than do short thick wires.

5 Conversely, short fat wires have <u>least</u> *(less)* resistance.

TEST 2

PART 1: SPEAKING AND WRITING

Page 48

SECTION 2: REPEAT SENTENCE

1 The Arts Magazine is looking for a new Assistant Editor.

2 The lecture will deal with the influence of technology on music.

3 Make sure you correctly cite all your sources.

4 There are hundreds of clubs and societies to choose from.

5 Does the college refectory offer vegetarian dishes on a daily basis?

6 All essays and seminar papers submitted must be emailed to your tutor.

7 He was not the only one to call for legal reform in the 16th century.

8 The Drama Society is now auditioning for parts in the student play.

9 There is a position available for a Junior Lecturer in Media Studies.

10 There will be a significant rise in tuition fees starting next year.

Page 49

FURTHER PRACTICE AND GUIDANCE: *PART 1, SECTION 2: REPEAT SENTENCE*

A

1b 2b 3b 4b 5a 6a 7b 8a

Pages 51–52

SECTION 2: DESCRIBE IMAGE

(Model answers)

A
This pie chart shows how many hours a year people spend on average visiting their local doctor in England. At 35 hours a year, people in the south-east spend the largest amount of time, with the east not far behind at 33 hours a year. People in the north-east and the north-west, at 13 and 15 hours respectively, spend the least time with their local doctor. People in the west visit their doctor for 17 hours a year, while the figure for the south-west is 20 hours.

B
This graph shows how many students on average are late for college on each day of the working week. It's noticeable, but not surprising, that Monday is the day when the largest number of students is late – as many as thirty. Friday has the second largest number of late students, with an average of about seventeen. Wednesday follows with about fifteen late-comers. Tuesdays and Thursdays are roughly the same, with the fewest late arrivals, numbering about ten.

C
This table compares how males and females over age sixteen use their time doing various things each day. It covers many kinds of activities, including how much time they spend sleeping, eating, and watching TV. One striking difference is that men have about five and a quarter hours' leisure time, whereas women have about half an hour less than this. The biggest difference is time spent doing housework. Women spend three hours a day doing housework, while men spend just under half that amount. Otherwise, there is not much difference between the time males and females spend on other activities.

D
This graph compares the proportion of households and businesses in the UK with Internet access and broadband connection to those in the rest of the European Union. It shows that the UK is about ten percent above the EU average for Internet access at home. Just over thirty percent of households in the EU have a broadband connection, while the UK is twelve percent above the EU average. For businesses, there is less difference. In fact, ninety percent of enterprises in both the UK and the EU have Internet access while, for broadband connections, the UK is only slightly higher.

E
The graph shows population change in the twelve years from 1998 to 2010. It shows both natural change, which I assume means births and deaths, and net migration and how these contribute to population growth. Between 1998 and 2002, there was a decline in growth due to natural change, but after that there was a steady rise during the rest of the period, peaking at an increase of just under 250,000. Figures for net migration peaked in 2005 at over 250,000, then fell to under 200,000 in 2009 before picking up again to reach about 225,000 in 2010. In general, the population rose over the period covered.

F
This pie chart shows how much time students spend reading various types of text. It is surprising to see that, given that they are students, only 7% of reading time is spent on reference books. 15% of their time is spent reading on the Internet. Newspapers take up the largest portion of students' reading time at 32%, closely followed by fiction at 26%. The third most popular kind of reading matter is magazines, which take up 20% of students' reading time.

Page 53

FURTHER PRACTICE AND GUIDANCE: *PART 1, SECTION 2: DESCRIBE IMAGE*

(Suggested answers)

A
1 A table.

2 A comparison between the way males and females over age sixteen spend their time each day.

3 For most categories, males and females spend similar amounts of time each day doing different activities.

4 The housework category shows the largest difference: females spend three hours a day doing housework, while males devote less than an hour and a half daily to this activity.

B

1 compares	4 approximately
2 instance	5 seen
3 on	6 average

Page 54

SECTION 2: RE-TELL LECTURE

(Model answers)

A

People on both the left and right wings politically have adopted de Tocqueville. He appealed to the left wing because he accepted democracy and he appealed to the right wing during the Cold War. Although he was an aristocrat, his views differed from his family and other aristocrats. He believed that, in the future, people would be more equal.

B

The instrument writers use affects their style. Writing with a quill took a long time so writers tended to write in short sentences. They had a balanced style and their output was small. Writing with a fountain pen led to a more flowing style. Writing with a typewriter produced a more journalistic style and writers produced much more work. Some people feel that writers who dictated their work, such as Henry James, became too conversational.

C

The lecturer said that art and technology can exist together. She said that photography forced artists to see in new ways and photographs can have a lot of emotional impact. Some people think photography is easier than traditional art. However, they don't realise that it takes skill to produce good photos and that many traditional artists, such as Vermeer, used technology to help them create their images.

SECTION 2: ANSWER SHORT QUESTION

1 coastguard	6 weather
2 May	7 (the) referee
3 download(ing)	8 (the) final
4 (an) X-ray	9 landscape(s)
5 shoplifting	10 a printer

Page 55

FURTHER PRACTICE AND GUIDANCE: *PART 1, SECTION 2: ANSWER SHORT QUESTION*

E 1	F 6	G 4	H 3	J 5
K 2	M 9	O 7	Q 10	S 8

Page 56

SECTION 3: SUMMARIZE WRITTEN TEXT

(Model answer)

Britain was slow to create a paid and organized police force, and before the 19th century, police work was done by unpaid individuals, or paid for privately or by local organizations.

SECTION 4: SUMMARIZE WRITTEN TEXT

(Model answer)

Irony is difficult to define, but it usually requires an audience combining some people who get the point and some people who don't, and because of this, it has an air of intellectual snobbery about it.

Page 57

SECTION 5: WRITE ESSAY

(Model answer)

These days, perhaps unfortunately, most people and many institutions of higher education are focused on the job market. It is the way things are, and if universities and colleges cannot provide the preparation for a career, or at least help you get a job that is better than one you would get without further education, they will soon go out of business. However, I don't think it is or should be a question of either one or the other.

On a personal note, I studied Latin at school, and both enjoyed it and found it to provide good mental discipline, as well as introducing me to a fascinating period of history along with some great poets and writers. I didn't study Ancient Greek, but I wish I had. While Latin and Greek may appear to be of no practical use, I believe, they do provide a solid foundation for learning any language and, indeed, for understanding how language works. Knowledge of Latin or Greek also improves your handling of your own language. So, they both fall into that category of training the mind, which I think is the first priority in education, and any subject which does this should be included in the school curriculum. Moreover, there is no reason why they should not be taught alongside more practical subjects such as computing.

In my opinion, during their time at school, students should be given as broad a range of subjects to choose from as possible. For a long time, the classical languages, especially Latin, were compulsory subjects in the same way as mathematics. I believe Latin and Greek should remain an option because education, after all, provides general preparation for life, not just for a specific job.

SECTION 6: WRITE ESSAY

(Model answer)

To begin with the reasons why more and more students are studying abroad, I can only draw on personal experience and other students I have spoken to. First, studying abroad is not necessarily cheaper. I am studying in England, which is rather expensive, whereas in my own country, education is free, the only expenses being your own upkeep, accommodation and, of course, the books you need.

Second, whether or not you get a better education at a foreign university depends, as in your own country, on which university you manage to get into – some are better than others. Therefore, the main reason for studying at a university abroad is, in my experience, the expectation of better job prospects. This has a lot to do with the economic climate in general. I believe I could receive a good education at home, but there are very few jobs for young people, and you don't want to end up driving a taxi after four years of study.

Having made the decision to study abroad, I think the advantages outweigh the disadvantages. First of all, you have to become proficient in another language – an education in itself. In my case, the language I have had to perfect is English, which has become the global language and therefore a huge asset in the job market, as well as introducing me to some of the best literature in the world.

Living in a different culture is also very interesting. The initial daily frustrations that occur through not fully understanding the way things are done, or said, in a new culture, plus a certain degree of homesickness are certainly disadvantages of going abroad to study. However, you soon make new friends and get over all that.

Page 58

FURTHER PRACTICE AND GUIDANCE: *PART 1, SECTION 6: WRITE ESSAY*

Paragraph 1: f
The first paragraph should begin with an introductory statement of the issue and indicate what the next paragraph will be about.

Paragraph 2: c
The second paragraph should discuss the advantages of studying abroad. These should be supported with reasons and/or examples.

Note that when you are asked to discuss the advantages and disadvantages of an issue, you may start with either one, although it is more usual to start with the advantages. For this reason, the answers for paragraphs 2 and 3 can also be reversed.

Paragraph 3: e
The third paragraph should discuss the disadvantages of studying abroad. These should be supported with reasons and/or examples.

As noted above, the contents of paragraphs 2 and 3 can be reversed: if paragraph 2 discusses the disadvantages, paragraph 3 will discuss the advantages.

Paragraph 4: g
The final paragraph of an essay should contain a summary. In this case, the summary will be of the advantages and disadvantages, in the same order they are presented in the essay. The conclusion should let the reader know your own view.

PART 2: READING

Page 60

MULTIPLE-CHOICE, CHOOSE SINGLE ANSWER

A: 3
1 is incorrect because legal scholarship aimed to have an effect on the present, not on the past. **2** is incorrect because no mention is made of this idea. **4** is incorrect because no mention is made of the desire to perfect the methods of historical research.

3 is correct because the writer says: *The idea here was to get as accurate a picture as possible of the law and its practice in ancient, especially Roman, times. Legal historians did this with a view to refining the laws and applying them to the present historical situation.*

B: 2
1 is incorrect because, although the eye is described as complex, that isn't given as a reason for studying other species. **3** is incorrect because it is contradicted by the text which says that the eye can change and remain useful if the changes are slight and gradual. **4** is incorrect because other species are examined to see what stages are possible, not because they have more complex eyes.

2 is correct because the writer says: *... the search for the stages through which an organ in any one species has come to perfection, which ideally would mean looking exclusively at its past generations, is rarely possible. Therefore, researchers are forced to examine species and genera of the same group to discover what stages or gradual developments are possible.*

Page 61

MULTIPLE-CHOICE, CHOOSE MULTIPLE ANSWERS

A: 3, 5, 7
1 is incorrect because the writer says that a new bride is not allowed to drink milk from her new family's cows. **2** is incorrect because she mustn't use the name of senior male relatives only. **4** is incorrect because a new bride has to avoid certain areas of the village, not the front entrance of her new home. **6** is incorrect because she has to avoid touching the drinking utensils.

3 is correct because the writer says: *A Xhosa bride in southern Africa, in contrast with her western counterpart, is expected to show both reluctance and sadness during her wedding ... .* **5** is correct because the writer says: *Further constraints are having to wear a handkerchief low over her forehead, never showing her bare head to her husband's relatives ... .* **7** is correct because the writer says: *Furthermore, she is not allowed to use the personal names of her mother-in-law, nor those of her husband's aunts and elder sisters.*

B: 1, 4, 5
2 is incorrect because this was true in the past. **3** is incorrect because it was only for a brief period in the 20th century that designers were mainly interested in aesthetic appeal. **6** is incorrect because modern designers focus on the function of furniture, rather than on the decorative aspect.

1 is correct because the writer says: *Function and economy, therefore, are of the utmost importance.* **4** is correct because the writer says: *... in the modern home, furniture should fulfil a specific purpose, and need as little care and attention as possible.* **5** is correct because the writer says: *Limited space must be used imaginatively, ...*

Page 63

FURTHER PRACTICE AND GUIDANCE: *PART 2: MULTIPLE-CHOICE, CHOOSE MULTIPLE ANSWERS*

1a
In the past, designers ... were not constrained by the limits of space, economy, or even practicality that inhibit the contemporary designer. The writer is saying that economy and practicality constrain modern designers.

2b
In the past, designers of furniture usually worked for royalty, the nobility, landowners and rich merchants ... fine furniture and interiors were designed to show off not only the riches of the owners ... The writer is implying that because furniture designers worked for the wealthy, only they could afford well-designed furniture.

3a
In the third paragraph, the writer describes modern furniture designs and says: *Function and economy, therefore, are of the utmost importance.*

4b
The writer states directly: *... in the modern home, furniture should fulfil a specific purpose, and need as little care and attention as possible.*

5a

By saying: *Limited space must be used imaginatively ...,* the writer implies that modern homes are small and that furniture must not take up much space.

6a

The writer both states directly and implies throughout the text that modern furniture designs favor function and practicality over aesthetics and decoration. Therefore, the decorative aspect is less important than the functional aspect.

Page 65

RE-ORDER PARAGRAPHS

A

Correct order: 1c 2a 3d 4b

B

Correct order: 1d 2c 3b 4a

C

Correct order: 1b 2a 3d 4c

Pages 67–68

READING:
FILL IN THE BLANKS

A

1 introduces (We need a verb to complement *to* later in the sentence: *introduce someone to something.*)

2 backgrounds (We need a noun to go with *academic, business* and *political* to describe where the students come from.)

3 equally (We need an adverb to say that the course is for two types of people.)

4 simply (We need an adverb to contrast the complexity of doctoral research with the simpler aim of improving understanding.)

B

1 aim (We need a noun to describe the reason for advertising.)

2 products (We need a noun to describe what is sold through advertising.)

3 purpose (*Serve the purpose* is a collocation.)

4 shows (We need a verb that means "depicts, contains a picture of".)

C

1 key (We need an adjective that means "very important".)

2 trends (We need a noun to describe the main forces at work in society.)

3 staff (We need a noun to contrast with "the student bodies".)

4 role (We need a noun to describe the function of the university.)

5 found (We need a verb to describe where we see ideas and social criticism.)

D

1 involved (If you are *involved in something,* you take part in it.)

2 practical (We need an adjective that means "suitable, appropriate".)

3 input (We need a noun that means "advice, opinion".)

4 safety (We need a noun to describe one advantage of employing an architect.)

E

1 financed (We need a verb that means "paid for".)

2 notes (Banks *issue notes.*)

3 rate (We need a noun that means "speed, pace".)

4 supplies (We need a noun to describe the new sources of gold.)

5 means (*Means of exchange* is a collocation.)

Page 69

FURTHER PRACTICE AND GUIDANCE: *PART 2: FILL IN THE BLANKS*

1 a singular noun

2 illustrates, products, shows, produces

3 a plural noun

4 aim, illustrates, purpose, point, shows, produces

5 *products*

6 a singular noun

7 illustrates, products, shows, produces

8 yes – *serve the purpose*

9 a verb in the third person singular

10 aim, products, purpose, point, produces

Pages 71–73

READING AND WRITING:
FILL IN THE BLANKS

A

1 appear (This means "come into existence".)

2 added (This means "put on as an extra feature".)

3 entirely (This means "completely".)

4 potential (If you *see the potential of something,* you realize the future possibilities it has.)

5 popularize (This means "make available to ordinary people".)

B

1 permanent (This means "lasting for a long time".)

2 plots (This refers to the stories in books and films.)

3 regarded (This means "thought of" and collocates with *as.*)

4 performance (*Public performance* is a collocation.)

5 content (This means "information".)

C

1 covered (This collocates with *with.*)

2 useful (This describes the oak tree and the passage later mentions some of its uses.)

3 remains (When villages and towns, etc., disappear, they leave behind *remains.*)

4 preserved (This means "kept in the same form or shape".)

5 levels (The text is referring to the levels at which different trees grew.)

D

1 whereas (This contrasts the feelers of butterflies with those of moths.)

2 mistaken (This collocates with *for.*)

3 liable (If something is *liable to do something,* it tends to do it.)

4 slight (This means "small, subtle".)

5 blends (*Blend in with* is a collocation.)

E

1 aside (If you *put something aside for the moment,* you ignore it temporarily.)

2 despite (This means "in spite of" and can be followed by a noun.)

3 decisions (This collocates with *made.*)

4 benefit (This means "advantage".)

5 courses (*Courses of action* is a collocation.)

F

1 described (This collocates with *as.*)

2 react (This collocates with *with.*)

3 travel (We use *travel* to talk about the motion of particles.)

4 complicated (This means "difficult, complex", and is then contrasted with a simple explanation.)

5 characteristics (This refers to the properties of the waves and particles; the ways they behave.)

PART 3: LISTENING

Page 74

SUMMARIZE SPOKEN TEXT

(Model answers)

A
It is not language change that the speaker is complaining about because this is in the nature of language and there is nothing to stop it. What matters to him is that, generally, standards of both spoken and written English have dropped among his students and, more seriously perhaps, among professional writers such as journalists.

B
Something comparable to today's newspapers began during the time of Julius Caesar, who set up the posting of news-sheets in the busiest meeting places in Rome. These contained the latest news concerning wars, sports, gossip, and so on. Scribes, who were often slaves, would act as news gatherers for those not in Rome, and could even make enough money out of it to buy their freedom.

C
Drawing a comparison with changes in fashion, the speaker examines the ups and more frequent downs in the reputation of the poet, Alexander Pope. Hugely popular in his own day, succeeding generations – the Romantics followed by the Victorians – found him not to their taste, and heavily criticized him and his poetry. It was not until the early 20th century that his work became appreciated and popular again.

Page 75

MULTIPLE-CHOICE, CHOOSE MULTIPLE ANSWERS

A: 3, 4
1 is incorrect because no mention is made of beans. **2** is incorrect because flat boards were part of the press. **5** and **6** are incorrect because the large presses used on olives and grapes were unsuitable for printing.

3 and **4** are correct because the speaker says: ... *the common screw presses used for crushing oil seeds and herbs, or even for doing more domestic chores such as pressing fabrics, adapted for printing.*

B: 2, 3, 6
1 and **5** are incorrect because pianos and pianolas are mentioned in the context of life before recorded music. **4** is incorrect because this is mentioned as something that changed the sound of the orchestra.

2 is correct because the speaker says: *New technologies ... can alter the sound of music and, in the case of electronic recording systems, affect the economics and distribution of music.* **3** and **6** are correct because the speaker says: ... *with the Internet, sites to download music from, file-sharing, and so on, we have access to more music than ever before – and a lot of it for free.*

C: 1, 4
2 and **3** are incorrect because these were Rousseau's beliefs before he wrote *The Social Contract*. **5** is incorrect because this idea wasn't suggested in *The Social Contract*.

1 is correct because the speaker says: ... *because it is easier to survive by joining forces with others, people form societies to better fight anything that might endanger their situation.* **4** is correct because the speaker says: *In such conditions, man is brutish and competitive by nature, and there is no law or morality.*

Page 76

FURTHER PRACTICE AND GUIDANCE: *PART 3, SECTION 2: MULTIPLE-CHOICE, CHOOSE MULTIPLE ANSWERS*

1 printing presses
2 crushing oil seeds and herbs, and pressing fabrics
3 crushing olives and grapes
4 wood
5 They were large and had too much pressure.
6 flat boards
7 iron presses

Page 78

FILL IN THE BLANKS

A	B
1 imported	1 nervous
2 mill	2 convey
3 provided	3 sensory
4 availability	4 functions
5 production	5 reflexes

C

1 state
2 struggle
3 source
4 engages
5 recruitment
6 biased
7 originate

Page 79

HIGHLIGHT CORRECT SUMMARY

A: 3
The speaker says: *Experts believe that we store memories in three ways. First, there is the sensory stage which is to do with perception and lasts only a fraction of a second, ... These first perceptions and sensations are then stored in the short-term memory, which is the second stage. Finally, important information or information that has been reinforced by, for example, repetition, is then filtered into the long-term memory.*

B: 1
The speaker says: *The first approach, which prevailed up until the middle of the 20th century, was that the Revolution was part of the age-old battle between parliament and the monarchy, ... the second approach saw it as a working-class revolution, ... In other words, they saw it as a class war, and a forerunner of the French Revolution and those that came after. Historians who supported the third approach saw that things weren't as clear cut as the others thought. ... they focused on the details of the period immediately leading up to its outbreak and allowed for its unpredictability.*

Page 80

MULTIPLE-CHOICE, CHOOSE SINGLE ANSWER

A: 2

1 is incorrect because the speaker says: *The criteria mentioned seem a bit fuzzy to me.* **3** is incorrect because the speaker says: *Also, you can strike the first blow and still plead self-defence.* **4** is incorrect because the speaker says that you have to try to convince a jury that you acted reasonably in the situation.

2 is correct because the speaker says: *It seems to depend on … the relative strengths of those involved.*

B: 3

1 is incorrect because the speaker says that the editor may view the work as if they themselves had written it. **2** is incorrect because no mention is made of editors understanding authors' difficult lives. **4** is incorrect because the speaker says editors might *take no account of the author's original intentions*, not that they find it difficult to see them.

3 is correct because the speaker says: *Editors might, from their experience as writers, possibly unconsciously, try to make over the submitted novel as they themselves would have written it.*

C: 5

1 is incorrect because the speaker says we only tend to think of people who speak more than one language as being "bright", not that they actually are brighter. **2** is incorrect because the speaker says they often find one language more suitable than another for expressing certain kinds of thoughts and feelings, not that they have difficulty expressing emotions. **3** is incorrect because the writer refers to mental exercise, not physical exercise. **4** is incorrect because the idea of having a split personality is mentioned, not the idea of having an attractive personality.

5 is correct because the speaker says: *And it's true that we tend to think of people who can speak two or more languages as being bright.*

Page 81

SELECT MISSING WORD

A: 4

The text is about photography. In the beginning, cameras were very large, but then they became smaller. This meant that the camera user was less obvious and could move around while taking pictures. So, the missing words are: *as they took pictures*.

B: 2

The text is about the aspirations of young people. It talks about the careers they aspire to and the benefits of those careers. However, it is also important to think about whether young people will actually be able to pursue their ideal career. So, the missing word is: *realistic*.

Page 82

FURTHER PRACTICE AND GUIDANCE: *PART 3, SECTION 2: SELECT MISSING WORD*

A: 1

Only *about an hour* can go with the verb *last*.

B: 2

Parts of the world describes where the crop failures occurred.

C: 3

Comments and questions are taken *from an audience*.

D: 2

Funds can be borrowed. Borrowed money must usually be paid back over time and at an interest rate set by the lender. The speaker believes the funds they need can be borrowed *at low interest rates*.

E: 3

Some students feel that online courses are *less enjoyable* than traditional classes, due to their lack of community.

Page 84

HIGHLIGHT INCORRECT WORDS

A

In the 19th century, few people could afford to travel abroad; it was expensive and there weren't the massive (*mass*) transport systems that we have today. So curiosity about foreign lands had to be satisfied through books and drawings. With the advent of photography, a whole new version (*dimension*) of "reality" became available. Publishers were not slow to realize that here was a large new market of people eager (*hungry*) for travel photography and they soon had photographers out shooting the best known European cities, as well as more exotic places further afield (*away*). People bought the pictures by the millions, and magic lantern shows were presented in schools and leisure (*lecture*) halls. Most popular of all, however, was the stereoscopic picture which pretended (*presented*) three-dimensional views and was considered a marvel of Victorian technology.

B

Classified advertisements placed by individuals in newsprint (*newspapers*) and magazines are not covered by the Advertising Standards Authority's "court (*code*) of practice". If you happen to buy goods that have been wrongly described in such an advertisement, and have lost money as a result, the only thing you can do is bring a case against the person who placed the advertisement for misrepresentation or for breach of contrast (*contract*). In this case you would use the small claims procedure, which is a relatively cheap way to sue for the recovery of a debt. If you want to pursue a claim, you should take into account whether the person you are suing will be able to pay damages, should any be rewarded (*awarded*). Dishonest traders are wary (*aware*) of this and often pose as private sellers to expose (*exploit*) the legal loopholes that exist: that is, they may claim they are not in a position to pay damages.

WRITE FROM DICTATION

1 Like humans, owls can see in three dimensions.

2 Modern art now does better than stocks as an investment.

3 Commercial necessity was the reason given for the decision.

4 Grants are available to those in financial difficulty.

Page 85

FURTHER PRACTICE AND GUIDANCE: *PART 3, SECTION 2: WRITE FROM DICTATION*

1 is intended primarily for

2 remnants of ancient glaciers

3 account for / of all workplace illnesses

4 Evidence suggests / changes shape in response to

TEST 3

PART 1: SPEAKING AND WRITING

Page 86

SECTION 2: REPEAT SENTENCE

1 You will be informed of the results by e-mail.

2 Please have copies of your seminar papers in the library a week in advance.

3 Most students are not eligible to claim housing benefit.

4 If you want to quit the student union, tell the registrar.

5 Does the university have an ice-hockey team?

6 Without doubt, his primary motive was economic.

7 The modern approach to the problem is to stress the symbolic side of human nature.

8 Many privately-owned firms have been eaten up by larger corporations.

9 I'm afraid Professor Jones doesn't suffer fools gladly.

10 Most of these criticisms can be shown to be false.

Page 87

FURTHER PRACTICE AND GUIDANCE: *PART 1, SECTION 2: READ ALOUD*

1 The <u>starting point</u> of <u>Bergson's</u> <u>theory</u> is the <u>experience</u> of <u>time</u> and <u>motion</u>.

2 <u>Time</u> is the <u>reality</u> we <u>experience</u> most <u>directly</u>, but this <u>doesn't mean</u> that we can <u>capture</u> this <u>experience</u> <u>mentally</u>.

3 The <u>past</u> is <u>gone</u> and the <u>future</u> is yet to <u>come</u>.

4 The only <u>reality</u> is the <u>present</u>, which is <u>real</u> to us through our <u>experience</u> of it.

Page 88–89

SECTION 2: DESCRIBE IMAGE

(Model answers)

A

This graph shows how popular several new EU member states and other parts of the world have become among holidaymakers during the period 2003–2007. By far the greatest increase has been in visitors to Latvia, a number which grew by more than 1,100% during this time period. Slovakia and Poland show the next largest increases, while China and Israel were at the bottom showing a growth of about 160%.

B

This graph shows that there has been a steady decline in the readership of national daily newspapers in Britain during the period 1978 to 2009. The percentage of readers has declined by about 30%, which is roughly a fall in readership of 10% every ten years.

C

In the ten years covered by the graph, overall sickness absence has fallen, though it remained higher in the public sector than in the private sector. In 2000, both private and public sector worker levels were above 3 percent, with public sector workers at a high of about 3.7 or 3.8 percent and private sector workers at about 3.2 percent. By the end of 2010, just above 3 percent of public sector employees were absent from work, compared with only slightly more than 2 percent of private sector employees. The gap between the two sectors was at its widest in the final quarter of 2008. So, on average, sickness rates are higher in the public than the private sector.

D

This graph shows e-security problems faced by businesses in the UK in 2001, 2003 and 2005. Virus infections and disruptive software remained the biggest problems in all the years covered, with 35% of businesses having such incidents in 2005, compared to 41% in 2001 and 50% in 2003. The next most common type of problem was staff misuse of information systems, rising from about 12% in 2001 to about 22% in 2003 and 21% in 2005. Unauthorised access by outsiders remained constant in 2003 and 2005 at about 16%, up on 2001's 13%. Finally, theft or fraud involving computers was at its highest in 2003 at about 12%, having risen from 6% in 2001 and then dropping to 8% in 2005.

E

The graph compares expenditure per household between the countries of the UK, and some specific regions of England. England as a whole is just above the average, while Northern Ireland, Scotland and Wales spend less than the average. Wales spends the lowest, at almost fifteen percent below the average, in contrast to the capital, London, at over fifteen percent above the national average, making it the biggest spender. Apart from London, South East and East England, the rest of the country spend below average.

F

The picture shows a view of a city, possibly taken from a hill or a very tall building. In the foreground, there are many small, low buildings. It might be a slum area, where very poor people live. In the background you can see skyscrapers, which may house wealthier people, or it may be a business district. It could be in South America, but could be anywhere really, where poor people come to the cities looking for work and a better life.

Page 90

FURTHER PRACTICE AND GUIDANCE: *PART 1, SECTION 2: DESCRIBE IMAGE*

(Suggested answers)

A

1 part of a city

2 low houses of poor quality / a slum / badly-built housing / etc.

3 skyscrapers / office buildings / well-built, modern buildings / etc.

4 any major city which has this type of contrasting architecture, e.g. Sao Paulo in Brazil

B
1 of **2** In **3** there **4** looks **5** In **6** by **7** in

Page 91

SECTION 2: RE-TELL LECTURE

(Model answers)

A
The lecturer questions the idea that species are so perfectly adapted to the climate and environment they inhabit that they cannot be moved to another set of conditions and survive. The main argument is that species are more adaptable than we think; using rats as an example of adaptability to show both plants and animals can survive a change of climate and environment.

B
The subject is motivation and success and how an understanding of what it is would benefit both business and education. Incentives are not the answer because it is a mental attitude that involves being prepared to work hard and above all learn from mistakes. Nor is it a question of talent since those who are gifted also need to put in the hours to develop their talent. In fact, hard work can outdo talent.

C
The speaker says that while it is good to know what our likes and dislikes are, and when you are studying literature, the fact that you like a book is not a good criterion for judging it as literature. Saying you like or dislike a work – whether it's music or art or literature – is not valid or useful criticism.

Page 92

SECTION 2: ANSWER SHORT QUESTION

1 a portrait
2 in a city
3 an eclipse / a solar eclipse
4 West
5 (at the) till / checkout
6 a basement apartment
7 a keyboard
8 (a) negative (feeling)
9 a decade
10 plumber

SECTION 3: SUMMARIZE WRITTEN TEXT

(Model answer)

Comparing the standard of living among countries using national income in dollars as a measure can be misleading, because official exchange rates are often set artificially.

SECTION 4: SUMMARIZE WRITTEN TEXT

(Model answer)

The writer compares personal photographs, which record the past and evoke feeling of nostalgia, with news photographs, which must have an immediate emotional impact to make us believe they show a present reality.

Page 93

FURTHER PRACTICE AND GUIDANCE: *PART 1, SECTION 3: SUMMARIZE WRITTEN TEXT*

1e 2c 3a 4d

Page 94

SECTION 5: SUMMARIZE WRITTEN TEXT

(Model answer)

This text is about plagiarism and how it is difficult to define legally because it has a different meaning for different cultures and within cultures at different times, using Shakespeare as an example.

SECTION 6: WRITE ESSAY

(Model answer)

Tourism is a huge industry and those countries that attract millions of visitors every year are geared towards catering to these tourists. Most people only have about two weeks to spend abroad and a holiday that is organized seems the most suitable to them. There are those, too, who prefer to be free to go off the beaten track and experience the local culture as fully as possible. I think both types of tourist have something to offer the local communities they visit, and with some benefit to themselves.

Organized tourism, which usually means staying in a hotel with all meals provided and excursions to places of historical and cultural interest thrown in, obviously benefits local communities economically. Hotels get built, restaurants open, and employment increases – though it may only be seasonal. Visitors get a taste of the local culture, but it would be difficult to measure how much they bring to it, apart from money. A negative aspect of this is that the impact of mass tourism on a community may destroy the traditional culture, not to mention the landscape.

On the other hand, those who like to move about freely from place to place and soak themselves in the local culture may not bring the economic benefits that mass tourism does, but in their efforts to understand local customs and ways of life, may bring greater understanding of their own culture to the country they are visiting. Of course, this is not something that can be measured. Also with more time on their hands, contacts and friendships may be established which benefit all concerned.

Personally, I think the second type of tourism is the best, providing cross-cultural understanding while leaving the cultures intact, but mass tourism is here to stay, and provides greater economic benefits to local communities.

PART 2: READING

Page 95

MULTIPLE-CHOICE, CHOOSE SINGLE ANSWER

A: 3
1 is incorrect because no change to farming is mentioned. **2** is incorrect because fathers and sons fought in different regiments, but did not fight against each other. **4** is incorrect because in fact local rivalry was prevented.

3 is correct because the writer says: *… Dingiswayo reorganized his army along the lines of age rather than old local allegiances.*

B: 4
1 is incorrect because teenagers up to 16 were allowed half a pint of milk a day, while some other groups were allowed a pint. **2** is incorrect because people in the country could get eggs without coupons, but they still had to pay for them. **3** is incorrect because the text mentions a general improvement in health standards, not a healthier diet.

4 is correct because the writer says: *... Then there was the green book for pregnant women, ... and this allowed them first choice of fruit, a daily pint of milk and a double supply of eggs ... .*

Page 96

FURTHER PRACTICE AND GUIDANCE: *PART 2: MULTIPLE-CHOICE, CHOOSE SINGLE ANSWER*

1T 2F 3T 4F 5F 6T

Page 97

MULTIPLE-CHOICE, CHOOSE MULTIPLE ANSWERS

A: 1, 2, 4, 5
3 is incorrect because the writer says: *Legend has it that Napoleon is responsible for making the European countries which he conquered keep to the right, ... So France, obviously, and Spain, ... used this system, ...* **6** is incorrect because the writer says: *... over the years other countries adopted the practice to make crossing borders easier and safer. The latest European country to convert was Sweden, in 1967.* So Germany must have adopted driving on the right before 1967.

1 is correct because the writer says: *Japan does too ... .* **2** is correct because the writer says: *In fact, those that drive on the left make up about twenty-five per cent of the world's countries and are, apart from the UK itself, ...* and Scotland is part of the UK. **4** is correct because the writer says: *... as late as 2009, Samoa switched from driving on the right ... .* **5** is correct because the writer says: *... apart from the UK itself, mostly countries that were British colonies: India, South Africa, ...*

B: 1, 2, 4
3 is incorrect because it's possible that he didn't take any of the photos himself. **5** is incorrect because before the war he was a well-known portrait photographer.

1 is correct because the writer says: *Lincoln granted him permission to travel anywhere ... .* **2** and **4** are correct because the writer says: *But no one else could have organized the large army of photographers needed to cover the broad sweep of the war and provided access to many leading generals and politicians.*

Page 98

RE-ORDER PARAGRAPHS

A

Correct order: 1d 2b 3a 4c

B

Correct order: 1d 2a 3b 4c

C

Correct order: 1c 2d 3b 4a

Page 100

FURTHER PRACTICE AND GUIDANCE: *PART 2: RE-ORDER PARAGRAPHS*

1a 2d 3a 4b 5c

Pages 101–102

READING: FILL IN THE BLANKS

A
1 associate (We need a verb. *Associate* collocates with *with*.)
2 responsible (We need an adjective. *Responsible* collocates with *for*.)
3 translations (We need a plural noun to describe the versions of the stories.)
4 despite (We need a word that will contrast the childlike atmosphere and the political perception.)

B
1 mistake (*Make a mistake* is a collocation.)
2 notion (We need a noun that means 'idea'.)
3 interests (Your *economic interests*)
4 mark (If something is *off the mark*, it is incorrect.)
5 fit (If something *fits the case*, it is appropriate for that situation.)

C
1 rate (*Rate of change* is a collocation.)
2 dying (*Dying out* is a phrasal verb which means "disappearing".)
3 less (We need a comparative form to go with *than*.)
4 trained (We need an adjective which collocates with *in*.)

D
1 lie (We need a verb which means "are found, are located".)

2 discovered (We need a verb to describe the actions of the Europeans.)
3 notable (We need an adjective which collocates with *for*.)
4 system (*Military system* is a collocation.)
5 estimated (We need a verb which means "calculated".)

E
1 reason (*Reason* collocates with *for*.)
2 establish (*Establish the cause of (death)* is a collocation.)
3 knowledge (*Medical knowledge* is a collocation.)
4 involves (We need a verb which means "includes as part of the process".)

Pages 103–105

READING AND WRITING: FILL IN THE BLANKS

A
1 invention (As an artificial process, photography was invented, not discovered.)
2 brought (*Bring to fame* is a collocation.)
3 interest (*Interest* collocates with *in*.)
4 accident (*By accident* is an idiom which means "accidentally, without meaning to".)
5 public (*Make something public* is an idiom which means "tell people about something".)

B
1 board (*A board* is a flat piece of wood.)
2 served (This means "acted as".)
3 Alternatively (We use this word when we present an option.)
4 late (*Late in the day* is an expression.)
5 grasp (This collocates with *concept*.)

C
1 method (This means "way of doing something".)
2 roughly (This means "approximately".)
3 called (The pad *was called* an ink ball. If the gap had been followed by *as*, then *known* would have been correct.)

4 consisted (This collocates with *of*.)

5 approach (You take an *approach to a problem* when you try a particular way to find a solution.)

D

1 wrapped (When an item of clothing such as a cloak goes around you, you are *wrapped in* it.)

2 traditional (Both men and women in Persia wore trousers as part of their cultural traditions.)

3 way (If something *finds its way* somewhere, it eventually goes there.)

4 adopted (This means "started using".)

5 made (*Make a comeback* is an idiom which means "become popular again".)

E

1 milder (This refers to the weather being less severe than it was.)

2 decided (Here, this means "convinced, persuaded".)

3 mashed (*Mash up* is a phrasal verb which describes how they broke beans, peas and lentils into pieces.)

4 breeds (Each individual kind of a domesticated animal is known as a *breed* (*of dog, of sheep, etc.*).)

5 alternating (This describes the agricultural cycle the Romans used.)

F

1 as (This collocates with *known*.)

2 pointed (*Pointed towards* means "gave an idea of the future development of".)

3 models (The objects behind described are *models* of the human head.)

4 controlled (This collocates with *by*.)

5 realize (This means "understand".)

PART 3: LISTENING

Page 106

SUMMARIZE SPOKEN TEXT

(Model answers)

A

In the interview, a professor talks about psycho-geography, saying it is not an academic discipline. It is basically the study of the psychological effects of the environment on us, especially the urban environment, and its aim is to get us to be more attentive to and critical of our surroundings and

the atmosphere and emotions they evoke.

B

The speaker tells us how difficult it is to talk of the history of the novel if we don't have a definition of what the novel is and does. This is complicated by the various types of novels and their subject matter. He does say, though, that the English novel, as we understand novels today, began in the late 17th century.

C

This is about the problem of consciousness and the possibility – or impossibility – of knowing for certain how another person thinks or feels. We may, through our own experience and observing others, make rational and sometimes accurate guesses, but we can never really know for sure.

Page 107

MULTIPLE-CHOICE, CHOOSE MULTIPLE ANSWERS

A: 1, 4

2 is incorrect because the speaker says: *... it must also be demonstrated that ... they have adequate opportunities for physical education*, but this does not mean they necessarily have to do a sport. **3** is incorrect because the speaker says: *Furthermore, while there is no formal assessment, officers from the LEA will come and inspect what is being done and look at the child's exercise books.* **5** is incorrect because no mention is made of a record of attendance.

1 and **4** are correct because the speaker says: *Schedules, lesson plans and book lists must be shown, ...*

B: 3, 6

1 and **4** are incorrect because there is no mention of China or India bringing rice to Europe. **2** is incorrect because the writer's only mention of Greek is that the word rice *... is derived from the Aramaic ourouzza and came to us by way of Greek and Arabic.* **5** is incorrect because, although rice was grown in Italy, it was brought by the Spanish and not by Italians.

3 and **6** are correct because the speaker says: *... it was the Arabs who introduced rice to their Spanish territories in the 7th century, but it didn't spread to the rest of Europe until much later when, in the 15th*

century, Spaniards began to cultivate their own short-grain variety at Pisa in Italy.

C: 2, 3

1 is incorrect because contemporary writers do not only write about institutions. **4** is incorrect because the questions they ask are not irrelevant, although they may be about a small specialized area. **5** is incorrect because the speaker says: *In the 19th century, there were still writers who used the same freedom of enquiry as the ancients, and are all the more readable – and relevant – because of it.*

2 is correct because the speaker says: *... modern writers on politics might concentrate on one particular institution in that system – the House of Lords in England – or on voting patterns within a country.* **3** is correct because the speaker says: *Many writers on politics these days are university-based and so have to have specialized interests, ...*

Page 108

FILL IN THE BLANKS

A	**B**
1 opinions	**1** causal
2 attached	**2** linked
3 institution	**3** generalizations
4 colleagues	**4** patterns
5 reputation	**5** analysis
6 staff	**6** modify
	7 support

C

1 categorize

2 sociologist

3 letters

4 influence

5 customs

6 account

Page 109

FURTHER PRACTICE AND GUIDANCE: *PART 3, SECTION 2: FILL IN THE BLANKS*

1 behavior

2 university

3 recognized

4 productive

5 critical

6 colleagues

7 relatively

Page 110

HIGHLIGHT CORRECT SUMMARY

A: 2

The speaker says: *I'm a marine biologist – and ... I'm interested in the Strandlopers, ... In fact, it was through my early interest in all things to do with the sea that I first heard of them. ... the Strandlopers lived off the sea and seashore gathering food such as mussels, oysters, crabs, and so on, just as I did. ... we do have archaeological evidence such as pottery, discarded shells, the bones of seals and large fish, and so on. ... they might have used a primitive form of fishing line ... Anyway, the more we search the more we discover ... I find it endlessly fascinating.*

B: 1

The speaker says: *To reach some kind of understanding of a period in the past ... requires a creative act of the imagination ... What must it have been like to be a peasant under a feudal baron? ... So, you have to imagine the terms under which life was lived in those days ... Now, of course, every age views the past from its own present ... which is why each age has to write its history over again. It's not so much that more facts or evidence come to light – if they do – but that sensibilities change too.*

Page 111

FURTHER PRACTICE AND GUIDANCE: *PART 3, SECTION 2: HIGHLIGHT CORRECT SUMMARY*

1a 2b 3b 4a 5a

Page 112

MULTIPLE-CHOICE, CHOOSE SINGLE ANSWER

A: 3

1 is incorrect because contour lines were used in the 16th century and the Ordnance Survey wasn't set up until 1791. **2** is incorrect because before the 16th century contour lines weren't used. **4** is incorrect because they were first used on a map of France and there is no mention of a military purpose.

3 is correct because the speaker says:

The first time land contours were used was on a map of France, ...

B: 4

4 is correct because the speaker says: *... in the 14th century, English merchants were obliged to have them outside their shops.*

C: 3

1 is incorrect because the speaker says there were no root crops to feed the animals in winter, not that there were no root crops at all. **2** is incorrect because the speaker says: *Spanish and Portuguese explorers had brought back such novelties as potatoes, tomatoes, ... it took people some time to accept some of these new foods, as they feared they were poisonous.* **4** is incorrect because the speaker says: *... including exotic spices to add flavor to the usual diet.*

3 is correct because the speaker says: *By the 16th century, however, choice in foodstuffs had grown ... .*

Page 113

SELECT MISSING WORD

A: 2

The text is about how future climate change may affect people. It describes the extent of possible warming, and how the effects will vary from region to region. It then lists effects on humans, starting with effects on water resources, so the missing words are: *food production and health.*

B: 3

The text is about how parents discipline their children. It discusses various forms of discipline, including corporal punishment, and the effects on children's relationships at school. The final sentence contrasts less harsh methods with corporal punishment, and talks about the effect on children's attitudes towards their school and people at school, and so the missing word is: *peers.*

Page 114

HIGHLIGHT INCORRECT WORDS

A

"No news is good news" may be true for most of us most of the time – after all, we don't look forward to unpleasant things happening to us – but "Bad news is good news" is true for those who work in the news media, and, I suspect, for the rest of us, at least some of the time. It is tied up with stories and our seemingly unsatisfied (*insatiable*) need for stories. Have you ever been grasped (*gripped*) by a story where nothing goes wrong for the characters? There's an accident (*incident*) in a Kingsley Amis novel that nicely illuminates (*illustrates*) this: the main character Jake comes home to find his wife chatting to a friend about a hairdresser both women know who has moved with his family to somewhere in Africa. Jake listens in, expecting tales of cannibalism and such like, but no, the friend has just received a letter saying they love the place and are settling in nicely. Jake leaves the room in disgrace (*disgust*).

We demand to be entertained, and while we don't object to a happy ending, the characters have to have experienced loss, pain and hardship in one form or another along the way to have earned (*deserved*) it.

B

Leisure travel was, in a sense, a British invention. This was mostly (*mainly*) due to economic and social factors; Britain was the first country to become fully industrialized, and industrial society offered greater (*growing*) numbers of people time for leisure. This, coupled with improvements in transport, especially the railways, meant that large numbers of people could get to holiday resorts in a very short time.

Modern mass tourism of a sort we can easily recognize today began in 1841 when Thomas Cook organized the first packet (*package*) tour, in which everything was included in the price (*cost*) – travel, hotel and entertainment. To cater for the large numbers of new holiday-makers, holiday camps were established, both on the coast and in the countryside, and they became immensely popular. Their popularity declined, however, with the rise of cheap overseas tours, which gave many people their first opportunity to travel about (*abroad*).

WRITE FROM DICTATION

1 This has been a major source of confusion for academics.

2 None of the alternatives is satisfactory.

3 The aim of the course is to provide a broad theoretical basis.

4 Has all the evidence been properly examined?

Page 115

FURTHER PRACTICE AND GUIDANCE: *PART 3, SECTION 2: HIGHLIGHT INCORRECT WORDS*

1 A team of marine biologists studying whale carcasses – the dead bodies of whales – has <u>found</u> (*learned*) that they create a unique environment, one that is rich in animals and bacteria, including several new species.

2 When a whale dies, its body slowly sinks to the ocean <u>floor</u> (*bottom*), where it becomes food for a vast ecosystem.

3 One whale carcass contains more <u>nutrients</u> (*nutrition*) than would normally filter down through the water column in 2,000 years.

4 Using a submersible robot, the team collected collarbones of whales from the seafloor and <u>raised</u> (*brought*) them to the surface.

5 Back in the lab, the team found the bones were covered in bacteria and other organisms, more than 10 of which had never been <u>catalogued</u> (*identified*) before.

TEST 4

PART 1: SPEAKING AND WRITING

Page 116

SECTION 2: REPEAT SENTENCE

1 You are not permitted to take reference books out of the library.

2 The seminar will now take place a week on Tuesday.

3 You don't have to be on Professor Smith's course to attend this lecture.

4 The library will be closed for three days over the bank holiday weekend.

5 I think we should get together over the weekend to discuss this assignment.

6 There's an hourly bus service from the campus into town.

7 This is the third time you've asked for an extension on this project.

8 They say Professor Jones's lectures are always interesting, and funny.

9 Being a student representative on the union really cuts into my study time.

10 I've got a tutorial in an hour and I haven't had any time to prepare for it.

Page 117

FURTHER PRACTICE AND GUIDANCE: *PART 1, SECTION 2: REPEAT SENTENCE*

1b 2a 3b 4a 5a 6b 7b 8a

Pages 118–119

SECTION 2: DESCRIBE IMAGE

(Model answers)

A
This chart shows the various means that can be used to prevent unwanted material on computers and the percentage of people who use them. By far the most common method used, by about 23% of people, was putting blocks or filters on their e-mail accounts. About 19% did the same for their Internet browser or search engine, while about 10% use passwords. Other methods favored by less than 10% include never giving out personal details, and either monitoring children's use of the Internet, or putting locks on certain sites.

B
This graph shows the pump price for unleaded petrol and diesel in the UK from 1999 until 2008. The first thing to notice is that the line for diesel is always higher than for premium unleaded, which means it's generally more expensive. The other thing to notice is that the price for both fuels roughly doubled from 1999 to 2008, going from about 62 or 63 pence a litre to more than 120 pence a litre in the case of diesel. Prices for both seemed to peak in 2008, but fell dramatically later that same year, diesel ending on a price of 100 pence per litre and petrol on a price of about 90 pence per litre.

C
The picture shows a number of wooden houses on the bank of a river or lake. At first, I thought no one could live there because the houses don't look very sturdy, but then I noticed the clothes hanging out to dry. Obviously the people who live there must be quite poor.

There are boats in the picture, which might be used for fishing or for transport. The trees look a bit like palm trees, so maybe this is somewhere tropical.

D
This pie chart illustrates the various means of transport people who live outside the city use to get to work by percentage. The largest number of commuters, just over 30%, use the train while 27% travel by car. Surprisingly, very few people use only the bus or the underground, so most bus and underground users must be included in the 29% who use more than one form of transport to get to work.

E
This graph shows projected sales of soft drinks for the Morgan Drinks Company in millions per year from 2018 to 2024. The graph shows that the company expects to sell 20 million bottles of still water in 2018, rising to over 30 million by 2024. Fizzy water, on the other hand, will increase from thirty million bottles to about 38 million bottles in 2020, and then fall gradually. Sales of fruit drinks will remain stable at around 45 million bottles a year.

F
The map shows which parts of the world are most densely forested, and shows two types of forest – evergreen and deciduous. The most densely-forested area is in South America. At about the same latitude, there are thick forests in parts of Africa. I imagine in both these cases they are tropical rainforests. Central America and the northern parts of Canada are also densely forested, as are the northern parts of Europe and Asia, from Scandinavia and across Siberia to Mongolia. In the east, parts of China and Indonesia show the most forested areas.

Page 120

FURTHER PRACTICE AND GUIDANCE: *PART 1, SECTION 2: DESCRIBE IMAGE*

1 This graph shows the pump price for unleaded petrol and diesel in <u>Europe</u> from 1999 until 2008. <u>the UK</u>

2 The first thing to notice is that the line for diesel is always <u>lower</u> than for premium unleaded, which means it's generally more expensive. <u>higher</u>

3 The other thing to notice is that the price for both fuels roughly doubled from 1999 to 2008, going from about 62 or 63 pence a litre to more than 120 pence a litre in the case of petrol. diesel

4 Prices for both seemed to peak in 2008, but fell dramatically later that same year, diesel ending on a price of 100 pence per litre and petrol on a price of about 80 pence per litre. 90

Page 121

SECTION 2:
RE-TELL LECTURE

(Model answers)

A
This lecture is about Machiavelli and his book *The Prince*, and how he got a bad reputation as a ruthless man who will do anything to get what he wants. The lecturer's aim is to try and persuade us to look at the book in its historical context to see why he wrote it and to show that his reputation is undeserved. Machiavelli loved his home town, Florence, and was prepared to do anything to protect it. At the time, it was threatened by several enemies, so only harsh measures would do.

B
The lecturer talks about the subject of happiness and how, although it was once mainly the concern of philosophers, it has now become an academic subject and a concern of governments, who try to incorporate it into policy. The speaker is a bit cynical about how the theories about happiness have been presented by non-philosophers, and how the conclusions they come to are mostly obvious to the average person.

C
After a brief mention of the megalopolis, the lecturer focuses on the small city state, particularly ideal cities like those imagined by Plato and da Vinci. He puts forward possible reasons why the number of citizens was limited to about five thousand, suggesting that small numbers made voting easier and were easier to feed on food produced locally, instead of having to import it.

SECTION 2:
ANSWER SHORT QUESTION

1 (the) Suez (Canal)

2 (in) a freezer

3 (a/your) driving/driver's licence

4 (to) a gym, gymnasium

5 (an) aqualung

6 (a) supermarket

7 radiology

8 (to) an art gallery / (to) a museum

9 liters

10 (your/the) wrist

Page 122

SECTION 3:
SUMMARIZE WRITTEN TEXT

(Model answer)

This is about the effect of information technology on the structure of society according to some analysts, with IT experts becoming the elite and many blue-collar workers losing their jobs.

SECTION 4:
SUMMARIZE WRITTEN TEXT

(Model answer)

Although the English are known as tea drinkers, in the 17th and 18th centuries, they went to coffee houses, where they would discuss ideas and do business.

Page 123

SECTION 5: WRITE ESSAY

(Model answer)

While it is true that many, if not most, households in the developed world are full of gadgets and labor-saving devices, and it is also true that it appears that people have less free time, I'm not sure how closely related the two things are. Is it really the case that all this modern technology is directly responsible for us having less free time?

In the home, having a dishwasher, rather than doing the dishes by hand, probably gives you the time to do another household chore and not necessarily the time to sit down and watch a TV show or read a book. At work, modern technology has certainly made things faster. At the most basic level, to e-mail a business document takes seconds, whereas before computers it would take far longer. However, this again seems to create time for more work, not less. Perhaps labor-saving means less effort rather than less work.

As for the quality of life, I believe that, on the whole, having this technology has made things better in many ways. Computers, after all, have entertainment value as well as being tools for work. However, if you believe that having a decent amount of free time in which to do the things you want is an important aspect of quality of life, then you'll probably feel that all this technology has made things worse and perhaps even more complicated.

To conclude, the only other complication I can see is when the technology is new to you and you have to learn how to use it. Computers are a fact of life now and children learn very quickly, often better than their parents, how to use them.

SECTION 6: WRITE ESSAY

(Model answer)

A recent trend in the entertainment world has been to adapt classic works of literature for the movies or TV. Although the results of this are often very popular, not everyone agrees that this is a good thing. I'd like to argue that it depends on the quality of the adaptation.

Some people feel that adapting classic works for the movies or TV brings these works to a wider audience, introducing people to works they might not otherwise have experienced. Adaptation, they claim, broadens our horizons and gives us access to higher culture. This is true, as long as the adaptation retains the key elements of the original work.

Other people feel that adapting classic works detracts from the originals, and that, in fact, the movie or TV version of a classic work may become better known than the original. Adaptation, they claim, lowers our cultural standards. This view, however, assumes that written works are necessarily of better quality than works produced for the screen, which is not necessarily the case.

In my opinion, neither view is correct on its own. The truth is somewhere in the middle. One can point to cases that support both points. Some adaptations have been highly successful in faithfully presenting the original work, while other adaptations have failed miserably, and should probably have never been attempted.

Page 124

FURTHER PRACTICE AND GUIDANCE: *SECTION 6: WRITE ESSAY*

Paragraph 1: C
The first paragraph begins with an introductory statement outlining the issue, and indicates what the rest of the essay will discuss.

Paragraph 2: B
The second paragraph indicates one view on the issue. The phrase "some people" is used to identify the first group.

Paragraph 3: D
The third paragraph describes the opposing view. The phrase "other people" indicates that this paragraph must come after "some people".

Paragraph 4: G
The final paragraph contains a summary that indicates the author's stance. In this case, the summary indicates that the writer does not believe that either stance presents the whole truth about the issue.

Not used: A, E, F
A The fact that young people are increasingly reading electronic books is not relevant to the prompt.

E How young people become acquainted with shared cultural references is not relevant to the prompt.

F This detail is not relevant to the prompt.

PART 2: READING

Page 125

MULTIPLE-CHOICE, CHOOSE SINGLE ANSWER

A: 2
1 is incorrect because the writer says: *The problem is that people often choose a career for the wrong reasons. For instance, some people follow in the footsteps of a parent,* ... . **3** is incorrect because the writer says: ... *some people follow in the footsteps of a parent, ... inheriting the family business. Others make exactly the opposite decision,* ... .

4 is incorrect because the writer says: *People may also persuade themselves to pursue a career for which they are unsuited ... as a result of meeting people they admire.*

2 is correct because this is given as the right reason for choosing a career as the writer says: ... *we should do those things for which we have a natural talent.*

B: 2
1 is incorrect because although life stories of famous men are mentioned, the text does not say that ancient Roman literature was mainly composed of them. **3** is incorrect because although satire is mentioned, the text does not say that ancient Roman literature was mainly composed of it. **4** is incorrect because there is no mention of Roman literature being censored.

2 is correct because the writer says: *Culturally, partly through native genius and partly through absorbing the achievements of the older and richer culture of Greece, its literature became the basis of European values,* ... .

Page 126–127

MULTIPLE-CHOICE, CHOOSE MULTIPLE ANSWERS

A: 3, 4, 6
1 is incorrect because he wrote papers on barometers. **2** is incorrect because the writer says: *Before Luke Howard invented his system for classifying clouds, they had simply been described by their shape and color as each person saw them* ... . **5** is incorrect because Howard used the term "city fog", not "smog".

3 is correct because the writer says: *Before Luke Howard invented his system for classifying clouds, they had simply been described by their shape and color as each person saw them* ... . **4** is correct because the writer says: ... *in the 20th century his cloud classification system was adopted, with some additions, as the international standard* ... . **6** is correct because the writer says: *Howard had realized that cities could significantly alter meteorological elements.*

B: 2, 5
1 is incorrect because the writer does not mention the use of hobbies as therapy. **3** is incorrect because the writer discusses how people might use hobbies to create a particular impression, not that

they reveal your true character. **4** is incorrect because the writer is not talking about people who do extreme sports, but about people who claim to do extreme sports.

2 is correct because the writer says: *When does a hobby ... cease to be a hobby or a pastime and become something a bit more serious, such as something you realize can be turned into financial gain* ... . **5** is correct because the writer says: *Most people's hobbies turn out to be easy and stress-free pastimes* ... .

Page 128

FURTHER PRACTICE AND GUIDANCE: *PART 2: MULTIPLE-CHOICE, CHOOSE MULTIPLE ANSWERS*

1a
This is supported by: *He wrote papers on barometers.*

2b
This is supported by: *Before Luke Howard invented his system for classifying clouds, they had simply been described by their shape and color* ... .

3a
This is supported by: *Howard believed that all clouds belonged to three distinct groups; cumulus, stratus and cirrus.*

4a
This is supported by: *This system came to be used ... with some additions, as the international standard. This* refers to Howard's system.

5b
This is supported by: *One of these he called "city fog". Nowadays we call it "smog"* ... .

6b
This is supported by: *Howard had realized that cities could significantly alter meteorological elements.*

Pages 129–130

RE-ORDER PARAGRAPHS

A
Correct order: 1c 2a 3d 4b
B
Correct order: 1e 2b 3d 4c 5a
C
Correct order: 1c 2e 3a 4d 5b

Pages 131–132

READING:
FILL IN THE BLANKS

A

1 final (We need an adjective. The *final rounds* of a competition are those that happen towards the end of the competition.)

2 place (*Take place* is a phrase which means "happen, occur".)

3 event (We need a noun to refer to the World Cup.)

4 period (The text is talking about the time over which the competition happens.)

5 host (The *host nation* is the country where an international sporting event is taking place.)

B

1 center (If something *takes center stage*, it is the focus of people's attention.)

2 effect (We need a noun to refer to the result of new ideas.)

3 end (If something *reaches a dead end*, it can't progress or develop any further.)

4 lead (We need a verb. If something *leads you in an unexpected direction*, it produces an unexpected result.)

5 familiar (We need an adjective to contrast older ideas with new combinations of ideas.)

C

1 behave (We need a verb. *Behave* collocates with *in the same way*.)

2 choices (We need a noun to refer to the decisions about money we make.)

3 financial (We need an adjective to specify the kind of mind-set (set of opinions) which is being discussed.)

4 conclusion (*Come to a conclusion* is an idiom.)

D

1 told (We need a verb. You are *told* things by other people.)

2 waste (*Go to waste* is an idiom.)

3 down (*Hand down* is a phrasal verb which means "give something to your children, to the next generation".)

4 away (*Throw away* is a phrasal verb which means "dispose of, get rid of".)

5 dispose (*Dispose* collocates with *of*.)

E

1 fight (A duel was a kind of fight.)

2 legal (We need an adjective to refer to the fact that it was not lawful to fight duels.)

3 kept (If you *keep to* rules, you obey them.)

4 weapon (We need a noun to refer to swords and pistols.)

Page 133

FURTHER PRACTICE AND GUIDANCE: *PART 2, READING: FILL IN THE BLANKS*

1 a 3rd-person verb in the present tense

2 choices, conclusion, economical, financial, ideas

3 a plural noun

4 answer, behave, conclusion, economical, financial

5 an adjective

6 answer, behave, choices, conclusion, ideas

7 a noun

8 behave, economical, financial

9 yes, *come to the same conclusion*

Pages 134–136

READING AND WRITING:
FILL IN THE BLANKS

A

1 respond (*Respond* collocates with *to* later in the sentence.)

2 known (*Known* collocates with *as*.)

3 chance (If there is *no chance to escape*, it isn't possible to escape.)

4 cause (A *cause* is something that makes something else happen. In this case, it refers to whatever makes us feel threatened.)

5 symptoms (This refers to the outward signs of a disease.)

6 towards (*The first step towards* doing something is the start of a process.)

B

1 estimated (*It is estimated that* means that people calculate or guess the amount of something.)

2 left (*Left* means "remaining, still in existence".)

3 stricter (Laws can be *strict*.)

4 labelled (When a product has information on it that tells you it is recyclable, it is *labelled as* recyclable.)

5 cost (*At great cost* is an idiom.)

C

1 legal (The next sentence goes on to refer to a *legal* context where anti-social behavior is defined.)

2 includes (Graffiti is given as one example of what constitutes anti-social behavior.)

3 age (An *age group* is a set of people who are all the same age.)

4 alike (If something affects young and old *alike*, it affects both groups in the same way.)

5 responsibility (*Take responsibility for* is a collocation.)

D

1 appear (If our actions *appear* to be selfless, that's what they seem to be like.)

2 caused (If something *causes you to do* something, it makes you do it, or forces you to do it.)

3 risk (*At risk* is a collocation.)

4 similar (*Under similar circumstances* means "in the same situation".)

5 selfish (We need an adjective to contrast with *altruistic* in the previous sentence.)

E

1 cultivate (We *cultivate the land* when we grow things on it.)

2 souvenirs (We need a noun to describe in general what people on pilgrimages brought home from their trips.)

3 trip (This is a synonym for *tour* in the phrase *Grand Tour*.)

4 educating (If you *educate someone in* something, you teach them about it.)

5 something (The meaning here is that the Grand Tour was like a pilgrimage in some ways. *Have something of the X about it* is a phrase meaning "resemble X in some ways".)

F

1 history (If something *has a long history*, it has existed for a long time.)

2 state (*State* here means "condition".)

3 planted (If an area has had trees placed in it, it has been *planted* with them.)

4 engineered (If something is *brilliantly engineered*, it is built in a very clever way.)

5 cooling (The water that came along the thin channels reduced the temperature.)

PART 3: LISTENING

Page 137

SUMMARIZE SPOKEN TEXT

(Model answers)

A

In the interview, a professor of English is asked whether English is an easy subject at university, because all you have to do is read books. The professor argues that this is not true, saying that not only do students have to read a lot of books in a short time, but they also develop critical abilities and gain an understanding of the cultural context surrounding the books they read.

B

The speaker draws on personal experience to describe the behavior of crowds. He tells us of how he got caught up in a demonstration that turned violent and how he felt about this and how his feelings changed during the demonstration. He concludes that in crowds the individual is lost in the group mind and follows where the crowd goes, which gives one a sense of freedom from responsibility.

C

This is about John Milton the poet, but the speaker believes you can get a better idea of what Milton believed socially and politically by reading his prose writings. He wrote about many subjects, including divorce, but the most relevant to us today is his pamphlet or essay on freedom of expression and publication, and which is against all forms of censorship.

Page 138

MULTIPLE-CHOICE, CHOOSE MULTIPLE ANSWERS

A: 2, 4, 5

1 is incorrect because this is not described as a health problem.

3 is incorrect because noise may interfere with spoken communication, not with speech as such.

2 is correct because the speaker says: *Traffic noise is one of the health hazards, as it can lead to other problems, like noise-induced hearing impairment.* **4** is correct because the speaker says: *... while this doesn't drive you mad in the medical sense, it is intensely annoying and can lead to mental health problems.* **5** is correct because

the speaker says: *There is increasing evidence that noise ... can give rise to serious health and social problems. Some of which, such as its effects on people's behavior and anger levels, ...*

B: 2, 3, 4

1 is incorrect because although Saint Lucia is mentioned, which is in the Caribbean, no mention is made of a Poet Laureate of the Caribbean. **5** is incorrect because the speaker says: *But I think Germany might have – no, it wasn't Germany. Somewhere else, but I don't remember.*

2 is correct because the speaker says *... and Ireland and Scotland.* **3** is correct because the speaker says: *He was the Poet Laureate of Saint Lucia.* **4** is correct because the speaker says: *But he was or is the American Poet Laureate, isn't he?*

C: 4, 5

1 is incorrect because travel is only mentioned in the example of recovering from jet-lag. **2** is incorrect because countryside is only mentioned in the context of urban change. **3** is incorrect because time zones are only mentioned in the example of recovering from jet-lag. **6** is incorrect because although changes in government are mentioned, they are not mentioned as a difficulty.

4 is correct because the speaker says: *It is in the smaller, everyday things that you might experience what is known as culture shock, although it's not really a shock, but puzzling all the same. For example, the precise way to behave at a supermarket checkout may have changed.* **5** is correct because the speaker says: *And in ordinary conversation, the frames of reference have changed, and quite often you find that you don't really know what people are talking about, even though they are speaking your native tongue.*

Page 139

FILL IN THE BLANKS

A

1 topics	4 rightfully
2 ironic	5 victims
3 imprisoned	6 relations

B

1 overload	5 miserable
2 cope	6 trend

3 discard	7 affluent
4 consumers	

C

1 reaction	4 contemporary
2 negative	5 internal
3 Initially	6 source

Page 140

HIGHLIGHT CORRECT SUMMARY

A: 3

The speaker says: *I want to take a quick look at how material culture ... affects the non-material culture, our customs, behavior, beliefs, attitudes, and so on. Now, of course, it works both ways ... Take, for example, genetic science. While many, if not most, people welcome the advances made in this field ... many, too, object to the idea of cloning.*

B: 1

The speaker says: *Ernest Hemingway ... was badly wounded, hospitalized, and fell in love with a nurse. He wrote a novel about a man who was badly wounded in the First World War, was hospitalised and who fell in love with a nurse. The Spanish Civil War and the Second World War followed as did books about his experiences in them. Now, how much can we draw on a writer's biography to explain his work? It should, I believe, be irrelevant to the judgement you bring to the merits of the individual work.*

Page 141

MULTIPLE-CHOICE, CHOOSE SINGLE ANSWER

A: 1

2 and **4** are incorrect because the speaker says: *The division of literary works into genres ... makes life easier for the person browsing in a bookshop. He or she can go directly to where their favorite kind of book is shelved, be it science fiction, gothic, romance, and so on.* **3** is incorrect because the speaker says: *... for the most part, such writers: are writing fantasies.* **5** is incorrect because the speaker says: *However, some genre writers, particularly writers of detective and police fiction, ...*

1 is correct because mainstream fiction is contrasted with genre fiction.

B: 4

1 is incorrect because the speaker says: *Each year, about six million people in Britain consult their doctors because they feel stress or anxiety, and it is estimated that at least another six million suffer from stress-related illness but do not seek medical advice.* **2** is incorrect because the speaker does not say this is easy and says: *I suppose, too, that it's possible for someone to train themselves to be able to take higher levels of stress by repeatedly putting themselves in a stressful situation – to build up a tolerance for stress.* **3** is incorrect because the speaker says: *But stress is a fact of life for all of us ... .*

4 is correct because the speaker says: *Long working hours, fear of losing their jobs, the difficult journey to and from work in crowded trains and buses, all contribute to increased levels of stress.*

C: 3

1 is incorrect because the speaker says: *Research into the human genome has recently made it clear that both sides are partly right.* **2** is incorrect because the speaker says: *On the nature side, we have what we get from our genes ... such as temperament.* **4** is incorrect because the speaker does not claim that *all* non-physical traits are inherited.

3 is correct because the speaker says: *... some now claim that such traits as intelligence and personality are also encoded in our genes.*

Page 142

SELECT MISSING WORD

A: 3

The text is about how students should go about research in the library. The speaker describes various ways of finding information, then suggests looking in the reference shelves and the newspaper section. However, in newspapers, it might be more difficult to find the precise information needed. So, the answer is: *the article you're looking for.*

B: 2

This text is about the nature of touch. The speaker describes active and passive touching and says that the way touch works is complicated. So the answer is: *still poorly understood.*

Page 143

HIGHLIGHT INCORRECT WORDS

A

When societies were still mostly rural and agricultural, waste dispersal *(disposal)* was hardly an issue, partly because people tended to make use of everything and partly because there was plenty of space to bury rubbish. It was when societies became predominantly urban and industrious *(industrial)* that problems arose – mainly to do with wealth *(health)*. City authorities had a hard time trying to find effective *(efficient)* ways of getting rid of all the rubbish. One of these was to get people to set *(sort)* out their rubbish into different types, just as these days we are encouraged to separate our rubbish into different categories for easier removal and recycling. So, for example, kitchen rubbish was set aside and used for feeding animals. However, fears of disease put an end to that. In fact, it wasn't until the 20th century that all waste was simply thrown together and put *(ploughed)* into landfills.

B

Archery, the practice or art of shooting with a bow and arrow, has played an important part in English history, being the major *(main)* weapon of the foot-soldier and instrumental in winning many battles in wars with the French – with whom we seemed to be continuously *(constantly)* at war during the Middle Ages. The English featured *(favored)* the longbow over the short bow and the crossbow, the latter being the main firearm of militias *(militaries)* on the European continent. The crossbow fired a metal bolt released by a trigger, rather like a gun, and had the farthest *(longest)* range of any of the bows, but the main advantage of the longbow was its accuracy. The importance placed on archery is illustrated by the fact that medieval kings in England encouraged the practice and one of them, Edward III, went so far as to bar *(ban)* all sports on Sundays and holidays except archery. Because there were no standing armies in those days, and in the event of war rulers had to call on the populace, everything was done to make sure there were large numbers of competent, if not expert archers, to recruit.

WRITE FROM DICTATION

1 The field of social history has always been difficult to define.

2 All essays must be accompanied by a list of references.

3 Authoritarian regimes were more common in the past than they are today.

4 The new law was harder to impose than the government thought.

Page 144

FURTHER PRACTICE AND GUIDANCE: *PART 3, LISTENING: WRITE FROM DICTATION*

1 blamed, price hikes

2 technically challenging, near the surface.

3 typically does not keep, tried to withdraw

4 similarities between, their respective

LISTENING SCRIPTS

TEST 1

Page 8

SECTION 2:
REPEAT SENTENCE

You will hear some sentences. Please repeat each sentence exactly as you hear it. You will hear each sentence only once.

1 Please come to the next seminar properly prepared.

2 You'll find the economics section on the second floor of the library.

3 Next time, we'll discuss the influence of the media on public policy.

4 There is plenty of cheap accommodation off-campus.

5 The lecture on child psychology has been postponed until Friday.

6 The meeting will take place in the main auditorium.

7 You must establish a day and a time with your tutor.

8 There will be no extensions given for this project.

9 New timetables will be posted on the student noticeboard.

10 All students are encouraged to vote in the forthcoming elections.

Page 14

SECTION 2:
RE-TELL LECTURE

You will hear a lecture. After listening to the lecture, please retell what you have just heard from the lecture in your own words. You will have 40 seconds to give your response.

A
So, continuing our series of lectures on Modernism, we now turn to architecture and, in particular, to the work of Frank O. Gehry. Now, I'm not going to go into his career in detail; it is enough to say that early on he was, like other modernist architects, tied to the rectangle, the straight line, and so on. Often their buildings would have this basic shape and they would just, um, add bits of decoration like splashes of color or pointless balconies. Soon enough, Gehry wanted to break away from straight lines and grid-like designs. He wanted the freedom to experiment with other shapes – curves and unusually-angled roofs. What helped him with this was the computer, which allowed him to visualize and experiment with complex shapes, and to work on the whole design as one piece, without the added decoration being thrown in as an afterthought. Architecture as art, if you like … or, or sculpture even. He himself said that he had struggled with crossing the line between architecture and sculpture.

Now, I want to talk about one building in particular … um … the Guggenheim Museum in Bilbao, which I think you'll agree is a masterpiece.

B
Now, you might think it strange that in a lecture on biology, I will be talking a lot about mathematics … um … If I may digress a bit … When I was a student, mathematics, the language of clear abstraction, had nothing to do with life sciences like biology, the sphere of messy organic forms, cutting up frogs in the lab, and so on … um … In fact, I started doing biology precisely to avoid maths and physics. So, I've had a lot of catching up to do.

We are all aware of how the sciences have come to inter-relate more and more, and not only will mathematics impinge more and more on biology but also, I am told, in the 21st century, the driving force behind mathematics will be biology. This is partly because mathematicians are always on the look out for more areas to conquer. But a far greater reason is that the subject has been boiled down to physics and chemistry – obvious attractions for mathematicians.

A number of mathematical fields can be applied to biology. For example, knot theory is used in the analysis of the tangled strands of DNA, and abstract geometry in four or more dimensions is used to tell us about viruses. Again, neuroscience appears to be maths-friendly and equations can also explain why hallucinogenic drugs cause the users to see spirals.

So, if mathematicians are taking such a keen interest in biology, the least we can do as biologists is return the compliment.

C
Most of what the general public knows about daily life in ancient Rome comes from art, architecture and literature, which tell us more about the elites, especially … um … the goings-on of the emperors … but how much do we know of the lives of ordinary Romans? Did they have a voice, apart, that is, from what we can gather from graffiti? The usual picture is one of time spent at festivals, baths and, typically, the games. However, for many Romans, terrible living conditions, poverty, debt and the chance of being sold into slavery at any moment – that is, if they weren't slaves already – left no time or energy for such forms of entertainment, or for any interest in politics, for that matter.

Indeed, after the death of Augustus, executive power was taken from the elected assemblies of the Roman people. Now it was the emperor's job to look after the people, and his generosity often depended on the mood and behavior of the people – on how often and how violently they protested and rioted. One example would be Claudius ensuring a steady grain supply, even in winter, after rioters pelted him with stale crusts of bread. There is an anecdote about, um, Hadrian. While touring the provinces, an old lady approached him with a complaint; he made excuses and tried to get away. She said that if he wouldn't give her a hearing, he shouldn't be emperor. She got her hearing.

SECTION 2:
ANSWER SHORT QUESTION

You will hear some questions. Please give a simple and short answer to each one. Often just one or a few words is enough.

1 Which section of a newspaper gives the editor's opinion?

2 What instrument would you use to examine very small objects or life forms?

3 What is a destructive program that spreads from computer to computer?

4 What term is used for animals such as humans that usually give birth to live young: mammals or reptiles?

5 What do you call a system of government in which people vote for the people who will represent them?

6 What do we call the piece of paper that proves you have bought an item?

7 What do you call the document that gives details about your qualifications and work experience?

8 How would you describe an economy based largely on farming?

9 What is the study of the stars and planets called?

10 In business and advertising, what does PR stand for?

PART 3: LISTENING

Page 36

SECTION 1: SUMMARIZE SPOKEN TEXT

You will hear a short lecture. Write a summary for a fellow student who was not present at the lecture. You should write 50–70 words.

You will have 10 minutes to finish this task. Your response will be judged on the quality of your writing and on how well your response presents the key points presented in the lecture.

A

Interviewer: I understand that one major concern of yours in running a successful company, especially in the current economic climate, is the question of worker loyalty. Are you saying that such a thing no longer exists and, if so, what are some of the reasons for this, and how important is loyalty to the smooth and successful running of a company such as yours?

Interviewee: Well, I do think it's important, but I also realize that we can't go back to the old-fashioned sense of loyalty where an employee would spend his whole working life with one company or business. Our grandparents', even our parents', generation expected long-term employment, and their loyalty was rewarded with health care and a pension. This is no longer the case. Many companies are no longer willing, or perhaps even able, to provide such a financial package. Besides, to a younger generation, sticking at the same job all your life isn't a very exciting or inspiring prospect.

Some reasons for this might be the shortening of contracts, outsourcing, automation, and people holding down more than one job. In other words, we've all had to adapt to the realities of a rapidly changing, fast-paced economy. However, all this is not to say that loyalty is dead, rather it has changed emphasis. Today it is more about trust, in that an employee will promise to bring his skills and engage fully in his work for as long as she or he is there. People change jobs a lot more these days, but I still believe that a company is better off with at least a core of people who stay for the long term.

B

I'd now like to turn to the Roman, um, Latin writers of the period. Their achievements in the other arts – architecture, painting and sculpture – were rather second-rate, and mostly in imitation of the Greeks. And, it's true that Latin writers also wanted to emulate the Greeks and used their writers as models, but somehow the language wouldn't allow it. What I mean to say is, the particular qualities of the Latin tongue made for the excellence of their writings, especially the poetry. For one thing, Latin is capable of great compression – that is to say, it can convey in five or six words what we would need twice the number to say.

What also helped Latin writing flourish was the nature of Roman education. Whatever its faults as they would appear to us, its linguistic and literary emphasis seemed designed to produce orators and writers. A drawback of the system was that education was only available to the richer classes of society, and so Roman literature is mainly a product of those classes. This in turn meant that the subject matter was fairly limited and narrow in its social reach – though there were exceptions.

C

Some economists argue that financial aid to developing countries is, in the long run, inefficient and even counter-productive. However, there are two main types of aid that we will deal with here. First, there is long-term aid to countries such as Ethiopia and Somalia, where there are recurrent problems such as drought and poor agricultural production, and where there is little or no industry to speak of – problems that won't go away with an injection of money.

Then there is emergency aid, which also appeals for contributions from the public, when a disaster of one kind or another strikes. Recent examples would be the earthquake in Haiti, and the tsunami in Japan. In the case of emergency aid, it arrives in the first instance as food, clothing, shelter, and medical aid, all of which are of immediate practical use and great benefit.

With countries that have long-term developmental problems, just pumping in money is not enough and, sad to say, a lot of the money doesn't go where it should. What is more important is providing know-how: teaching the skills and expertise needed to help develop the economy and social services such as health, sanitation, and so on. It is also necessary to help build the institutions – a bureaucracy, if you like – that can organize and run these services.

Page 37

FURTHER PRACTICE AND GUIDANCE: *PART 3, SECTION 1: SUMMARIZE SPOKEN TEXT*

Listen to each of the following extracts from a lecture in turn. Make notes as you listen. At the end of each extract, pause the CD and use your notes to summarize the extract in your own words.

Extract 1:

Some economists argue that financial aid to developing countries is, in the long run, inefficient and even counter-productive. However, there are two main types of aid that we will deal with here. First, there is long-term aid to countries such as Ethiopia and Somalia, where there are recurrent problems such as drought and poor agricultural production, and where there is little or no industry to speak of – problems that won't go away with an injection of money.

Extract 2:

Then there is emergency aid, which also appeals for contributions from the public, when a disaster of one kind or another strikes. Recent examples would be the earthquake in Haiti and the tsunami in Japan.

In the case of emergency aid, it arrives in the first instance as food, clothing, shelter, and medical aid, all of which are of immediate practical use and great benefit.

Extract 3:

With countries that have long-term developmental problems, just pumping in money is not enough and, sad to say, a lot of the money doesn't go where it should. What is more important is providing know-how: teaching the skills and expertise needed to help develop the economy and social services such as health, sanitation, and so on. It is also necessary to help build the institutions – a bureaucracy, if you like – that can organize and run these services.

Page 39

SECTION 2: MULTIPLE-CHOICE, CHOOSE MULTIPLE ANSWERS

Listen to the recording and answer the question by selecting all the correct responses. You will need to select more than one response.

A

The heyday of the English landscape garden was the 18th century, and it stood for many things: the appreciation of natural beauty, of course, but also the idea of a civilized life, good taste, one's personal philosophy, and one's social status. Gardens also – though it is hard for us to credit – became expressions of their owners' political affiliations.

Until the picturesque style emerged as part and parcel of the Romantic Movement, gardens had been strictly formal, laid out with mathematical precision following the Italian and French examples. There then came a backlash against this rigid formality, led by, among others, the poet Alexander Pope. Pope and his allies argued for a more natural nature.

Lord Burlington was a major figure in the landscape garden movement, and he was famously influenced by his love of the Italian architect, Andrea Palladio, along with the picturesque or romanticized landscapes of Italian classical painting. With these in mind, he scattered his gardens and parks with classical Greek and Roman temples and statues. In other words, he wanted to make the garden look like those paintings.

B

Woodblocks used for pictorial illustration became fairly common in 15th century Europe, but had been used long before that for printing designs on textiles. Most of these were simple in design and quite crudely cut, but some were skillfully drawn and cut, while others even contained pictorial imagery.

Records show that woodblock printing on fabrics was practised by the Egyptians as early as 2000 years BC. The oldest existing printed fabric, which is Egyptian, dates from the 4th century. At the same time, the craft seems to have been widely established, even commonplace, elsewhere: for example, in India, Mexico and Peru, where the same techniques continue to be practised today. And the technique was almost certainly used by both the Japanese and the Chinese too.

C

Political parties in most democracies not only have to win more votes than their rivals to get into power, they also have to persuade the electorate that it is worth their going out to vote in the first place. In the UK, turnout is frequently low, and one reason cited is … the weather! Some countries, therefore, have made voting compulsory; it is against the law not to vote and failing to vote is a punishable offence.

In Austria, for example, failure to vote results in an automatic fine, as it does in Australia. As a consequence, voter turnout is rarely less than 92% in both these countries. Other countries have penalties that affect the individual in more practical ways. In Greece, for example, although it is no longer acted on, passports were confiscated or not granted; and in Bolivia, non-voters may be banned from using banks or schools for up to three months.

The punishment in countries such as France, Germany, the UK, and so on is seeing the government you didn't elect raise your taxes.

Page 40

SECTION 2: FILL IN THE BLANKS

You will hear a recording. Write the missing words in each blank.

A

Almost everyone has heard of the London Stock Exchange, but relatively few know anything about the London Metal and Commodity Exchanges – yet these markets have a greater influence on world economies because they set global prices for some of the essential raw materials for industry and food manufacture.

The LME provides three basic services to the world's non-ferrous metal trade. First, it is a market where large or small quantities of metal of a guaranteed minimum standard can be bought and sold on specific trading days. Second, it acts as a barometer of world metal prices. And third, it is a "hedging" medium: that is, it can help traders get some protection from price fluctuations that occur for economic, political or financial reasons.

B

It isn't necessary to have a specialized knowledge of, say, the intricacies of counterpoint, or even to be able to read music to understand it. Usually, getting the point of a piece of music, its emotional and dramatic impact, is immediate or simply requires you to become more familiar with it. Of course, prolonged study of music and its composition, as in any other field, will increase your understanding, but not necessarily your enjoyment. Now, I realize that it can require a good deal of willingness on our part to risk new sensations, and there is a lot of music that will seem unfamiliar and alien to you on a first hearing.

C

Before farming was introduced into Scotland, people lived by hunting, fishing, and gathering wild foodstuffs. This way of life meant that they usually didn't settle permanently in one place, but were to an extent nomadic, moving about in search of a livelihood, perhaps returning to the same places at certain times of the year. It is believed that the islands of Orkney were known to these people, but, so far, only a few flint tools have been found to verify this. This is because coastal erosion has destroyed many ancient sites and these may have contained relics of some of these earliest pioneering colonists.

Page 41

SECTION 2:
HIGHLIGHT CORRECT
SUMMARY

You will hear a recording. Choose the paragraph that best relates to the recording.

A

A cliché, as you know, is an overused and worn out phrase – and … um … these are to be avoided like the plague in your essays. Indeed, someone once said, I quote, "there is no greater danger to either education or thinking than the popular phrase". Let me digress a little further; originally a cliché was a printer's term, back in the days when letters were set one by one, for a ready-made block of type of frequently used phrases, usually in the newspaper business. So … there you are … um … clichés were also known as stereotypes.

Now, if you think of graphic design as a language with its own vocabulary, grammar, and so on, it too must have its clichés. Obvious examples would be, um, the twin Greek masks of comedy and tragedy that symbolize the theater and, more popularly known, the heart as a symbol of love, especially on Valentine cards, and so on. Far from being a terrible fault – as it would be in literature – the visual cliché is essential in the world of graphic communication. This is certainly true when it comes to advertising and propaganda. The visual cliché can give immediate life to an idea and a clear meaning to what could be a mere abstraction.

B

All whales, dolphins, and porpoises are social animals, although the degree of sociability varies greatly from one species to another.

Differences of behavior have not evolved by chance. Living in close proximity to other animals has certain costs and benefits, so we can expect the group size adopted by a species to be the most suitable for its environment and lifestyle. River dolphins, for example, have a fairly simple social system, forming small groups of just a few animals – rarely more than ten. On the other hand, many of the oceanic dolphins may roam the seas in groups of thousands. Also, there can be differences within species: for example, with sperm whales, females and juveniles form groups while adult males are solitary.

Some of the reasons for living in groups include greater efficiency in searching for and catching food, benefits for mating, learning, defence, and sensory integration. Now, sensory integration is the means by which each animal contributes to the information gained by the group as a whole, and this plays an important part in defence and in the search for food. For example, if one animal discovers a shoal of fish or a hungry shark, it can immediately pass on this information to the others in the group so that all may benefit. A single animal or small group may remain unaware of the food or predator, and so miss a meal or suffer an attack.

Page 44

SECTION 2:
MULTIPLE-CHOICE, CHOOSE
SINGLE ANSWER

Listen to the recording and answer the multiple-choice question by selecting the correct response. Only one response is correct.

A

I suppose the reason I got into geology was, well, as a kid I was fascinated by fossils – the fact that they went back countless years, long before there were any people on the planet. That was exciting and, um, they were beautiful too. And one thing led to another. What fascinates me … let me give you an example: suppose we dredge up from the sea floor some silt washed down by a river and, um, suppose that for political or other reasons we can't enter the country through which that river runs. Well, by

careful study of the particles of that silt, we can form a pretty accurate picture of the nature of that country. Not just the rocks, I mean, but the vegetation and animal life of the area. I sometimes think what we do is a bit like, um, Sherlock Holmes. You know, he takes a look at a man's shoes and can tell you which field in which county in England he's been in, and when. That sort of detective aspect of the work is always interesting and exciting. OK, we do spend time in the lab and at the computer, but we do get out and about, and go to interesting places for fieldwork.

B

What troubles me when I'm asked the question, "Can creative writing be taught?" – usually asked in a skeptical tone of voice – is not that I can't find an answer, but trying to figure out why I'm being asked. What do they want me to say? "No, of course it can't. I just like taking people for a ride. I'm a con artist."

Obviously, you can't teach someone to have a talent for storytelling, or a love of language, or how to write extremely well, but there are important lessons to be gotten across that will improve their writing and, at the very least, make it publishable.

For me, the best starting point is the habit of close reading, really close, and responding to the language. Forget about grand themes and ethical content, whatever, for the moment and ask if the author writes badly or well. So, writing can be taught through reading, through literature. Then I'd say, when it comes to your own writing, that you need to learn how to edit: to know when to say, "You don't need that word or that sentence. And that whole paragraph can go." It's one of the most important lessons a writing class can teach. As for producing a Tolstoy or a Dickens … well, people like that tend to get there by their own route.

C

It is not often I get the chance to talk about the psychology of pop music, or rather the lyrics and the effect they have on young people. I must say at the outset that I'm not at all sure about the findings of a recent survey I've been studying, conducted over a period of 30 years. In short, it claims that late adolescents and college students are more narcissistic than ever before. This might well be true, and it might also be true that pop lyrics are becoming more self-absorbed, negative and violent. But this might reflect the psychology of the writers and performers more than their listeners. Also, as the writers of the study are alarmed to discover, this radical increase in narcissism comes with higher levels of loneliness and depression which, if you think about it for a second, is hardly surprising. Furthermore, they have detected a link with heightened anger and problems maintaining relationships.

Now, a couple of points: first, adolescents are pretty much self-absorbed anyway, but it's rarely pathological; also, you can read almost anything you want into song lyrics from any era. Again, people nowadays find it easier to express themselves emotionally than their counterparts did 30 years ago. Last, the survey suggests a complete personality change over the period covered, yet I doubt that personality traits can change so much from one generation to another or, for that matter, from one culture to another.

Page 45

SECTION 2: SELECT MISSING WORD

You will hear a recording about the brain. *At the end of the recording, the last word or group of words has been replaced by a beep.* Select the correct option to complete the recording.

A
We learn most about ourselves and the way we function, both physically and mentally, when things go wrong. For a long time it was thought that the brain acted as a whole in governing the body's functions. Then, in 1861, Paul Broca, a French anatomist and anthropologist, discovered that different parts of the brain perform different functions. After carrying out a postmortem examination on a patient who had had a severe speech impediment, he discovered, as he had expected, damage to a section of the left frontal lobe of the brain. The left side of the brain governs language ability. The patient's problem had been that he

could only utter one syllable, though he fully [BEEP]

You will hear a recording about money.

At the end of the recording, the last word or group of words has been replaced by a beep. Select the correct option to complete the recording.

B
The Chinese were, as far as we know, the inventors of paper money and, because it was so easy to move around compared with coins, it was named "flying money". They were also the first to experience an economic problem which has become all too familiar: by the 12th century, there was enough money in circulation to cause serious inflation.

In Europe, it wasn't until about 1400 that bankers in Spain and Italy began to honor "bills of exchange", which were a kind of private paper money not in general use. They were documents used by those involved in a business transaction in which payment was made through a third party to avoid the cost of foreign exchange. However, it is the Swedes who are generally credited with producing the first proper European bank [BEEP]

Page 46

SECTION 2: HIGHLIGHT INCORRECT WORDS

You will hear a recording. Below is a transcription of the recording. Some words in the transcription differ from what the speaker(s) said. As you listen, circle the words that are different.

A
When the European Economic Community was established in 1957, its aim was, in broad terms, to move towards closer political and economic co-operation. Today, the much larger European Union has a far-reaching influence on many aspects of our lives, from the conditions we work under, to the safety standards we must adhere to, and the environment in which we live.

In order to achieve the free flow of goods and services, workers and capital between the member countries, they needed to establish

mutual policies in areas as diverse as agriculture, transport, and working conditions. When they had agreed on these policies, they became law. Now, though, the EU is concerned with a far wider range of issues.

B
Stem cells are the body's master cells, the raw material from which we are built. Unlike normal body cells, they can reproduce an indefinite number of times and, when manipulated in the right way, can turn themselves into any type of cell in the body. The most versatile stem cells are those found in the embryo at just a few days old. This ball of a few dozen stem cells eventually goes on to form everything that makes up a person.

In 1998, James Thompson announced that he had isolated human embryonic stem cells in the laboratory. At last, these powerful cells were within the grasp of scientists to experiment with, understand, and develop into fixes for the things that go wrong.

SECTION 2: WRITE FROM DICTATION

You will hear some sentences. Write each sentence exactly as you hear it. Write as much of each sentence as you can. You will hear each sentence only once.

1 Hundreds of scientific papers have been published on global warming.

2 Political power only disappears when this stage has been completed.

3 Social networks are changing the way we communicate.

4 The cotton industry purchased all its raw cotton from abroad.

Page 47

FURTHER PRACTICE AND GUIDANCE: *PART 3, SECTION 2: HIGHLIGHT INCORRECT WORDS*

Listen to the recordings while reading the transcriptions. Circle the words in the transcription that do not match the recording.

1 One way to think about voltage is to imagine it as the pressure that pushes charges along a conductor.

2 The electrical resistance of a conductor would then be a measure of the difficulty of pushing those charges along.

3 Now, if we use an analogy of water flowing in a pipe, a long narrow pipe resists flow more than a short fat one does – a long narrow one has more resistance.

4 Currents work in the same way: long thin wires have more resistance than do short thick wires.

5 Conversely, short fat wires have less resistance.

TEST 2

Page 48

SECTION 2: REPEAT SENTENCE

You will hear some sentences. Please repeat each sentence exactly as you hear it. You will hear each sentence only once.

1 The Arts Magazine is looking for a new Assistant Editor.

2 The lecture will deal with the influence of technology on music.

3 Make sure you correctly cite all your sources.

4 There are hundreds of clubs and societies to choose from.

5 Does the college refectory offer vegetarian dishes on a daily basis?

6 All essays and seminar papers submitted must be emailed to your tutor.

7 He was not the only one to call for legal reform in the 16th century.

8 The Drama Society is now auditioning for parts in the student play.

9 There is a position available for a Junior Lecturer in Media Studies.

10 There will be a significant rise in tuition fees starting next year.

Page 49

FURTHER PRACTICE AND GUIDANCE: *PART 1, SECTION 2: REPEAT SENTENCE*

A

You will hear eight sentences. First, cover all the answer options below with a piece of paper. Then, after hearing each sentence, uncover the two answer options and circle the sentence you heard.

1 Of course, you can also choose to have your grades e-mailed to you.

2 Does the professor keep regular office hours?

3 I'll check again, but I'm pretty sure we're supposed to read Chapter Two.

4 I think the university's main campus is close.

5 If your parents come to visit you this semester, where will they stay?

6 When I was in school, I had many of the same problems you do now.

7 I thought the mid-term exam was worth only half our course grade.

8 Many of the most popular courses are available online.

Page 54

SECTION 2: RE-TELL LECTURE

You will hear a lecture. After listening to the lecture, please retell what you have just heard from the lecture in your own words. You will have 40 seconds to give your response.

A

Alexis de Tocqueville, as we have noted, appears to have had some appeal to both ends of the political spectrum – left and right – or rather, both have found him to be useful for their purposes in certain circumstances. His rational acceptance of the new forces of democracy brought about by the American and French revolutions made him an icon of left-wing liberals. However, during the Cold War – that is, from the end of World War II until the collapse of communism – he was adopted by some leading thinkers on the right. So, there are two sides to his political philosophy, and the man himself, that we need to look at.

Now, I would suggest that de Tocqueville's biography is important here. You must always bear in mind when reading him that he was an aristocrat, and one whose family had suffered in the French Revolution. He wasn't your typical aristocrat because his politics differed from others of his family and social rank. He abandoned the Catholic church and married beneath his class. Yet he never quite threw off the prejudices of

that class. However, and what is important, he did recognize and believe that the tendency of history, which in those days could be traced back to the Middle Ages, was towards the leveling of social ranks, and more equal and democratic conditions. The French Revolution had in the end brought Napoleon, whom he hated, but democracy would inevitably come to France. His trip to America was to see democracy in practice, make note of its shortcomings and errors, and then find safeguards against them.

B

What I want to look at today is the question of how much technology – if, um, a pen can indeed be called technology ... perhaps I should say the instrument of writing – affects a writer's style and level of production. I also want to consider other factors that may have an effect on prose style, such as personality, educational background, and so on.

Now, production levels aren't so hard to measure in relation to the writing instrument used. The quill pen, for instance, would need continual re-filling and re-sharpening, which led to a leisurely, balanced style of prose full of simple sentences. Writing took a lot longer than now and the great novelists of the 18th century – Fielding, Smollett, Richardson – had a relatively small output, though some of their books ran to enormous length.

By the middle of the 19th century, the fountain pen had been invented. It didn't need such constant re-filling, which can account for the more flowing, discursive style of, say, Dickens and Thackeray, as well as their tremendous output. Then came the typewriter, whose purpose, once you got the hang of it, was to speed up the writing process and was therefore much favored by journalists. This, it seems to me, gave rise to a short-winded style characterized by short sentences. A short prose style, if you like. Dictating machines and tape recorders led, as one novelist complained, to writers becoming too conversational, rambling and long-winded. Henry James, although he didn't use these machines, dictated his later novels and, well, some might agree with this accusation.

Well, it looks as though we're going to have to leave word processors, computers and, of course, the way film and its narrative techniques have affected writing style for another day.

C

It is almost impossible these days not to include photography in a course on the history of art. I disagree with people such as Walter Benjamin who suggest that technology and art don't go well together. Photography, with its realism, its accurate representation of the thing in front of you, initially deprived many artists of their subject matter, forcing them to look in new ways – no bad thing. True, mass produced images of, say, the Mona Lisa, obviously can't provide the same experience as seeing the real painting. On the other hand, there are photographs which, to my mind, are far more thought-provoking and have greater emotional impact than a painting of the same subject could.

Some people say that the traditional idea of an artist with a trained hand and eye is old-fashioned. They no longer believe that an artist needs specialist knowledge, but rather that he or she can simply point a camera at a scene and record it. However, on the one hand, that ignores the creative skill involved in producing photographs. On the other hand, it also ignores the fact that even in the past, painters used various technological aids. For example, the Dutch painter, Vermeer, used a *camera obscura* to help him create his images. We'll go into that later, but for now, I want to look at the documentary and cultural value of photography.

**SECTION 2:
ANSWER SHORT QUESTION**

You will hear some questions. Please give a simple and short answer to each one. Often just one or a few words is enough.

1 What emergency service is usually called when someone is in trouble at sea: ambulance or coastguard?

2 Name a month that falls between April and June.

3 What word describes moving a program or other material from a website to your computer?

4 What do we call a picture that a doctor takes to see inside your body?

5 What crime has someone stealing items from a shop committed: shopfitting or shoplifting?

6 If someone is feeling a little ill, they may say they are feeling "under the ..." what?

7 Who is the person in charge of a football match?

8 What do we call the last game in a sporting competition, which decides the champion?

9 What is the general term for paintings of the countryside or natural views?

10 Which of these would probably be found in an office: a printer, a blanket, or a nail brush?

Page 55

FURTHER PRACTICE AND GUIDANCE: *PART 1, SECTION 2: ANSWER SHORT QUESTION*

First read the answer options below. Then listen to ten questions. Write each question number (1–10) next to the correct answer. You will not use all of the answer options.

1 Where would you be most likely to find a whale: in a tropical forest, in the ocean or at the top of a volcano?

2 If someone found that their coat had a stain on it, where would they probably take it?

3 What are the things that hens lay called?

4 The people whose job it is to uphold the law and protect the public from criminals are called ...

5 On what geographical feature would someone be living if their country was surrounded by water on all sides?

6 What general part of the day is known as dawn?

7 What are the people who work the land, plant crops, and raise animals for food commonly known as?

8 If a button has come off a shirt, what would someone most likely use to put it back on?

9 What appliance do people use to keep their food cool and prevent it from spoiling?

10 To cross over from one side of a wide river to the other, without using a boat, what is usually required?

PART 3: LISTENING

Page 74

**SECTION 1:
SUMMARIZE SPOKEN TEXT**

You will hear a short lecture. Write a summary for a fellow student who was not present at the lecture. You should write 50–70 words.

You will have 10 minutes to finish this task. Your response will be judged on the quality of your writing and on how well your response presents the key points presented in the lecture.

A

Interviewer: Now, professor, recently you wrote a letter to a leading national newspaper complaining about falling standards in both written and spoken language among students, even graduates, and saying that you deplore the way English is being debased by change and dumbing down ...

Interviewee: Yes, I said that standards are falling and that very few graduates these days can write a comprehensible essay ... their grammar and syntax is all over the place ... um ... and I do have certain regrets over the way some words have now become unusable in their full meaning because they've been sloppily misused by those who should know better, such as journalists. So, because they use, say, "enormity" to mean something very big instead of something very wicked, I can no longer use the word in its correct sense without being misunderstood. And there are hundreds of other cases like this. But, of course, language changes, and meanings shift and change emphasis, and it's as useless to complain about that as it is to moan about the weather. The point I was making was that, at the earliest possible level, children should be made familiar with the basics of grammar and syntax, how to put sentences together, and so on. But I'm not suggesting going back to the days when, as I did, you had to analyze sentences in minute detail as if you were doing Latin. Though, of course, there is something to be said for having that kind of detailed understanding of the language.

B

Perhaps the first example of what could be called a newspaper was the *Acta Diurna* – roughly, "Daily News" – that Julius Caesar introduced in 59 BC. This was a handwritten news-sheet posted daily in the Forum at Rome and in other common meeting places around the city. Of course, a lot of the news would be out of date in the sense that, for example, it took a long time for reports of a victory in a distant country to get back to Rome. Nonetheless, a lot of the items included are similar to those found in more modern newspapers: news of battles, as already mentioned, as well as political and military appointments, political events, and even a social diary recording marriages, births, and deaths. One mustn't forget sport – if that is what you'd call it. Just like modern fans of football, sports-minded Romans could keep up with the latest results of the gladiator contests. People who lived in the provinces and wanted to be kept up to date would send scribes to Rome to copy the news and have them send it back by letter. Many of these scribes could make extra money by providing the news to more than one client. Quite a few of them were slaves and would go on to use the extra money earned to buy their freedom.

C

As you have probably noticed, fashions and tastes change quite noticeably over the years, most obviously perhaps in clothes, hairstyles and popular music. The reputations of writers and artists are no different, though the alternating periods of being in and then out of fashion are longer. A poet may no longer appeal to a large reading public for a number of reasons, though we must keep in mind that poetry is a minority taste and its readership is relatively small in the first place.

So, um, I want to look at the reputation of Alexander Pope. In his own lifetime, he was praised and idolized by both his friends and the literary world in general, though he did have some rather vicious enemies. Yet both friends and enemies seemed more concerned with either praising or attacking his character and morals than with properly assessing the poems themselves. The Romantics,

of course, had little time for him. Indeed, the Romantic movement, in poetry at least, was an attempt to make a complete break with the strict formality and rationality of the Augustan poets, of whom Pope was the most notable example. They did not regard him as a real poet and complained of his ignorance of nature in the sense of mountains, trees, and flowers.

The Victorians were even less responsive to Pope and this was probably the period when his reputation was at its lowest. In fact, it wasn't until the 1920s that Pope and the Augustan poets were re-evaluated, and given the attention and respect they deserved.

Page 75

SECTION 2: MULTIPLE-CHOICE, CHOOSE MULTIPLE ANSWERS

Listen to the recording and answer the question by selecting all the correct responses. You will need to select more than one response.

A

It now seems likely that the earliest printing presses were, in fact, simply the common screw presses used for crushing oil seeds and herbs, or even for doing more domestic chores such as pressing fabrics, adapted for printing. Other large wooden presses, such as those used for crushing the juice from olives and grapes – known as beam presses – had been around for centuries, but proved to be unsuitable for printing due to their size and their necessarily heavy pressure.

Most presses of this type work on the simple principle of direct vertical pressure, controlled by a central screw at the lower end of which was attached a flat board – what later became known as a platen. We know that many of these earliest printing presses were still in regular use in the 17th century, and the basic design remained almost unchanged until the 19th century, when they were replaced with iron presses.

B

Technological change has had a profound effect on the way music is made and how it sounds, as well as on the way we listen to it. New technologies – and I mean

this in the broadest sense, not just electronic devices – can alter the sound of music and, in the case of electronic recording systems, affect the economics and distribution of music. For example, the innovation of the valve trumpet in the 19th century changed the sound of the orchestra. Now everyone has easy access to a wide variety of music, but it is arguable whether this has increased our understanding of it. Before radio and recorded music, those who could afford it would have pianos or pianolas – mechanical pianos that played a roll of sheet music – so the basic ability to read notes off a page was more widespread. However, these days, regardless of whether or not we are musical experts, there is no doubt that music enhances life, and with the Internet, sites to download music from, file-sharing, and so on, we have access to more music than ever before – and a lot of it for free.

C

You may not know much, if anything, about Jean-Jacques Rousseau, but you have probably heard the well-known quote: "Man is born free, and everywhere he is in chains." In his early work, Rousseau argued that mankind was happiest and at its best in a "state of nature" – that is, before the creation of society and civilization. He saw society as artificial and corrupt, and that good people were corrupted by it. *The Social Contract* is perhaps the most enduring and well-known of his books, covering pretty well every aspect of Man in society. However, in this book, his attitude to the condition of Man in a state of nature changes. In such conditions, man is brutish and competitive by nature, and there is no law or morality. Therefore, because it is easier to survive by joining forces with others, people form societies to better fight anything that might endanger their situation. Rousseau's political philosophy has had a profound influence on later thinkers, even though, or perhaps especially because, it is open to many interpretations. But political philosophy is not everybody's cup of tea. In his own time, Rousseau was a bestseller, with novels such as *The New Heloise* and, especially, *Emile*, though even the latter is not free of his constant desire to improve society. It illustrates his ideas about the best form of education, which involves educating a child's emotions before their reason. This too had a profound influence on educational theorists.

Page 78

SECTION 2:
FILL IN THE BLANKS

You will hear a recording. Write the missing words in each blank.

A

Paper was first manufactured in Europe by the Spanish in the 12th century, although it had been imported since the 10th century. Around the year 1276, a mill was established at Fabriano in Italy. The town became a major center for paper making, and throughout the 14th century provided most of Europe with fine quality paper – which it has continued to produce ever since. By the 15th century, paper was also being manufactured in Germany and France, and it was not long before both countries became almost completely independent of material bought from overseas. With the increasing availability of paper in Europe, the production of identical printed pictures became almost inevitable.

B

The spinal cord – the link between the brain and the body – is a band of nervous tissue about the thickness of your little finger that runs through the backbone. Nerve cells called motor neurons convey electric impulses that travel from the brain to the spinal cord, branching off at the appropriate point and passing to the various parts of the body. Similarly, sensory neurons transmit messages from organs and tissues via the spinal cord to the brain. But the spinal cord also functions without the brain having to intervene; it alone controls those actions called spinal reflexes that need to be carried out very fast in response to danger.

C

The growth of the modern state brought with it the development of mass political parties and the emergence of professional politicians. A man whose occupation is the struggle for political power may go about it in two ways. First, a person who relies on their political activities to supply their main source of income is said to *live off* politics, while a person who engages in full-time political activities, but who doesn't receive an income from it, is said to *live for* politics. Now, a political system in which recruitment to positions of power is filled by those who *live for* politics is necessarily drawn from a property-owning elite, who are not usually entrepreneurs. However, this is not to imply that such politicians will necessarily pursue policies which are wholly biased towards the interests of the class they originate from.

Page 79

SECTION 2:
HIGHLIGHT CORRECT SUMMARY

You will hear a recording. Choose the paragraph that best relates to the recording.

A

In his great novel *Remembrance of Things Past* or *In Search of Lost Time*, Marcel Proust explored what are called "involuntary memories" – those that come to us quite suddenly without conscious effort, usually triggered by one of the senses. The fact that his book has two titles in English might suggest there is some doubt as to how our minds go about remembering things. In perhaps the most well-known such episode in the novel, the character Marcel is reminded of his childhood by the aroma produced when dunking a cake in a cup of tea. This is not far away from the belief that as we get older we can remember quite clearly incidents from years ago, but find it hard to remember what we did last week. Proust's insight into memory is certainly true of one way the mind works. But why and how do we remember what we do?

Experts believe that we store memories in three ways. First, there is the sensory stage which is to do with perception and lasts only a fraction of a second, taking in sight, sound, touch, and so on. These first perceptions and sensations are then stored in the short-term memory, which is the second stage. Finally, important information or information that has been reinforced by, for example, repetition, is then filtered into the long-term memory. Naturally, we tend to more easily absorb material on things we already know something about, as this has more meaning for us and can create a web of connections with related material that is already stored in the long-term memory.

B

I want to look now at the three main approaches historians have taken towards the English Revolution or Civil War. There is a fourth point of view, taken up by most schoolchildren when they first meet the subject, but it can hardly be called historical. On the one hand, schoolchildren tend to have a romantic image of the Cavaliers, who were supporters of the monarchy, as aristocratic, charming, flashily dressed, and up for a bit of fun. On the other hand, they tend to regard the Roundheads or Puritans, who were followers of Oliver Cromwell, as miserable, working-class, dressed in black, and insisting on a life without luxuries. It isn't difficult then to takes sides.

The first approach, which prevailed up until the middle of the 20th century, was that the Revolution was part of the age-old battle between parliament and the monarchy, with parliament representing the traditional rights of Englishmen against the attempt by the Royal Family to increase its power and dictate law. In reaction to this, the second approach saw it as a working-class revolution and an important stage in the development of capitalism. In other words, they saw it as a class war, and a forerunner of the French Revolution and those that came after. Historians who supported the third approach saw that things weren't as clear cut as the others thought. Instead of seeing the Revolution as the result of long-term trends in the country's history, and therefore almost unavoidable, they focused on the details of the period immediately leading up to its outbreak and allowed for its unpredictability. The two sides, also, weren't so clear cut, with some aristocrats supporting parliament and some members of the working class fighting on the side of the monarchy.

Page 80

SECTION 2: MULTIPLE-CHOICE, CHOOSE SINGLE ANSWER

Listen to the recording and answer the multiple-choice question by selecting the correct response. Only one response is correct.

A

How would you define "reasonable" as it is used in law? For example, you are allowed to use "reasonable force" when defending yourself. It seems to depend on how serious the situation was, whether it was possible to resolve it by peaceful means, whether you were ready to try those means and, finally, the relative strengths of those involved. Now, most men know, and they've probably grasped this from their earliest years in the school playground, that, when it comes to blows, fights don't stop until one of you is in no shape to do any damage to the other. The criteria mentioned seem a bit fuzzy to me. How can you convince a jury you were ready to try and talk your way out of it when the other person would have none of it and, besides, he was quick to land the first punch? Also you can strike the first blow and still plead self-defence. Of course, you again have the problem of convincing people that the threat was so great that you had no alternative, apart from getting beaten up yourself. Reacting calmly and rationally to a perceived threat is not easy to do.

B

Randall Jarrell, the great American critic and poet, once defined the novel as, "an extended piece of prose fiction with something wrong with it". Now, nothing is perfect and you don't have to look very hard to find something wrong – or perhaps just something you don't like – about any work of fiction you care to name. Where, we might ask, does the editor come into this? And is it beneficial to an author to have an editor who is also a novelist? You would think that being a writer themselves, familiar with the process of writing a novel and its demands, they would be able to get inside the head of the author, and be sympathetic and understanding of what needs to be done. This is

not an unreasonable assumption to make. However, is it not possible that there is an opposite side to this? Editors might, from their experience as writers, possibly unconsciously, try to make over the submitted novel as they themselves would have written it. The ideal, one supposes, is for the editor to see the book through the author's eyes, but if they apply their own creative talent to the job they might end up seeing it too much through their own eyes and, in this way, take no account of the author's original intentions.

C

It is claimed, by neuroscientists among others, that speaking two or more languages increases cognitive abilities and in some way re-wires the brain, as it were, in a way that positively affects how the brain works. And it's true that we tend to think of people who can speak two or more languages as being bright. Learning a language is, anyway, good mental exercise, not to mention its benefits in introducing you to other peoples and cultures. This is why all school curricula should include at least one compulsory language. Anyone who knows two languages will find that, in certain circumstances, they compete for position, the vocabulary of one getting in the way of the other. Often bi- or multilingual people find one language more suitable for expressing certain kinds of thoughts or feelings.

There is another view on being bilingual, not from a neuroscientist, but from someone whose business involves words and language. Brought up in a bilingual home, speaking Greek and French, and also fluent in English, she is old enough to remember when her native language, Greek, was also in effect two languages. There was the formal, correct form, *katharevousa*, which was taught and spoken in schools, written in newspapers and books, and so on, and the everyday *demotic* language you used with your friends. As for her view on bilingualism, she says that you end up with a split personality.

Page 81

SECTION 2: SELECT MISSING WORD

You will hear a recording about photography. *At the end of the recording the last word or group of words has been replaced by a beep.* Select the correct option to complete the recording.

A

These days nearly everyone with a mobile phone is able to take photographs or even make a video, but originally cameras were so large and heavy that photography's appeal as a pastime was limited to a few enthusiasts. Also, the time needed for the exposure meant that your subjects, if you were photographing people, had to remain still for what must have seemed like a very long time. Movement would come out as a blur in the picture or, if someone walked across the view of the lens, would not register at all, which is why early photographs of city streets appear deserted. In other words, all pictures had to be posed. However, as early as the 1880s, manufacturers in both Europe and America began producing miniature models, some of them small enough to be hidden in people's clothing. Cameras came in all shapes and sizes. Handbags, walking stick handles and tie-pins were among the oddest and were collectively known as "detective cameras". This was not because they were used in police work, but because the user could move about without attracting attention [BEEP]

You will hear a recording about career aspirations.

At the end of the recording, the last word or group of words has been replaced by a beep. Select the correct option to complete the recording.

B

Most, if not all, young men and women have dreams of the future which include themselves, their families, and possibly their country. At one time or another, they evaluate and criticize their own society, and think of the changes they would like to make. For most people, however, the biggest contribution they can make to their society's development and change is through the careers they will follow, rather than through direct political action. For the lucky few, their careers will be interesting as well as allowing them to make a measurable contribution to the growth of their country. This is why it is important to know something about the career aspirations of young people and the reasons for their interest in these ideal careers. At the same time, it is equally important to consider whether their aspirations are [BEEP]

Page 82

FURTHER PRACTICE AND GUIDANCE: *PART 3, SECTION 2: SELECT MISSING WORD*

You will listen to five speakers saying a sentence. For each speaker, choose the option that best completes their sentence.

A The museum of natural history offers tours every day. The tours are free and last [BEEP]

B Between 1972 and 1974, unusual weather patterns led to crop failures in many [BEEP]

C When you make a presentation, be sure to keep it short, and to take questions and comments [BEEP]

D Some members of the board have expressed concern about how much the new center will cost to build, but I'm confident we'll be able to borrow the funds [BEEP]

E Some students say that while courses offered on the Internet may be convenient, the lack of community associated with traditional classroom settings makes them [BEEP]

Page 84

SECTION 2: HIGHLIGHT INCORRECT WORDS

You will hear a recording. Below is a transcription of the recording. Some words in the transcription differ from what the speaker(s) said. As you listen, circle the words that are different.

A

In the 19th century, few people could afford to travel abroad; it was expensive and there weren't the mass transport systems that we have today. So curiosity about foreign lands had to be satisfied through books and drawings. With the advent of photography, a whole new dimension of "reality" became available. Publishers were not slow to realize that here was a large new market of people hungry for travel photography and they soon had photographers out shooting the best known European cities, as well as more exotic places further away. People bought the pictures by the millions, and magic lantern shows were presented in schools and lecture halls. Most popular of all, however, was the stereoscopic picture which presented three-dimensional views and was considered a marvel of Victorian technology.

B

Classified advertisements placed by individuals in newspapers and magazines are not covered by the Advertising Standards Authority's "code of practice". If you happen to buy goods that have been wrongly described in such an advertisement, and have lost money as a result, the only thing you can do is bring a case against the person who placed the advertisement for misrepresentation or for breach of contract. In this case, you would use the small claims procedure, which is a relatively cheap way to sue for the recovery of a debt. If you want to pursue a claim, you should take into account whether the person you are suing will be able to pay damages, should any be awarded. Dishonest traders are aware of this and often pose as private sellers to exploit the legal loopholes that exist: that is, they may claim they are not in a position to pay damages.

SECTION 2: WRITE FROM DICTATION

You will hear some sentences. Write each sentence exactly as you hear it. Write as much of each sentence as you can. You will hear each sentence only once.

1 Like humans, owls can see in three dimensions.

2 Modern art now does better than stocks as an investment.

3 Commercial necessity was the reason given for the decision.

4 Grants are available to those in financial difficulty.

Page 85

FURTHER PRACTICE AND GUIDANCE: *PART 3, SECTION 2: WRITE FROM DICTATION*

Each sentence below has some words missing. You will hear the complete sentences. Listen and write the missing words.

1 The course is intended primarily for non-science majors.

2 Many of the world's lakes are remnants of ancient glaciers.

3 Repetitive stress injuries account for nearly two-thirds of all workplace illnesses.

4 Evidence suggests that the human brain changes shape in response to the way it is used.

TEST 3

Page 86

SECTION 2: REPEAT SENTENCE

You will hear some sentences. Please repeat each sentence exactly as you hear it. You will hear each sentence only once.

1 You will be informed of the results by e-mail.

2 Please have copies of your seminar papers in the library a week in advance.

3 Most students are not eligible to claim housing benefit.

4 If you want to quit the student union, tell the registrar.

5 Does the university have an ice-hockey team?

6 Without doubt, his primary motive was economic.

7 The modern approach to the problem is to stress the symbolic side of human nature.

8 Many privately-owned firms have been eaten up by larger corporations.

9 I'm afraid Professor Jones doesn't suffer fools gladly.

10 Most of these criticisms can be shown to be false.

Page 87

FURTHER PRACTICE AND GUIDANCE: *PART 1, SECTION 2:*

The sentences that follow are from Text D on page 86. Listen to the sentences being read aloud. As you listen, underline the words that the speaker stresses.

1 The starting point of Bergson's

theory is the experience of time and motion.

2 Time is the reality we experience most directly, but this doesn't mean that we can capture this experience mentally.

3 The past is gone and the future is yet to come.

4 The only reality is the present, which is real to us through our experience of it.

Page 91

SECTION 2:
RE-TELL LECTURE

You will hear a lecture. After listening to the lecture, please retell what you have just heard from the lecture in your own words. You will have 40 seconds to give your response.

A
We appear to take it as a rule, or as a law of nature, that each species is adapted to the climate of its own home. For example, species from the Arctic, or even a temperate region, could not survive in a tropical climate, nor could a tropical species last long if it found itself at the South Pole. But it is true to say there's too much emphasis placed on the degree of adaptation of species to the climates where they live.

We assume that this adaptation – if all species are descended from a single form – must have taken place over millions of years, yet a large number of plants and animals brought from different countries remain perfectly healthy in their new home. Also, there are several examples of animal species that have extended their range, within historical times, from warmer to cooler latitudes and the other way round. Rats and mice provide good examples: they have been transported by man to many parts of the world and now have a far wider range than any other rodent, and they can be found living in the cold climate of the Faroe Islands to the north through the tropical zones to the Falklands in the south.

It is possible to see adaptation to any climate as a quality that is part of an inborn flexibility of the physical and mental constitution of most animals. Therefore, the ability to survive in the most

different climates by both man and his domestic animals, and the fact that elephants once existed in an ice age while living species live in tropical areas, should not be seen as deviations from the rule, but as examples of this flexibility being brought into action under particular circumstances.

B
Today, I want to look at some research that has been done into what motivates people and, um, particularly on what is called the 'mind set' – or more simply the mental attitude – that highly-motivated people have. And, of course, the attitude of those who aren't so motivated, or who lose their motivation. Now, it's obvious that motivation is crucial to performance, but that doesn't tell us where it comes from. Why is it that some people work hard and do well while others can work just as hard and don't, why some are committed to what they are doing and others aren't? Finding answers to this question would be extremely useful to educators, as well as in other areas of life. Businesses, for example, have long believed that financial incentives – bonuses, perks, pay rises – are the great motivators, and to an extent they can make a difference, but what we are calling the mind set is more important.

What has made it difficult to find out what the causes of motivation are, is that motivation and the capacity for hard work can be mistaken for talent – thinking it's a gift. Either you've got it or you haven't. People who believe this have a fixed mind set and are not only going to perform less well than they could, but it's also an attitude that will affect their whole outlook on life.

Some say that if talent is something people are born with and you're unlucky enough not to have any, then there's not much point in putting in all that extra effort for no real reward. However, research has shown that, if you put in the hours, practice brings the same level of achievement as talent. It's a question of changing this fixed attitude and adopting a growth attitude, which includes seeing mistakes and failures as opportunities to improve.

C
I suppose that it has always been the case for the majority of us that the first test of a work of art or literature or music is how much pleasure it gives us, and we don't want to bother with analysing why or how it has had such an emotional impact on us. It's always good to know what your pleasures are in the positive sense – and not as easy as some people think – as opposed to only really knowing what you don't like and complaining about it, though presumably there's some kind of pleasure to be had from that too. But now that you've chosen to take a course on the novel, I'm afraid that evaluating literature on the basis of how you feel about a book won't count as an intelligent critical response to the work being studied.

It is, however, useful to remind yourselves from time to time that we all fall for trash every now and again. For instance, you might actually enjoy listening to a catchy pop song, but you'd find it hard to explain in critical terms that it is good, or better than something else, just because it is enjoyable. So, you're here to sharpen up your critical knives, as it were, among other things of course.

Page 92

SECTION 2:
ANSWER SHORT QUESTION

You will hear some questions. Please give a simple and short answer to each one. Often just one or a few words is enough.

1 What is a painting of a person's head usually called?

2 Where would you find an urban area: in a city or in the countryside?

3 What do we call it when the Moon completely blocks out the light from the Sun?

4 What point of the compass is directly opposite East?

5 Where do you pay for your purchases at a supermarket?

6 What do you call an apartment that is below ground level: a basement apartment or a penthouse apartment?

7 What feature do pianos and computers have in common?

8 If you are feeling fed up, is it a positive or a negative feeling?

9 What do we call a period of ten years?

10 A specialist who repairs leaking water pipes is called a … .

PART 3: LISTENING

Page 106

SECTION 1:
SUMMARIZE SPOKEN TEXT

You will hear a short lecture. Write a summary for a fellow student who was not present at the lecture. You should write 50–70 words.

You will have 10 minutes to finish this task. Your response will be judged on the quality of your writing and on how well your response presents the key points presented in the lecture.

A

Interviewer: Professor, could you say a bit more about this psycho-geography you mentioned earlier?

Interviewee: Well, I could give you a short history of the subject, though, um, it's not a subject in the academic sense as far as I'm aware – or at least not at the college where I teach.

Interviewer: But what is it exactly? It sounds rather complicated, a mixture of, what, psychology and geography?

Interviewee: No, not at all. Well, the first theorist of it was a Frenchman, Guy Debord, and basically, in his words, it's the study of the effects of the geographical environment on the emotions and behavior of people. Put like that, of course, it doesn't sound like anything new – people have always been aware at some level of the effect of their surroundings on their emotions and way of life. And this includes not just buildings, but the landscape as a whole, the climate, and so on. But it is mainly an urban thing, and these days people who call themselves psycho-geographers tend to be harsh critics of the way modern city planners develop urban space. Really, I suppose, it asks people to pay more attention to their environment, be critical of it, and to note not just the aspects we've already mentioned but the atmosphere created by them as well.

I could go on and … um … tell you how to go about it, but all you have to do is go online and you'll find a site for almost any city you care to name. It's worth looking into.

B

It is almost impossible to talk about the *history* of the novel without starting with a definition of it, which is by no means easy to do. We all know what we ourselves mean by a novel and have our favorite novelists, whether they are from the heyday of Victorian fiction – Dickens, say, or George Eliot – or someone more modern or postmodern, for example, B. S. Johnson, who is famed for writing a novel that was bought in a box, with loose pages that you could read in any order. Again, you might be a fan of crime or detective fiction, which brings the added complication of genre. That is, does the fact that a work of fiction is comedy, tragedy, satire, ghost story, and so on, affect our definition?

Anyway, as far as the history of the English novel is concerned, we're on fairly solid ground when we date the first novels to the late 17th and early 18th centuries. The first that is still read as a novel in the way we read novels now is Bunyan's *Pilgrim's Progress*, which did have an enormous effect on English prose writing, but for me it would be Defoe's *Robinson Crusoe*. Now, people have tried to locate the beginnings even earlier than this, to Elizabethan prose writing and even further back, but I think this is to lose sight of what a novel is and does and confuses any kind of fiction with the true novel.

C

It was the philosopher Thomas Nagel, I think, who came up with the thought experiment of trying to imagine what it's like to be a bat – though I suppose any animal would do. The point is, of course, that you can't, just as you can't know what it's really like to be another person – I mean *know* rather than *imagine*. How much can we know of what goes on in another person's mind? We observe people, watch what they do, listen to what they say – and other sounds they may make – see how they respond to their environment, their likes and dislikes, what they eat, and so on. And from this we have learned to make fairly accurate predictions about how they'll behave in certain situations, yet we still can't be sure what thoughts have passed through their minds and certainly not what it feels like to them. We can guess, based on personal experience in similar situations, so we must assume that humans are alike enough for us to be reasonably certain that, for example, we experience the color red in roughly the same way, or in the same ways. But, again, to you red might bring to mind thoughts of blood and death, whereas to someone else warmth or excitement. And the differences can't just be cultural.

Page 107

SECTION 2:
MULTIPLE-CHOICE, CHOOSE MULTIPLE ANSWERS

Listen to the recording and answer the question by selecting all the correct responses. You will need to select more than one response.

A

There are two main reasons why parents decide to educate their children at home: either they dislike schools on principle, however odd those principles might be, or they don't believe their local schools provide an adequate education or the right sort of education for their children. If someone decides to teach their child at home – either by themselves or by employing a teacher – they have to convince their local education authority (LEA) that the teaching provided is satisfactory. Schedules, lesson plans and book lists must be shown, and it must also be demonstrated that the child is in fact learning and that they have adequate opportunities for physical education and meeting other children. Furthermore, while there is no formal assessment, officers from the LEA will come and inspect what is being done and look at the child's exercise books. If they are not satisfied, they may make out a school attendance order.

B

Certainly in Europe and the West we tend to think of bread as the staple food in our diet, as many proverbs and sayings, such as "bread is the staff of life" attest. Yet for the majority of the world's population the most important staple food is not wheat but rice, which is the seed of a different type of grass. The earliest evidence we have of rice being cultivated dates back to eight thousand years ago, when rice grains of that period were discovered in a village in China. By around six thousand years ago, the cultivation of both long-grain and short-grain rice had become well-established in China, and had just got going in India.

The word "rice" itself, however, is derived from the Aramaic *ourouzza* and came to us by way of Greek and Arabic. In fact, it was the Arabs who introduced rice to their Spanish territories in the 7th century, but it didn't spread to the rest of Europe until much later when, in the 15th century, Spaniards began to cultivate their own short-grain variety at Pisa in Italy.

C

The earliest writers on politics – and I'm thinking of Plato and Aristotle here – felt free to draw insights from all areas of human knowledge, unlike modern academic writers who tend to put things into smaller and smaller compartments, or focus more closely on one area of enquiry. For example, Plato would examine a whole political system and the philosophy that underlies it, whereas modern writers on politics might concentrate on one particular institution in that system – the House of Lords in England – or on voting patterns within a country. With this focus the bigger questions that the ancients dealt with – "What is the best form of government?" or "What is justice?" – tend to get left behind. Many writers on politics these days are university-based and so have to have specialized interests, and while they may make new and interesting discoveries in their special field, it is at the loss of a broader perspective – not to mention the loss of a general audience or readership. In the 19th century, there were still writers who used the same freedom of enquiry as the ancients, and are all the more readable – and relevant – because of it.

Page 108

SECTION 2:
FILL IN THE BLANKS

You will hear a recording. Write the missing words in each blank.

A

There have been many studies in America of the opinions and behavior of university lecturers and professors, and of well-known "free" or public thinkers who are not attached to a university or other institution, which show that those who are recognized as being more successful or productive as scholars in their field, or are at the best universities, are much more likely to have critical opinions. That is to say that they are more likely to hold liberal views – in the American use of that word – than those of their colleagues who are less creative or who have less of a reputation. The better a university is, as measured by the test results of its students or by the prestige of its staff, the more likely it has been that there will be student unrest and a relatively left-of-center faculty.

B

However simple or complex the chain of events in any given situation, when looked into it usually reveals a train of causal relationships – they are seen to be linked in some way. The methods of analysis aim to establish these relationships and provide a solid background for useful generalisations based on what at first appear to be separate events. The first step in this process is to collect facts and then see if any particular patterns emerge. If they do, it then becomes possible to form theories related to the facts, and this type of empirical theory forms a useful basis for analysis and prediction. However, on its own this theory is not enough; the essential second step is to test it by collecting more facts and by checking predictions against events. These new facts may mean you have to modify the theory, bearing in mind that new facts can only either disprove or support a theory – they cannot prove it to be right.

C

It is difficult to know how to place Montesquieu – if you're the kind of person who likes to categorize. Historian, political philosopher, sociologist, jurist or, if you think the *Persian Letters* a novel, a novelist – he was all these things. Perhaps, as some have, he could be placed among that almost extinct species, the man of letters. The books that

make up *The Spirit of the Laws* have had the most influence on later thinkers, and in them, as in his equally great *Considerations on the Causes of the Grandeur and Decadence of the Romans*, he makes his underlying purpose clear. It is to make the random, apparently meaningless variety of events understandable; he wanted to find out what the historical truth was. His starting point then was this almost endless variety of morals, customs, ideas, laws and institutions and to make some sense out of them. He believed it was not chance that ruled the world, and that, beyond the chaos of accidents, there must be underlying causes that account for the apparent madness of things.

Page 110

SECTION 2:
HIGHLIGHT CORRECT SUMMARY

You will hear a recording. Choose the paragraph that best relates to the recording.

A

Um … how did I get into anthropology? Well, I'm not an anthropologist, not trained in it anyway – in fact I'm a marine biologist – and it's more that I'm interested in the Strandlopers, the "beach walkers", if you like, than in anthropology generally. In fact, it was through my early interest in all things to do with the sea that I first heard of them. As a kid my favorite pastime was getting down to the beach and mucking about in rock pools and collecting anything the sea tossed up, and, um, the Strandlopers lived off the sea and seashore gathering food such as mussels, oysters, crabs, and so on, just as I did. So when I heard of them I thought, right, this is my kind of thing and I felt a kind of, well, affinity for them.

At first people thought they were a myth; I suppose because there didn't seem to be much evidence for their existence, but now we do have archaeological evidence such as pottery, discarded shells, the bones of seals and large fish, and so on. And those shells, we believe, became their first tools, and in some cases were also used as money and jewellery. Of course, before they had the implements, the, um, tools to hunt and fish, everything had to be caught by hand, so they kept mostly to shallow water. Then they might have used a primitive form of fishing line, perhaps the tendril of a climbing plant or a strip of animal skin with a bone or small piece of wood that would stick in the fish's throat. Anyway, the more we search the more we discover – most recently, caves on the coast have been discovered with ancient drawings. I find it endlessly fascinating.

B

To reach some kind of understanding of a period in the past – the Middle Ages, say – requires a creative act of the imagination not unlike that of a novelist getting inside the skins of their characters or establishing the environment they live in. What must it have been like to be a peasant under a feudal baron? What might his beliefs and politics have been? Did he, for example, think his situation was simply part of the natural order of things, or that it was grossly unfair and needed to be overthrown?

So, you have to imagine the terms under which life was lived in those days, and learn to feel in a different way about things by putting yourself into a world very different from your own. Now, of course, every age views the past from its own present and an 18th century historian's concept of the Middle Ages will be very different from that of one from the 21st century – which is why each age has to write its history over again. It's not so much that more facts or evidence come to light – if they do – but that sensibilities change too.

Page 112

SECTION 2:
MULTIPLE-CHOICE, CHOOSE SINGLE ANSWER

Listen to the recording and answer the multiple-choice question by selecting the correct response. Only one response is correct.

A

Map-making has a long and fascinating history – both before Ptolemy produced the first great map of the world and after, up to the beautiful simplicity of the London Underground map and the precisely-detailed Ordnance Survey maps, which cover almost every inch of the United Kingdom.

Ancient map-makers used to draw in hills, valleys and rivers to give an idea of the topography, the shape of the land. It wasn't until the late 16th century that contour lines were used – that is, lines that linked points of the land at the same height – but this was to show the relative depths and shallows of a river. The first time land contours were used was on a map of France, which took about forty years to complete, and was finished in 1783. The Ordnance Survey was set up in 1791 and their maps, as the name suggests, were originally made for military purposes, and the first one to be produced was of the county of Kent at a ratio of one inch to one mile.

B

Signs advertising business premises have been around for thousands of years and were used in ancient Egypt, Greece and Rome to attract customers; and they often used symbols to illustrate what kind of business it was – for example, bushes or branches of ivy meant the place was a tavern. Both of these, the tavern and its sign, were introduced into Britain by the Romans in the first half of the 1st century AD. In Europe in the Middle Ages signs became more common, then, in the 14th century, English merchants were obliged to have them outside their shops. However, the fashion was to have large swinging signs hung from a strut sticking out of the wall – and many public houses still have such signs – but so many accidents occurred, mostly involving people on horseback, that in the 17th century a law was brought in requiring shopkeepers to mount their signs flat against the wall of the premises, where they could do no harm.

C

The basic English person's diet in medieval times was made up of bread, cheese and beef, while ale was the drink for all ages and social classes except for the aristocracy, who drank wine. In winter there were no root crops to feed the animals, so they were killed in autumn and the meat salted to preserve it. People kept livestock even in the towns: cows were usually kept tied or tethered, but pigs were allowed to wander at will, feeding on the rubbish off the streets.

By the 16th century, however, choice in foodstuffs had grown, including exotic spices to add flavor to the usual diet. This had come about because European rulers wanting to increase their power and wealth and also, in fairness, in the spirit of enquiry and the quest for knowledge, had financed voyages of exploration overseas.

This opened up trade routes, bringing precious spices – and vast profits – from the East, and to the west Spanish and Portuguese explorers had brought back such novelties as potatoes, tomatoes, maize, peppers and chocolate. It must be said, though, that it took people some time to accept some of these new foods, as they feared they were poisonous.

Page 113

SECTION 2:
SELECT MISSING WORD

You will hear a recording about climate change. *At the end of the recording the last word or group of words has been replaced by a beep.* Select the correct option to complete the recording.

A

How much the Earth's climate will change in the future depends, among other things, on how quickly and to what extent the concentration of greenhouse gases in the atmosphere increases. If we take no action to limit future greenhouse gas emissions, it is estimated that there will be a rise in temperature of 0.2 to 0.3 °C every ten years. This is a far greater rate of warming than anything that has occurred over the past ten thousand years.

One set of predictions claims that some regions of the world will warm more quickly than others, and rainfall will also increase in some areas and decrease in others. These changes will affect the sea level, which could rise by 50cm over the next century. All this will affect humans through the effects it has on water resources, [BEEP]

You will hear a recording about parental discipline.

At the end of the recording, the last word or group of words has been replaced by a beep. Select the correct option to complete the recording.

B

When parents are asked how they handle their very unruly children, most will admit that they are likely to use physical forms of punishment. This is not to say that a parent generally hits their child each and every time they are bad. Nevertheless, parents generally use physical punishment as a last resort, after having unsuccessfully tried other forms of discipline with children who have become very bad. Those who believe in physical punishment, however, are unaware of the fact that it does not lead to better children. In fact, the opposite is true.

Research findings show that children from homes where corporal punishment is the norm exhibit more anti-social behavior than children whose parents seldom or never hit them. For example, children whose parents systematically use corporal punishment are more often than not behind any classroom disruptions. Such children not only create discipline problems at school, but they are also overly aggressive. In addition, they have extremely low self-esteem and a negative attitude to those around them. On the other hand, children whose parents use less harsh methods of discipline have a healthier attitude towards their school environment and [BEEP]

Page 114

SECTION 2: HIGHLIGHT INCORRECT WORDS

You will hear a recording. Below is a transcription of the recording. Some words in the transcription differ from what the speaker(s) said. As you listen, circle the words that are different.

A

"No news is good news" may be true for most of us most of the time – after all, we don't look forward to unpleasant things happening to us – but "Bad news is good news" is true for those who work in the news media, and, I suspect, for the rest of us, at least some of the time. It is tied up with stories and our seemingly insatiable need for stories. Have you ever been gripped by a story where nothing goes wrong for the characters? There's an incident in a Kingsley Amis novel that nicely illustrates this: the main character Jake comes home to find his wife chatting to a friend about a hairdresser both women know who has moved with his family to somewhere in Africa. Jake listens in, expecting tales of cannibalism and such like, but no, the friend has just received a letter saying they love the place and are settling in nicely. Jake leaves the room in disgust.

We demand to be entertained, and while we don't object to a happy ending, the characters have to have experienced loss, pain and hardship in one form or another along the way to have deserved it.

B

Leisure travel was, in a sense, a British invention. This was mainly due to economic and social factors; Britain was the first country to become fully industrialized and industrial society offered growing numbers of people time for leisure. This, coupled with improvements in transport, especially the railways, meant that large numbers of people could get to holiday resorts in a very short time.

Modern mass tourism of a sort we can easily recognize today began in 1841 when Thomas Cook organized the first package tour, in which everything was included in the cost – travel, hotel and entertainment. To cater for the large numbers of new holiday-makers, holiday camps were established, both on the coast and in the countryside, and they became immensely popular. Their popularity declined, however, with the rise of cheap overseas tours, which gave many people their first opportunity to travel abroad.

SECTION 2: WRITE FROM DICTATION

You will hear some sentences. Write each sentence exactly as you hear it. Write as much of each sentence as you can. You will hear each sentence only once.

1 This has been a major source of confusion for academics.

2 None of the alternatives is satisfactory.

3 The aim of the course is to provide a broad theoretical basis.

4 Has all the evidence been properly examined?

Page 115

FURTHER PRACTICE AND GUIDANCE: *PART 3, SECTION 2: HIGHLIGHT INCORRECT WORDS*

Listen to the recordings while reading the transcripts. Circle the words in the transcript that do not match the recording.

1 A team of marine biologists studying whale carcasses – the dead bodies of whales – has learned that they create a unique environment, one that is rich in animals and bacteria, including several new species.

2 When a whale dies, its body slowly sinks to the ocean bottom, where it becomes food for a vast ecosystem.

3 One whale carcass contains more nutrition than would normally filter down through the water column in 2,000 years.

4 Using a submersible robot, the team collected collarbones of whales from the seafloor and brought them to the surface.

5 Back in the lab, the team found the bones were covered in bacteria and other organisms, more than 10 of which had never been identified before.

TEST 4

Page 116

SECTION 2: REPEAT SENTENCE

You will hear some sentences. Please repeat each sentence exactly as you hear it. You will hear each sentence only once.

1 You are not permitted to take reference books out of the library.

2 The seminar will now take place a week on Tuesday.

3 You don't have to be on Professor Smith's course to attend this lecture.

4 The library will be closed for three days over the bank holiday weekend.

5 I think we should get together over the weekend to discuss this assignment.

6 There's an hourly bus service from the campus into town.

7 This is the third time you've asked for an extension on this project.

8 They say Professor Jones's lectures are always interesting, and funny.

9 Being a student representative on the union really cuts into my study time.

10 I've got a tutorial in an hour and I haven't had any time to prepare for it.

Page 117

FURTHER PRACTICE AND GUIDANCE: *PART 1, SECTION 2: REPEAT SENTENCE*

You will hear eight sentences. First, cover all the answer options below with a piece of paper. Then, after hearing each sentence, uncover the two answer options and circle the sentence you heard.

1 We're warning the client that the rates are increasing.

2 Much of his research objectives are driven by his natural curiosity and instincts.

3 The fire left the area almost completely devoid of vegetation.

4 I'll now demonstrate how the reaction can be arrested by adding a dilute acid.

5 The initial results are intriguing; however, statistically speaking, they are insignificant.

6 The opposition has so far been unresponsive to our proposal.

7 I believe that children should read aloud more.

8 The majority of the hardware we're using was built for a customer.

Page 121

SECTION 2: RE-TELL LECTURE

You will hear a lecture. After listening to the lecture, please retell what you have just heard from the lecture in your own words. You will have 40 seconds to give your response.

A

Machiavelli lived from 1469 to 1527. The philosopher Bertrand Russell referred to Machiavelli's most well-known book, *The Prince*, as a "gangsters' handbook". And while there's no doubt that certain people have read and used it as such, I think that if we put it into the context of when it was written, which was Italy, especially Florence, in the 15th and 16th centuries, it will be easier to judge Machiavelli's reasons for writing it.

Now, the Italy of that period was made up of a number of city states, often at war with each other. Add to that threats from foreign powers, especially France, and it was a very unstable and dangerous situation. Machiavelli loved his home city, Florence, and wanted to protect its culture, history and above all independence at all costs. One way to do this was to establish an army of Florentines loyal to the city state of Florence.

Much of Machiavelli's career was taken up with this issue. It must be remembered, though, that he led an active civic life, was deeply into politics, and was an ambassador for Florence. In this way, he got to meet and observe some of the key players of the time and through this came to understand the nature of power and how to hold on to it. *The Prince* was an attempt to teach Florence the lessons he had learnt.

B

There was a time when the subject of happiness was the business of philosophers, as part of their discussion of what makes for the good life. Then, much later, psychologists and sociologists got in on the act, and now, it seems, so has the government. I understand that governments should have the welfare and well-being of those it governs at heart from the purely practical point of view of keeping people quiet, at home enjoying their gadgets and comfort, rather than on the streets rioting. But surely it's not something you can legislate for.

Today there are numerous journals on the topic and it is even included in the curriculum at some universities and colleges. Surveys are done, statistics compiled, graphs drawn, yet all they seem to "prove" is what most people have concluded themselves from personal experience. An obvious example would be that having a lot of money doesn't necessarily make you happy. We all wish to be happy and have ideas about what it is we think would make us so. But we also know or suspect that it's not that easy. Most of us learn that it is a by-product of something else, usually being totally absorbed or involved in some task or pastime, and can only be reached that way. These activities, of course, must be worthwhile in themselves.

C

We have briefly looked at some of the problems involved in running a biggish city like, say, Melbourne, keeping the road and rail systems running, policing, providing food and housing, and so on. In another lecture, I'm going to deal with what we must now call the megalopolis – cities with populations of ten million or more. However, first I want to go back in history to when the population of cities could be numbered in the thousands rather than millions.

One of the earliest theorists of the city was, of course, Plato, who created an ideal city in his text, *The Republic*. The population of this city would be around twenty-five to thirty thousand at most. Oddly enough, the same figures were chosen by Leonardo da Vinci for his ideal cities. Now, of these twenty-five to thirty thousand inhabitants only about five thousand would be citizens. A reason for this might be that it is the largest number that could be addressed publicly at one time and by one person, and makes a voting system much easier to manage. Also, perhaps the numbers are kept deliberately low because a large population would be harder to control, or because, in practical terms, fewer inhabitants are easier to feed from local supplies without having to depend on outside sources.

SECTION 2: ANSWER SHORT QUESTION

You will hear some questions. Please give a simple and short answer to each one. Often just one or a few words is enough.

1 A famous canal links the Mediterranean Sea with the Indian Ocean. Is it the Corinth or the Suez Canal?

2 Where would you store meat you wish to keep frozen at home?

3 What is the most important document you would have to show if you wanted to hire a car?

4 Where would you go to work out on a treadmill?

5 What piece of equipment would you use to go diving in the sea, an aqualung or an aquaplane?

6 Where would you most likely go to buy some flour: a bakery, a florist or a supermarket?

7 Which hospital department would you go to for an x-ray: radiology or cardiology?

8 Where would you go to see an exhibition of sculpture?

9 Would you measure the volume of bottled water in liters or kilos?

10 What's the joint called where your hand is connected to your arm?

PART 3: LISTENING

Page 137

SECTION 1:
SUMMARIZE SPOKEN TEXT

You will hear a short lecture. Write a summary for a fellow student who was not present at the lecture. You should write 50–70 words.

You will have 10 minutes to finish this task. Your response will be judged on the quality of your writing and on how well your response presents the key points presented in the lecture.

A
Interviewer: Is it true you once said that English as a subject at university, um, literature, I mean, was a soft option – that it was just doing what you enjoy doing anyway, that is, reading books, um …

Interviewee: No, I didn't. In fact, I was arguing, and on occasion still have to argue, the opposite. This goes back to the very beginning of English as an academic subject. There was a demand for it, but the universities themselves didn't take it seriously as an academic discipline, so, to cut a long story short, they would only accept its place in the curriculum if it was made more difficult. What I said was that too many people *do* think of it as a soft option. If you want to find out just how rigorous a course it can be, ask any of my students. If you were to try to read the books on the list for one semester as a leisure activity you wouldn't get through them, let alone reading them with the proper attention, and then having to come up with a suitable and well thought out critical response. And, and, it's not just about the set books, there's the whole cultural context to take into account.

B
I became interested in – what would you call it? – the behavior, the psychology, perhaps – of crowds, after getting caught up, quite by accident, in a demonstration that turned into a bit of a riot. You may have seen it on the news not long ago. What interested me was, first my own reactions to the way the whole mood changed from peaceful demonstration to violence. Secondly, I wondered if everyone else was feeling the same as I was, and what that said about us and how we behave in crowds. Why is it that perfectly ordinary, respectable members of the public can start behaving in ways they wouldn't dream of doing when at home or among friends? A crowd, it seems to me, has a collective mind, each person there adds his or her mind to the collective mind, and willingly gives up all sense of judgement and responsibility. It gives you, I suppose, a feeling of freedom, of not having to be in control. It allows you the freedom, or you allow yourself the freedom to behave in ways that, if asked, you would say were against your principles, or made you feel guilty in some way – even criminal.

C
John Milton is best know for his poetry, especially *Paradise Lost*, but also for the more accessible, and shorter, *Lycidas*, and *L'Allegro* and *Il Penseroso*, plus one or two sonnets you will find in most anthologies – but an easier way into what he thought and believed in social and political terms, is through his prose writings. These were mostly pamphlets and tracts written in reaction to some political event or situation, but also included pamphlets on a wide variety of subjects including at least four on divorce, which for him was tied up with personal freedom. However, the text which has probably had the most relevance down the years and which can still be read with profit is the *Areopagitica*, which is a defence of freedom of expression and publication, and against censorship. It was written as a reaction to an attack on himself, in particular, a pamphlet on divorce he had written, and which some condemned as a "wicked book".

Page 138

SECTION 2:
MULTIPLE-CHOICE, CHOOSE MULTIPLE ANSWERS

Listen to the recording and answer the question by selecting all the correct responses. You will need to select more than one response.

A
Noises are defined as disagreeable sounds, but this suggests that they are no more than an annoyance, something to be put up with. There is increasing evidence that noise, on the scale that people who live in big cities have to deal with, is dangerous and can give rise to serious health and social problems. Some of which, such as its effects on people's behavior and anger levels, you might not have thought were caused by noise, and are health concerns. There is, of course, the almost constant noise of traffic, though this isn't a particularly modern problem. In ancient Rome, there were rules to minimize the noise made by the iron wheels of wagons, which battered the stones on the pavement, causing disruption of sleep. Traffic noise is one of the health hazards, as it can lead to other problems, like noise-induced hearing impairment. It is also highly distracting, interfering with speech communication and leisure time relaxation, and while this doesn't drive you mad in the medical sense, it is intensely annoying and can lead to mental health problems. Also, noise, whether you work in a place where loud machinery is operating or not, can have an effect on performance at work; though in itself not a health matter, this can lead to other problems.

B
Speaker 1: … yes, it's funny you should mention Merwin – until about a year ago I thought England was the only country that had a Poet Laureate. After all, it's a pretty

odd job, isn't it? No salary to speak of and just a barrel of wine or something as payment. But he was or is the American Poet Laureate, isn't he?

Speaker 2: That's right, but quite a few other countries have one too.

Speaker 1: I know, I looked into it a bit. Other countries in the UK for a start: Wales, as you'd expect, with their eisteddfods and long poetic tradition, and Ireland and Scotland. I think some places that were colonies or are in the Commonwealth have them – Canada, for example. And who's that wonderful Caribbean poet, um, the one that wrote *Omeros*?

Speaker 2: Derek Walcott.

Speaker 1: That's him. He was the Poet Laureate of Saint Lucia. But what about the rest of Europe? Don't the French have such a thing?

Speaker 2: No, I don't think so. They've got the Academy, and you get elected to that if you're considered the best in your field. But I think Germany might have – no, it wasn't Germany. Somewhere else, but I don't remember. By the way, you're a bit behind the times in thinking what they get paid is a barrel of wine. All that changed long ago, but one of the more recent ones asked to have it back.

C
Re-adjusting to life in your own country after living abroad for some time is a little like recovering from jet-lag after a long flight across several time zones. It takes time. And research indicates that after nine years living in a foreign country you never really do re-adjust. Of course, things have changed: governments have come and gone, what you knew as countryside has become a suburb, new technologies have changed the way people go about their daily lives, and so on. These changes may well have been taking place in your adopted country, but they were happening while you were there, so you could adapt as you went along. Those are not the main difficulties, however. It is in the smaller, everyday things that you might experience what is known as culture shock, although it's not really a shock, but puzzling all the same. For example, the precise way to behave at a supermarket checkout may have changed. And in

ordinary conversation, the frames of reference have changed, and quite often you find that you don't really know what people are talking about, even though they are speaking your native tongue.

Page 139

SECTION 2: FILL IN THE BLANKS

You will hear a recording. Write the missing words in each blank.

A
Privacy and the right to privacy are increasingly becoming hot topics in the media, which is a touch ironic, given that it is often the media that is responsible for invasion of privacy. This is not just about those whose careers put them in the public eye, but ordinary people who through no fault of their own have come to public notice because of some event that has attracted the attention of the media. It might be that a member of their family has been imprisoned for some crime, rightfully or wrongfully, or perhaps they are the victims of some natural disaster. Some people argue that those who have chosen to be in the public sphere, and have teams of public relations people to make sure they get as much public attention as possible – actors, rock stars, politicians and the like – have given up their right to privacy and get everything they deserve.

B
There is such a thing as information overload. There is just so much information out there now that we can't cope with it or fully absorb it, or even decide which bits of it we want to keep in our minds, or which to discard. There is a similar thing going on with the range of choices we have as consumers. There is so much stuff out there – so much to choose from, that, according to some experts, this situation is making us miserable. Most of us believe that the more we have to choose from the better, yet apparently our dissatisfaction with this wealth of choice, or rather the anxiety it produces, is part of a larger trend. It seems that, as society grows more affluent and people become freer to do what they want, the unhappier they become.

C
Post-modernism is broadly speaking a reaction against the movement or the period, or perhaps simply the values and beliefs of modernism. Most people, even those who seem to know what it is or was about, tend to define it in negative terms by telling us what it isn't, or doesn't do. Initially the term had a fairly limited application and referred to a new anti-modernist style of architecture. But it spread like a virus to include almost all aspects of contemporary culture. One thing we can be sure about is that it wanted to get rid of what were called the grand narratives by which we explained how the world – and history – got us from the past to the present. Another feature of post-modernism is its belief that truth and reality are human-centered and internal. That is, the primary source of truth in the present age is the self. This, I believe, has now all passed and been thrown in the rubbish bin of history. Yet it is difficult to know whether the age of information technology confirms the passing of post-modernism or is a consequence of it.

Page 140

SECTION 2: HIGHLIGHT CORRECT SUMMARY

You will hear a recording. Choose the paragraph that best relates to the recording.

A
I want to take a quick look at how material culture, that is, the things or objects we value and use, tools, technology, etc., affects the non-material culture, our customs, behavior, beliefs, attitudes, and so on. Now, of course, it works both ways: if you were, say, eighteen years old when mobile phones became widespread or when almost every home had a computer, you must have noticed a fairly significant change in people's attitudes and behavior, including your own. These two technological innovations were readily accepted and considered very much a positive contribution to culture.

On the other hand, there is the way in which our attitudes and beliefs have an effect on the material culture. Take, for example, genetic science. While many, if not most, people welcome the advances made in this field – from the discovery of DNA to the genome project and cracking the genetic code, with its promise of finding cures for diseases that have plagued mankind throughout history – many, too, object to the idea of cloning. This is not just because they fear, without reason, that it will mean creating a race of identical people if it gets into the wrong hands, but simply because it is, in their opinion, unnatural. It goes against everything they believe in. Similarly, there are many who object to genetically modified food, even when they are told it might be the only way to feed a rapidly growing global population.

B

Ernest Hemingway was famously masculine. We can see this in the topics he wrote about: all those fights and bullfights, all those wars, all that hunting and fishing. All this, it is thought, was overdoing it and must point to some deep insecurity in the man. Perhaps he felt that the conventional image of a writer as a person who doesn't do a lot more than sitting at a desk, not visibly contributing much socially or economically to society as a whole was unmanly and carried a certain amount of guilt and shame with it?

During the First World War, he was badly wounded, hospitalized, and fell in love with a nurse. He wrote a novel about a man who was badly wounded in the First World War, was hospitalised and who fell in love with a nurse. The Spanish Civil War and the Second World War followed as did books about his experiences in them. Now, how much can we draw on a writer's biography to explain his work? It should, I believe, be irrelevant to the judgement you bring to the merits of the individual work.

Biographies of writers can be fascinating, especially if they lived as hard and fast as Hemingway, but, unfortunately, these days many people prefer the biography to the actual work. It is odd that the very reason a person would want to read a biography of a writer – that the subject has achieved fame and distinction in his field – should be the excuse for not reading his works.

Page 141

SECTION 2: MULTIPLE-CHOICE, CHOOSE SINGLE ANSWER

Listen to the recording and answer the multiple-choice question by selecting the correct response. Only one response is correct.

A

The division of literary works into genres – or texts that deal with a particular subject, or a subject in a particular way – makes life easier for the person browsing in a bookshop. He or she can go directly to where their favorite kind of book is shelved, be it science fiction, gothic, romance, and so on. Many writers of genre fiction are immensely popular and successful, Stephen King and J. K. Rowling to name only two. But, for the most part, such writers aren't depicting the world we live in and are writing fantasies. However, some genre writers, particularly writers of detective and police fiction, are unhappy about being categorized in this way. Genre fiction, they say, has come to be seen as inferior to what is called mainstream or literary fiction. In other words, detective fiction isn't taken seriously as literature, and yet crime novels do deal with the raw stuff of everyday life. They are, in fact, closer to the harsh reality of the modern world than most mainstream fiction. But, the critics say, while they do deal with the usual stuff of novels – character, emotion, psychology, social comment, and so on – it seldom goes very deep, and besides, most detective fiction, like certain mass-produced romantic novels – though not to anywhere near the same extent – follow a formula.

B

In small doses, stress can have quite a positive effect. It can make you feel more alive, even exhilarated. I suppose everyone has a set level at which stress becomes unbearable, at which point they cease to function properly. I suppose, too, that it's possible for someone to train themselves to be able to take higher levels of stress by repeatedly putting themselves in a stressful situation – to build up a tolerance for stress. Indeed, some jobs absolutely require this. But stress is a fact of life for all

of us and, as the figures show, its effect is largely negative.

Each year, about six million people in Britain consult their doctors because they feel stress or anxiety, and it is estimated that at least another six million suffer from stress-related illness but do not seek medical advice. Long working hours, fear of losing their jobs, the difficult journey to and from work in crowded trains and buses, all contribute to increased levels of stress. Then there are domestic problems, such as a large mortgage on the house, children who want to drop out of school and join rock bands, not enough time to spare to be with the family.

C

The nature-nurture debate is still going on. It is not a question of taking sides because we know that both play an important part in what makes us who we are. It is more a question of emphasis – which of them has the greatest influence.

On the nature side, we have what we get from our genes, our inherited traits – eye color and other physical traits, for example, but also, some believe, non-physical ones, such as temperament. For example, you might be quick to anger, or have a nervous temperament, and this even extends to sense of humor. On the nurture side, there is what we get from our environment and our upbringing, what we learn.

Research into the human genome has recently made it clear that both sides are partly right. Nature gives us inborn abilities and traits while nurture takes these genetic tendencies and shapes them as we grow and learn and mature. This is an important point as it means, contrary to the belief of some, that we are not wholly determined by our genes. Scientists have known for years that eye and hair color are determined by specific genes, but some now claim that such traits as intelligence and personality are also encoded in our genes.

Page 142

SECTION 2: SELECT MISSING WORD

You will hear a recording about using the library. *At the end of the recording, the last word or group of words has been replaced by a beep*. Select the correct option to complete the recording.

A

Too many students search for material by going to what they think is the right shelf in the library, finding little or nothing and then reporting back to their tutor that there's nothing on it in the library. If you have some authors and titles in mind, look them up in the catalogue – they may not be where you think – and look at adjacent entries in the catalogue and on the shelves. The catalogue may lead you to restricted loan collections, reserve stacks or departmental collections, which may not always be obvious. You should also check the subject catalogue, trying to think of related terms. Other places to look would be the references shelves and newspaper section, though a problem here is finding [BEEP]

You will hear a recording about the sense of touch.

At the end of the recording, the last word or group of words has been replaced by a beep. Select the correct option to complete the recording.

B

Scientists distinguish two basic ways in which we receive information from the outside world through the sense of touch: active and passive, or to put it more simply, touching and being touched. Being touched, or passive tactile awareness, includes sensing external pressure and temperature acting on parts of the body, and this gives us clues as to the nature of our environment. Active touching is when we explore our surrounding with our hands, feet, mouth, and so on. Because it's difficult to guess what some objects are really like with the eyes alone – for example, their weight, hardness or softness, roughness or smoothness, etc. – touching them gives us a much fuller understanding of the objects around us. Yet, how touch works is very complex and [BEEP]

Page 143

SECTION 2:
HIGHLIGHT INCORRECT WORDS

You will hear a recording. Below is a transcription of the recording.

Some words in the transcription differ from what the speaker(s) said. As you listen, circle the words that are different.

A

When societies were still mostly rural and agricultural, waste disposal was hardly an issue, partly because people tended to make use of everything and partly because there was plenty of space to bury rubbish. It was when societies became predominantly urban and industrial that problems arose – mainly to do with health. City authorities had a hard time trying to find efficient ways of getting rid of all the rubbish. One of these was to get people to sort out their rubbish into different types, just as these days we are encouraged to separate our rubbish into different categories for easier removal and recycling. So, for example, kitchen rubbish was set aside and used for feeding animals. However, fears of disease put an end to that. In fact, it wasn't until the 20th century that all waste was simply thrown together and ploughed into landfills.

B

Archery, the practice or art of shooting with a bow and arrow, has played an important part in English history, being the main weapon of the foot-soldier and instrumental in winning many battles in wars with the French – with whom we seemed to be constantly at war during the Middle Ages. The English favored the longbow over the short bow and the crossbow, the latter being the main firearm of militaries on the European continent. The crossbow fired a metal bolt released by a trigger, rather like a gun, and had the longest range of any of the bows, but the main advantage of the longbow was its accuracy. The importance placed on archery is illustrated by the fact that medieval kings in England encouraged the practice and one of them, Edward III, went so far as to ban all sports on Sundays and holidays except archery. Because there were no standing armies in those days, and in the event of war rulers had to call on the populace, everything was done to make sure there were large numbers of competent, if not expert archers, to recruit.

SECTION 2:
WRITE FROM DICTATION

You will hear some sentences. Write each sentence exactly as you hear it. Write as much of each sentence as you can. You will hear each sentence only once.

1 The field of social history has always been difficult to define.

2 All essays must be accompanied by a list of references.

3 Authoritarian regimes were more common in the past than they are today.

4 The new law was harder to impose than the government thought.

Page 144

FURTHER PRACTICE AND GUIDANCE: *PART 3, LISTENING: WRITE FROM DICTATION*

Each sentence below has some words missing. You will hear the complete sentences. Listen and write the missing words.

1 The airline blamed the recent round of airfare price hikes on higher costs for aviation fuel.

2 Because deep-drilling is technically challenging, most geothermal energy exploration is limited to reservoirs of steam or hot water located near the surface.

3 A bank typically does not keep all its customers' money on hand, which means that if a majority tried to withdraw their funds at the same time, the bank would be unable to pay them.

4 Although there are some similarities between the two countries, the United States and Canada are very different in terms of their respective climates, resources, and population sizes.